SWINBURNE: THE CRITICAL HERITAGE

# THE CRITICAL HERITAGE SERIES

GENERAL EDITOR: B. C. SOUTHAM, M.A., B.LITT.(OXON.)
*Formerly Department of English, Westfield College, University of London*

---

*Volumes in the series include*

| | |
|---|---|
| JANE AUSTEN | B. C. Southam |
| BROWNING | Boyd Litzinger, *St. Bonaventure University* and Donald Smalley, *University of Illinois* |
| BYRON | Andrew Rutherford, *University of Aberdeen* |
| COLERIDGE | J. R. de J. Jackson, *Victoria College, Toronto* |
| HENRY FIELDING | R. Paulson, *The Johns Hopkins University, Baltimore* and Thomas Lockwood, *University of Washington* |
| THOMAS HARDY | R. G. Cox, *University of Manchester* |
| HENRY JAMES | Roger Gard, *Queen Mary College, London* |
| JAMES JOYCE | Robert H. Deming, *University of Miami* |
| D. H. LAWRENCE | R. P. Draper, *University of Leicester* |
| MILTON | John T. Shawcross, *University of Wisconsin* |
| SCOTT | John O. Hayden, *University of California, Davis* |
| TENNYSON | J. D. Jump, *University of Manchester* |
| THACKERAY | Geoffrey Tillotson and Donald Hawes, *Birkbeck College, London* |
| TROLLOPE | Donald Smalley, *University of Illinois* |

# SWINBURNE

## THE CRITICAL HERITAGE

*Edited by*

CLYDE K. HYDER

*Professor Emeritus of English*
*University of Kansas*

NEW YORK

BARNES & NOBLE, INC.

*First published in Great Britain 1970*
*Published in the United States of America 1970*
*by Barnes & Noble, Inc., New York, N.Y.*

© *Clyde K. Hyder 1970*

*SBN 389 03971 3*

*Printed in Great Britain*

*For*
*Two Distinguished Students*
*of Swinburne*

CECIL Y. LANG
JOHN S. MAYFIELD

# General Editor's Preface

The reception given to a writer by his contemporaries and near-contemporaries is evidence of considerable value to the student of literature. On one side we learn a great deal about the state of criticism at large and in particular about the development of critical attitudes towards a single writer; at the same time, through private comments in letters, journals or marginalia, we gain an insight upon the tastes and literary thought of individual readers of the period. Evidence of this kind helps us to understand the writer's historical situation, the nature of his immediate reading-public, and his response to these pressures.

The separate volumes in the *Critical Heritage Series* present a record of this early criticism. Clearly for many of the highly-productive and lengthily-reviewed nineteenth- and twentieth-century writers, there exists an enormous body of material; and in these cases the volume editors have made a selection of the most important views, significant for their intrinsic critical worth or for their representative quality—perhaps even registering incomprehension!

For earlier writers, notably pre-eighteenth-century, the materials are much scarcer and the historical period has been extended, sometimes far beyond the writer's lifetime, in order to show the inception and growth of critical views which were initially slow to appear.

In each volume the documents are headed by an Introduction, discussing the material assembled and relating the early stages of the author's reception to what we have come to identify as the critical tradition. The volumes will make available much material which would otherwise be difficult of access, and it is hoped that the modern reader will be thereby helped towards an informed understanding of the ways in which literature has been read and judged.

B.C.S.

# Contents

# CONTENTS

# Preface

More clearly than that of most writers, the critical reception of Swinburne shows how changes in current social and religious views may
affect literary judgment. It shows, too, how the vogue of older poets
may influence the attitude towards a new one: when John Morley
looked in vain for the note of 'enlarged meditation', he was looking
for something that was congenial to the age of Wordsworth and the
age of Tennyson but that the twentieth century does not consider
indispensable. Few authors have been more responsive to criticism,
in one way or another, than Swinburne. For such reasons his inclusion
in the 'Critical Heritage' series seems logical.

When asked to edit this volume for that series, I wondered whether
in my *Swinburne's Literary Career and Fame* (1933) I had not already
said nearly all I could say on the subject. During the centenary of
*Poems and Ballads* I had also published *Swinburne Replies*, a critical
edition of the three works in which Swinburne formally answered
critics. But I reflected that, with the publication of *The Swinburne
Letters* and other books, new material has come to light, that my per-
spective would be somewhat different, and that repetition, even if
sometimes unavoidable, would be largely confined to the Introduction;
after all, I had not previously edited writings about Swinburne. If it
seems that my chief indebtedness must be to earlier studies of my own,
in making them I acknowledged debts to others. I have renewed my
acquaintance with material already familiar and consulted some previously neglected or inaccessible, including an unpublished thesis
submitted at New York University in 1964 by Roger Leo Cayer,
'Algernon Charles Swinburne's Literary Reputation: A Study of the
Criticism of Swinburne's Work in England from 1860 to 1960'. I
found it useful to compare Dr. Cayer's impressions with my own,
particularly for the thirty years not covered in my earlier book. The
plan of the 'Critical Heritage' series limits selections chiefly to those
appearing in Swinburne's lifetime. Though my Introduction takes
some account of later critical attitudes, it does not evaluate scholarly
and biographical writings, mostly belonging to the twentieth century.

PREFACE

My chapter on Swinburne in *The Victorian Poets: A Guide to Research*
ed. Frederic E. Faverty (second edition: Harvard University Press,
1968), discusses them.[1]

My appreciation of two eminent admirers of Swinburne is in-
adequately suggested on the dedicatory page. Professor Cecil Y. Lang
of the University of Virginia has invariably shown himself a cheerful
and appreciative helper and friend, one whose edition of *The Swinburne Letters* has earned for him a recognized position among scholars.
To Mrs. Lang, incidentally, I am grateful for her translation (No. 24).
Mr. John S. Mayfield, Curator of Manuscripts and Rare Books at the
Syracuse University Library, who not only has made important discoveries relating to Swinburne but also has assembled a remarkable
collection of Swinburniana, generously given to that library, has again
patiently answered inquiries. I should not omit mention of help
received from the Watson Library of the University of Kansas, especially
from those in charge of the Interlibrary Loan Service and of Special
Collections, and from an obliging colleague, Professor Mattie Crum-
rine. It may be superfluous to add that this book owes no shortcomings
to others but is, like Hamlet's father, sent to its account with all its
imperfections on its head, not on theirs.

C. K. H.

[1] Some readers should be warned that about ten of the Swinburne pamphlets listed in
Wise's *Bibliography* are spurious and that others are under suspicion. The Bonchurch
Edition of Swinburne's *Works*, edited by Gosse and Wise, is misleading in arrangement
and omissions and is often corrupt.

# Introduction

## I

Swinburne's literary career was, at least in part, the story of a man's conflict with his generation, a generation with social and literary standards very different from our own. The *Saturday Review* was a leader of the attack on *Poems and Ballads* (1866). Some statistics that appeared in that periodical on 12 January 1867 emphasize one point of difference: of the more than four thousand new publications of 1866, 849 were religious books; fiction came second, with only 390 titles. At that time an author's role was considered an exalted one. Carlyle, for instance, had described men of letters as having a mission comparable to that of priests. Even at the risk of seeming platitudinous, one must affirm that every generation finds it hard to be tolerant of points of view cherished by previous generations. In appraising the reception of Swinburne's work, one must make allowance for varying outlooks in the twentieth and the nineteenth century, when reviewers were conscious of the need for social discipline and were not afraid of seeming moralistic or appearing to take themselves seriously.

Swinburne objected strenuously to contemporary literary standards. As early as February 1858 he mentioned a desire to review himself and describe his 'models—i.e., blasphemy and sensuality. . . . I flatter myself the last sentence was worthy of the *Saturday Review*.'[1] A few years later this passage would have seemed to him strangely prophetic. So would have some parts of a hoax[2] he attempted to foist on the *Spectator*, to which he was contributing in 1862—a review of an imaginary French poet. Of a supposititious poem he mockingly observed, 'Filth and blasphemy defile every line of it.' The hoaxing review was not published, but Swinburne's published review of Baudelaire's *Les Fleurs du Mal* and his letter to the *Spectator* defending *Modern Love*, a sequence of poems by his friend George Meredith, also indicate antagonism to accepted literary criteria. A more personal antagonism may appear in some answers to his critics—answers often cited in the pages that follow. In other ways he seemingly took account of criticism, as when he wrote a play in a vein unusual to him. Did his critics contribute to his occasional truculence or an increasing sense of isolation? Perhaps, but Swinburne himself wrote (October 31, 1882) of 'a thousand onslaughts which have never for one hour affected my own peace of mind or impaired my self-reliance and self-respect'.

In spite of his awareness of contemporary prepossessions and in spite of some reviewers' statements about *Chastelard* (1865), Swinburne could not have anticipated the violence of the attack on *Poems and Ballads* and its lasting effect on later criticism. In an autobiographical letter to E. C. Stedman,[3] he expressed the belief that he had 'probably been more be-written and belied than any man since Byron'. As with Byron, most of the hostility sprang from a challenge to social conventions and disregard of moral and religious sensibilities. Again as with Byron, the poet's personality and conduct, as well as legends about them, imparted a bias to criticism, and both gossip and fictional portrayal were injurious to the poet's reputation in England and the United States. In England, Swinburne's next important volume, *Songs before Sunrise* (1871), was more fairly reviewed than *Poems and Ballads*, though it brought to the fore the charge of Red Republicanism and strengthened the charge of blasphemy; but in America, where the reception of Swinburne's first four books did not differ markedly from their reception in England, *Songs before Sunrise* attracted little attention. In a country which was already a republic, the poet's ideal republic seemed no daring novelty, and America had even less concern than England, the home of Mazzini for some years, with abstractions related to Italian politics. Swinburne's second poetic drama on the Greek model, *Erechtheus* (1876), aroused warm enthusiasm, but since American reviewers neglected that book, too, there was, for a longer period than in England, little to offset the memory of *Poems and Ballads*. In both countries that memory continued to affect judgment, but later reviewers stressed aesthetic defects as objections on moral grounds became fainter. In both England and America, the vogue of Tennyson was re-enforced by that of Longfellow and others, whose kind of poetry was strikingly different from Swinburne's and affected criticism of his. Though accusations of sensuality persisted and though memories of the outcries of 1866 continued to influence much criticism to an even later time, in 1904 the first volume of Swinburne's *Collected Poems* was received with a tolerance that indicated the public was forgetting those outcries.

Swinburne's first book, *The Queen-Mother and Rosamond* (1860), contained two plays, the titles referring to Catherine de' Medici and to Henry II's mistress, Rosamond Clifford. The poet himself described it as 'of all still-born books, the stillest'. The two English notices of 1861 (Nos. 1, 2) illustrate a not uncommon blindness to the merits of new authors whose faults may be obvious. In June 1865 *Fraser's Magazine*, reviewing the book along with *Atalanta in Calydon*, considered the two plays obscure and in some passages indecent, and the *Edinburgh Review* was even more severe in July 1871. Since American reviewers of 1866 reviewed it with later works, especially *Poems and Ballads*, their judgments were equally harsh.

The *Queen-Mother and Rosamond* was transferred from Pickering, the original publisher, to Moxon. The transfer was probably arranged at the instance of Richard Monckton Milnes (Lord Houghton), who had been a friend of Edward Moxon, his own publisher, before Moxon died in 1858. Moxon had published the work of several great poets, including Wordsworth and Tennyson, and, as would have impressed Swinburne even more, had been Charles Lamb's friend and publisher. Unfortunately the company went into a decline after Moxon's death and reached a new low under the manager appointed in 1864, J. Bertrand Payne, whose dealings in 1866 Swinburne had cause to resent.

Moxon published Swinburne's first great success, *Atalanta in Calydon* (1865). In reviewing that play, the *London Review* hailed Swinburne as the possible successor of Tennyson, and the *Saturday Review* (No. 4) welcomed him to an honourable position among the younger poets. J. Leicester Warren (the poet Lord de Tabley) was chagrined when the editor of the *Fortnightly Review*, George Henry Lewes, interpolated in his review a statement that Swinburne may 'be counted henceforward among the contemporaneous *minor* poets' (my italics). Reviewers praised the brilliance of Swinburne's technique but qualified their praise by mention of overelaboration and an involved style in the dialogue (the *Athenaeum*) and luxuriance (the *Saturday Review*). The *Spectator*, though granting that the play is full of true poetry, considered 'the intellectual form and nexus of the play . . . unreal and also inadequate to the richness of the workmanship', a comment paralleled in criticism of Swinburne's subsequent books.[4]

More than one writer noted the modern and personal tone of *Atalanta*, but it was Swinburne's friend Lord Houghton who most pointedly referred to its 'bitter and angry anti-theism'. One recalls Christina Rossetti's reading the play appreciatively but pasting strips of paper over lines dealing with 'the supreme evil, God'. (Miss Rossetti later felt somewhat hesitant about sending Swinburne a copy of her *Called to Be Saints*, but Swinburne acknowledged the book with 'consummate graciousness'; and the two poets continued to admire each other.) In a later generation, Maurice Baring remembered that a woman who gave him a copy of *Atalanta* explained that the denunciation of God in it 'only applied to the Greek gods'.[5] The *Spectator* and *The Times* were aware that the religious tone of the play was not Greek.

Charles Eliot Norton, in his anonymous review in the *Nation*, may have been the only American reviewer to make this observation.[6] His friend James Russell Lowell overlooked the modern and personal note in *Atalanta*, choosing to dwell on the artificiality of all attempts to reproduce the classical style.[7] As a passage in *Under the Microscope* reminds us, Lowell's remarks greatly annoyed Swinburne.

Some of the later commentators on *Atalanta*, influenced by the reception of *Poems and Ballads*, looked for and found religious heterodoxy in the play. Florence Nightingale did not worry about its 'message':

Do read if you have not read Swinburne's *Atalanta in Calydon*. Forgive it its being an imitation of a Greek play. . . . But read it. The Atalanta herself, though she is only a sort of Ginn and not a woman at all, has more reality, more character, more individuality (to use a bad word) than all the *jeunes premières* in all the men novelists I ever have read—Walter Scott, Bulwer-Lytton, and all of them. But then Atalanta is not a sound incarnation of any 'social or economic principle'—is she? So men will say.[8]

Thinking of the excitement caused by *Atalanta*, 'A. Fogey' (Andrew Lang) in 1894 wrote of Swinburne's recognition by undergraduates, one of whom had quoted the poet, in a Latin essay, as *poeta ille noster* and who on being asked by the teacher, T. H. Green, whether he meant Milton had boldly replied, 'No, I mean Swinburne.'[9]

The play was, then, regarded as a poetic if not exactly a dramatic success, and the critical verdict was gratifying to its author. The first edition of five hundred copies, he noted, was soon exhausted and a second edition was required. Still regarded by some critics as Swinburne's masterpiece, it has been second in popularity only to *Poems and Ballads*.[10] Swinburne complained that though his father had made an advance to have the book printed, Moxon had paid him nothing. But on 10 December 1865 he wrote enthusiastically to a friend: 'I have already the wildest offers made me for any-thing I will do; and expect soon to have in effect the control of a magazine.'[11]

Swinburne's next book, *Chastelard* (1865), was in reality, like many poems in *Poems and Ballads*, composed before *Atalanta*. William Tinsley recalled that 'in 1860 or a year or two later' Swinburne had sold the manuscript to Tinsley Brothers but had later persuaded that publisher to release it.[12] Apparently as early as March 1864 D. G. Rossetti had written to Alexander Macmillan ('Scotch Macmillan' Swinburne called him in some verses denouncing various critics)[13] about the 'astonishing beauty' of Swinburne's early poems and had offered to submit *Chastelard* to him. Macmillan thought it 'a work of genius' but some parts of it 'very *queer*—very' and had rejected both it and the 'minor poems'—apparently some that were to appear in *Poems and Ballads*. When *Chastelard* was finally published by Moxon the majority of reviewers were not friendly—a fact often overlooked because of the more violent onslaught on *Poems and Ballads*. The *Reader* anticipated popularity for the play, though noting that 'passionate, burning kisses meet us on every page' and that, were it not for elegance of expression, the constant exhibitions of passion would deserve severe rebuke.[14] The *London Review* considered the play successful even 'though the love-ravings almost pass the bound of propriety'. The *Spectator* found 'a radical deformity of his poetry' to be 'want of moral and intellectual relief for the coarseness of passion and for the deep physical instincts of tenderness or cruelty on which he delights to employ his rich imagination', so that the reviewer closed the book 'with a sense of profound thankfulness that we have at last got out of the oppressive atmosphere in that forcing-house of sensual appetite into the open air'. The *Athenaeum* (No. 5), though it praised the beauty of the poet's diction and the dramatic quality of some passages, thought the language of the chief characters 'inherently vicious'. 'We decline to show by quotation how often the Divine Name is sported with in scenes which are essentially voluptuous.' Some objected to the inter-pretation of Mary's character—for instance, the *Gentleman's Magazine* and the *Fortnightly Review*.[15] The *Saturday Review*,[16] with a final note of disapproval, was inclined to judge Swinburne's excess leniently but found the play lacking in variety and contrast: 'He leaves those lofty seats of passion, where the mind is exhilarated and inspired . . . and betakes himself into tropical swamps of passion, where everything is sweltering in fierce and consuming heat, where there are uncouth destructive monsters, and where even the flowers and plants are of a size and form to fill men with fear.'

When *Chastelard* was issued in America by Hurd and Houghton, reviewers made similar objections. Lowell dismissed it cavalierly before passing on to *Atalanta*. Writing anonymously in the *Nation*,[17] Henry James described the play as dramatically faulty because of substituting colour for design. The poet's understanding of Mary ends with 'his very lively appreciation of the graces of her body'. Swinburne owned a vigorous poetic temperament but, as James was to realize in his own experience, constructing a good play is difficult even for those who possess a variety of literary gifts.

The reception of *Chastelard* pointed towards the approaching storm. But Swinburne was not disposed to compromise. His *Selection from the Works of Lord Byron* is introduced by one of his best critical essays, yet the book was denounced by the *Spectator*, the *Pall Mall Gazette*, the *Westminster Review*, and other periodicals,[18] some of which reviewed it along with *Poems and Ballads*. It contains a passage that sounds defiant:

At the first chance given or taken, every obscure and obscene thing that lurks for pay or prey among the fouler shallows and thickets of literature flew against him; every hound and every hireling lavished upon him the loathsome tribute of their abuse; all nameless creatures that nibble and prowl, upon whom the serpent's curse has fallen, to go upon his belly and eat dust all the days of his life, assailed him with their foulest venom and their keenest fangs. . . .

## II

Swinburne's friends realized that trouble might follow publication of his early poems. 'I have heard "low mutterings" from the lion of British prudery,' wrote George Meredith, 'and I, who love your verse, would play savagely with a knife among the proofs for the sake of your fame.'[19] Both D. G. and W. M. Rossetti counselled deletions. Lady Trevelyan urged Swinburne to

be wise in which of your lyrics you publish. Do let it be a book that can really be loved and read and learned by heart, and become part and parcel of the English language, and be on everyone's table without being received under protest by timid people. . . . You have sailed near enough to the wind in all conscience in having painted such a character for a hero as your Chastelard, slave to a passion for a woman he despises, whose love (if one can call it love) has no element of chivalry or purity in it.[20]

Swinburne replied that he was unable to decide what poems to omit and that 'whatever I do will be assailed and misconstrued'.[21] Ruskin, too, was disturbed by the prospect. On 8 December 1865, he wrote to Lady Trevelyan of having seen Swinburne and 'heard some of the wickedest and splendidest verses ever written by a human creature. He drank three bottles of porter while I was there. I don't know what to do with him or for him, but he mustn't publish these things.'[22]

When Moxon brought out *Poems and Ballads* the next year, the most forcible attack on it was John Morley's, appearing anonymously in the powerful *Saturday Review* for 4 August 1866 (No. 6). Yet Edmund Goose in his biography of Swinburne vastly exaggerated the importance of this one article when he attributed to it the fate of *Poems and Ballads*, as well as the author's subsequent literary fortunes. The reception of *Poems and Ballads* represents the verdict of a generation, not of an individual. Morley's review could not have influenced certain others, those which appeared on the same day, for instance. Furthermore, since Morley was himself a freethinker, he was silent about what other reviewers attacked as blasphemy or paganism. The poet himself recognized a more formidable enemy when he referred to 'the goddess Grundy' or 'the raddled old Columbine Cant'.

Two other attacks on *Poems and Ballads* also bear the date of 4 August. One in the *Athenaeum*, unsigned but written by Robert Buchanan (No. 7), alleged that Swinburne was insincere, 'unclean for the sake of uncleanness', and had pictured sensuality as the chief good. In tone more insulting than Morley's, Buchanan's review likened Swinburne to Petronius's Gito, 'seated in the tub of Diogenes, conscious of the filth and whining at the stars'. While literary historians are familiar with Buchanan's later writings on the 'fleshly school', his authorship of the *Athenaeum* review is usually overlooked. Neither Swinburne nor his friends identified him as the reviewer. The anonymous writer in the *London Review* of 4 August (No. 8) was more fair-minded than Buchanan, but asserted that Swinburne had taken pains to shock the decencies, drawing upon the most depraved stories of the ancient world, in a volume 'depressing and misbegotten—in many of its constituents so utterly revolting'. 'Anactoria' and 'Dolores' are 'especially horrible', 'Anactoria' ending in 'raving blasphemy' and 'Dolores' 'a mere deification of incontinence'. This reviewer regrets the necessity for such a harsh verdict and proceeds to mention happier aspects of *Poems and Ballads*.

In their disapproval the three reviews of 4 August are not

unrepresentative. After reading many such reviews, however, one may continue to be startled by reviewers' intemperate language. 'Swinburne's Folly' in the *Pall Mall Gazette* of 20 August described the poet as 'publicly obscene'. 'There are many passages . . . which bring before the mind the image of a mere madman, one who has got maudlin drunk on lewd ideas and lascivious thoughts.' Even after such statements the reviewer praised some poems and expressed the view that the volume should not be suppressed, though he thought about a third of it should be eliminated.

Sensuality, paganism, and blasphemy were the emphatic complaints. Occasionally there were references to the poet's treatment of women, hardly viewed in a domestic role. 'Dolores', for instance, does not suggest an exalted conception of marriage:

> Time turns the old days to derision,
> Our loves into corpses or wives;
> And marriage and death and division
> Make barren our lives.

Admiration for skilful technique and power of imagination, for command of language and rhythm, was yoked to disparagement for thinness of substance, monotony, or disproportion between form and thought. In his friendly unsigned review of *Atalanta* in the *Edinburgh Review* of July 1865 Richard Monckton Milnes had mentioned stylistic characteristics that could raise a suspicion of poverty of thought; John Morley was not the first person to apply the phrase to Swinburne. An underlying assumption was that form and thought can be easily dissociated.

J. Bertrand Payne, of the house of Moxon, professed to have heard that *The Times* planned to attack *Poems and Ballads*. Mudie's Library withdrew it from circulation. The publisher, too, decided to withdraw it, giving rise to a rumour that some poems had been suppressed in the issue bearing the imprint of John Camden Hotten, the dishonest and disreputable publisher to whom Swinburne, after consulting Bulwer-Lytton, decided to transfer the volume.

The first defence of *Poems and Ballads*, in the *Examiner* for 22 September 1866 (No. 10), is attributed to Professor Henry Morley, then of University College, London, who found 'a terrible earnestness' in *Chastelard* and *Poems and Ballads*.[23] He said that those critics who had denounced *Poems and Ballads* had done so 'because it does not paint the outside of the Sodom's apple of like colour with the ashes that it shows

within'. Neither Swinburne himself nor W. M. Rossetti wholly
accepted the point of view expressed in the *Examiner*, in spite of
Swinburne's argument (in his 1862 review of *Les Fleurs du Mal*) that
the moral of a poem may be implicit. In 1894 Robert Louis Stevenson
recalled the magical spell of *Poems and Ballads*, which he linked with
that of Meredith's 'Love in the Valley' and Yeats's 'Lake Isle of Innisfree'.
In 1868, when he was eighteen, Stevenson had made a comparison
somewhat similar to one made by the *Examiner*: 'In the latter [Swin-
burne], although we have all the fiery maddening pleasure of sin
burning on the paper, there is still a tang of bitter remorse, a loathsome
something that draws the veil aside and lets us see the white ashes gushing from the Sodom's apple, and the clanking bones of the skeleton
below the fair, white, smooth skin and flesh on which the sensual poet
gloats. To read Swinburne long would either make you mad or moral.
... Swinburne's sensualism is too deep; it works its own cure.'[24]
Richard Le Gallienne in 1906 called 'Dolores', 'Faustine', and 'Laus
Veneris' 'an inspired prophecy against the diabolism of the beauty of
women', and James Douglas wrote of 'Dolores' as 'one of the most
poignantly moral lyrics in the language'.[25] But if one supposes that
'Dolores' was written as a moral poem, one might recall Swinburne's
mention of 'four more jets of boiling and gushing infamy' being added
to the 'perennial and poisonous fountain of Dolores'.[26]

During the last part of October there appeared Swinburne's own
defence, *Notes on Poems and Reviews*. As he explained, his new publisher,
Hotten, had urged him to write it. In a letter to Hotten he insisted that
the book was not an answer to critics 'but rather a casual set of notes
on my poems, such as Coleridge and Byron (under other circumstances)
did on theirs'.[27] In this pamphlet Swinburne declared that he had no
apology to offer and would prefer to take no notice of the abuse of his
poems. He professed not to understand 'such sudden thunder from the
serene heavens of public virtue'. In response to allegations of indecency
and blasphemy, he insisted that his book was 'dramatic, many-faced,
multifarious'. A letter to W. M. Rossetti indicates that there was more
logic than candour in this defence; for while the objectionable poems
indisputably are dramatic, they are also rooted in Swinburne's convictions and sensibility. Swinburne supplies interpretations of the two
called 'especially horrible'—'Anactoria' and 'Dolores'—indicating a
relationship between 'Dolores' and 'Hesperia' and 'The Garden of
Proserpine', the last two of which were not among the poems
harshly criticized. He touches upon 'Faustine', 'Laus Veneris', and

'Hermaphroditus', but he does not mention two poems that were bitterly assailed, 'Les Noyades' and 'The Leper'. Though *Notes* (No. 11) has seemed to some recent students to be slightly disingenuous, most modern readers have applauded Swinburne's declaration that 'the question at issue is wider than any between a single writer and his critics. . . . Literature, to be worthy of men, must be large, liberal, sincere; and cannot be chaste if it be prudish.'

Swinburne's 'clear and defiant exposition of faith', as he described it, could not be expected to placate the reviewers. The *Examiner* did preface extended quotations from it with a statement that Swinburne's explanations would only humiliate those who required them, but the *Pall Mall Gazette* and the *Quarterly Review* were among several periodicals which found unsatisfactory Swinburne's explanation that the poems are dramatic. Why dramatize such subjects? The *Spectator* maintained that 'Mr. Swinburne fastens on such subjects [the morbid and sensual] and feasts on them with a greedy and cruel voracity, like a famished dog at raw meat'.[28] On 10 November *Punch* declared: 'Having read Mr. Swinburne's defence of his prurient poetics, *Punch* hereby gives him his royal licence to change his name to what is evidently its true form—SWINE-BORN.'

Without any prompting from Swinburne, W. M. Rossetti had decided to enter the fray in behalf of his friend. Avoiding mere contentiousness and not attempting to deny the limitations and vulnerable aspects of the volume, he embarked upon a cool and sensible analysis of the currents of thought and influence in *Poems and Ballads*, a title which he used in the title of his little book (No. 12). The moderation of its tone tended to conciliate those who disagreed with its conclusions. Among the admirers of its literary tact was the *Saturday Review*, which, along with the *Spectator* and the *London Review*, agreed with the author regarding Swinburne's literary genius but reaffirmed their objections to his subject-matter.[29]

When the volume was issued in the United States by G. W. Carleton of New York, 'Laus Veneris' was made the opening poem, and the title was changed to *Laus Veneris, and Other Poems and Ballads*, a title emphasizing 'the praise of Venus'. It was not surprising that President Noah Porter of Yale University referred to 'such lecherous priests of Venus as Algernon Swinburne'.[30] At this time the much-revered New England writers dominated the literary landscape. The highly respected Lowell wrote to E. C. Stedman on 26 November 1866: 'I have not seen Swinburne's new volume—but a poem or two from it which I have seen shocked me, and I am not squeamish. . . . I am too old to have a painted *hetaira* palmed off on me for a Muse, and I hold unchastity of mind to be worse than that of body. . . . *Virginibus puerisque?* To be sure! Let no man write a line that he would not have his daughter read. When a man begins to lust after the Muse instead of loving her, he may be sure that it is never the Muse that he embraces. The true Church of poetry is founded on a rock, and I have no fear that these smutchy back-doors of hell shall prevail against her.'[31]

On 29 November the publisher Carleton, who stated that he had published *Laus Veneris, and Other Poems and Ballads* on 3 November, was advertising a new printing—'the sixth thousand'—and announced the sale of the American edition of *Notes on Poems and Reviews* for ten cents a copy. Between 29 December 1866 and 10 January 1867 he made six times the statement that he had been unable to meet the demand. Since Carleton sent Swinburne no royalties, Longfellow later informed the poet that he had been cheated out of a large sum.[32] Gosse's statement that Carleton finally withdrew the book because of criticism cannot be true, since copies of later dates than 1867, with his imprint, are known. Some American readers learned about the English reception of *Poems and Ballads*, for John Morley's review was reprinted in the *Eclectic Magazine*, and the one in the *London Review* reappeared in *Littel's Living Age*.[33] On 3 November the *New York Times* condemned the book as combining the lowest lewdness with the most outrageous blasphemy, though conceding the power and beauty of Swinburne's language; but that paper also declared that 'the indecent literature of the day' would include *Adam Bede* and Charles Reade's latest novel. A passage in this review illustrates why Swinburne later wrote to E. C. Stedman that he had read in American journals remarks about his 'debility and puny proportions': 'He is a weak young person physically, and if we must allow his claim to be possessed with seven devils of uncleanness, we must also maintain that they have left him only a dreamy Don Juan after all. One sickens of his incessant efforts to be mistaken for a libertine.'

Feeling that he understood the allusions in *Poems and Ballads* better than some readers, George Henry Boker, the Philadelphia writer now remembered chiefly for his play *Francesca da Rimini*, wrote in a letter to the Southern poet Paul Hamilton Hayne: 'The fellow is morally so foul—not sensuous or sensual, but absolutely foul. . . . You cannot understand a tenth part of the horrible allusions in Swinburne's poetry.

I confess that my physical stomach turns at the beast, despite his genius:
—nay, that makes him the greater monster.'[34]

The most notable American defender of *Poems and Ballads* was the
Shakespearean scholar Richard Grant White, writing in the *Galaxy* for
1 December 1866. Though White admitted that no previous poet had
sung the praise of Venus with such frankness and fervour, he refused
to admit that Swinburne's poetry contained anything 'vulgar, or
coarse, or even immodest'. An unusually fair review also appeared in
the *Nation*, which deprecated Swinburne's choice of characters but
insisted that his greatness as an artist was indisputable.[35]

W. M. Rossetti remembered, as an example of the hostility to *Poems
and Ballads*, that the owner of an expensive painting had a cat eliminated
from it because Swinburne, in discussing the painting, had praised the
animal.[36] Nothing quite so picturesque can be told of Swinburne's
admirers, who included many of the young. The poet James Thomson
felt sure that any book incurring the displeasure of the *Saturday Review*
ought to be hailed with rejoicing.[37] The future author of *The City of
Dreadful Night* was of course to assume a leading position among the
poetic pessimists. A more important man of letters, Thomas Hardy,
who also had a dark view of the cosmic scheme, may have needed no
confirmation of his views, for his 'Hap'—a sonnet about the baffling
ways of 'Crass Casualty'—is dated 1866. After Swinburne's death
Hardy wrote the most effective poetic tribute to him, 'A Singer
Asleep', remembering the impact of *Poems and Ballads*,

> It was as though a garland of red roses
> Had fallen about the hood of some smug nun.

'A Refusal' (1924) dealt with the scruples of 'the grave Dean of Westminster' in accepting for the Abbey the memorializing of certain poets
—Byron, next Shelley, and, to cap the climax,

> Then—what makes my skin burn,
> Yea, forehead to chin burn—
> That I ensconce Swinburne!

Hardy himself was to be more successful than Swinburne in being
'ensconced'.[38]

Comments by well-known men of letters are cited in No. 14. These
do not include some by Swinburne's lesser followers, such as Philip
Bourke Marston and John Payne, or later admirers, such as John

Davidson or Alfred Noyes, and take no account of a poetic revolution that reached to distant lands, affecting such poets as Adam Lindsay Gordon and Henry Clarence Kendall in Australia and Sir Alfred Lyall in India, to say nothing of dozens of now forgotten poets.

George Saintsbury's mention (No. 26) of having read *Poems and Ballads* at Oxford reminds us of the enthusiasm of university students. Gosse has recorded that at Cambridge young men joined hands and marched along chanting 'Dolores' or 'A Song in Time of Revolution'.[39] Swinburne welcomed the admiration of the young and playfully assumed the role ascribed to him: '. . . please imagine me stalking triumphant through the land and displaying on every Hearth and in every Home the banner of immorality, atheism, and revolution' (from a letter of 22 December 1872).[40]

*Poems and Ballads* was henceforth the book predominantly associated with the name of Swinburne. Something of its vogue may be judged by the number of printings. According to Wise, who was fallible as well as sometimes untrustworthy, there were six 'editions' by 1873 and thirty-nine between 1875 and 1916.[41]

## III

It will hardly seem strange that critics objected to Swinburne's ideas or to the alleged absence of ideas. Matthew Arnold probably expressed a point of view congenial to his time (and to many in ours) when he conceived of great poetry as dealing with ideas that are in the broadest sense 'moral'—'the powerful and beautiful application of ideas to life' being a central aim. The nineteenth century was also inclined to let its judgment of art be much affected by knowledge of the artist. When, as late as 1905, Paul Elmer More confessed his temperamental lack of sympathy with Swinburne, he added, 'I should feel much easier in my appreciation of the *Poems and Ballads* if I knew how far they were based on the actual experience of the author.'[42] Instead of attempting to establish that the poet's nature is irrelevant to judgment of his work, one may assume that good poetry implies that its author possesses beauties of personality, if not of character, that are hidden rather than obvious. However that may be, authors cannot escape being judged by their conduct or supposed conduct, as repeated controversies about Byron remind us.

Henry Adams's admiring and vivid portrait and Bayard Taylor's letter (No. 3) give varying impressions of Swinburne's personality. A brief statement by William Hardman in December 1862 shows why the poet's conversation could strike some observers as offensive: '. . . although almost a boy, he upholds the Marquis de Sade as the acme and apostle of perfection, without (as he says) having read a word of his works. Now the Marquis de Sade was a most filthy, horrible, and disgusting rascal, a disgrace to humanity. . . . No one is fonder of good sound bawdry than I (or you), yet the Marquis completely bowls me over. . . . The assembled company evidently received Swinburne's tirades with ill-concealed disgust, but they behaved to him like a spoiled child.'[43] After he read them, as well as before, Sade's novels appealed to Swinburne's sense of humour, however misguided, and his jokes about the Marquis became chronic and more tiresome than, for example, his many allusions to Dickens's Mrs. Gamp. One may account for such an effect at least partly by the poet's algolagnia—a pathological tendency to associate eroticism and pain, which was noted by some early readers—in 'Dolores', for instance, and as a non-Sapphic intrusion in 'Anactoria' (a poem of which as late as 1909 Arnold Bennett wrote that Swinburne had enshrined 'in the topmost heights of its [England's] literature a lovely poem that cannot be discussed').[44] Swinburne had acquired a morbid interest in flagellation as a result of his floggings at Eton, and his frustration in a love affair may well, as Georges Lafourcade, his French biographer, suggested, have prevented a more mature emotional development. But Lafourcade was misled by Edmund Gosse's account of this affair, and some facts deserve incidental attention. Several years ago John S. Mayfield proved Gosse's identification of Swinburne's early sweetheart as Jane Faulkner to be incorrect, since she was only ten years old in 1862 (when Gosse said Swinburne proposed to her) and did not marry till 1871. Cecil Y. Lang has plausibly identified Swinburne's cousin, Mary Gordon, later Mrs. Disney Leith, as the object of his affection, and shown that Gosse misread 'The Triumph of Time' as a record of his emotional experience,[45] also reflected in other poems.

Changing attitudes towards Swinburne's expression of his eccentric sexual sensibility, which, after all, is expressed in only a small quantity of his work, underline a striking change in the interests and outlooks of two different generations. While in 1866 W. M. Rossetti indicated disapproval of Swinburne's association of eroticism and pain, that association was made the corner-stone of Lafourcade's interpretation in *La Jeunesse de Swinburne* (1928). In 1938 Lafourcade contributed to the *London Mercury* an article in which he reaffirmed his view of Swinburne's 'modernity' and the sincerity of his inspiration because of having given expression to his peculiar sexual sensibility.[46] But it seems more important that Swinburne wrote of many kinds of love, sometimes nobly, than that he occasionally voiced a tendency peripheral in human experience.

Swinburne's brief friendship with Adah Isaacs Menken, the much-married and somewhat tawdry performer in *Mazeppa* at Astley's Theatre, who associated with a number of literary men, is also a source of legend. A photographer took a picture of her and the poet together and sold a number of copies. Swinburne's relatives objected, and early in 1868 steps were taken to stop the sale. Scurrilous publications like the *Hornet* and the *Tomahawk* catered to the scandal-loving public by dealing with the 'liaison'. Numerous writers have suggested that Adah Menken inspired 'Dolores', though there is no evidence that Swinburne had met the actress before the poem was written and some evidence that he had not.[47] The name Dolores (in Latin, 'pains', 'sorrows') was obviously chosen for Swinburne's Anti-Madonna, 'Our Lady of Pain', because of its meaning, not because the name was sometimes used by (or for) the actress. In her album Swinburne inscribed some French verses entitled 'Dolorida', but evidence shows that they had been previously composed;[48] furthermore, Alfred de Vigny, a poet whose work Swinburne knew, had used the title 'Dolorida' for a poem, and so that title is less likely to have had any personal reference for Swinburne. An American author, Fulton Oursler, wrote a novel, *The World's Delight* (1929), concerned with the career of Adah Menken, in the last four chapters of which Swinburne has an important role. There is no factual basis for the incidents described.

Another American novelist, Mrs. Gertrude Atherton, took legend seriously, for she admitted that she had in mind the supposed effect of alcohol on Swinburne's inspiration when she wrote her novel *The Gorgeous Isle* (1908), introducing a poet named Byam Warner, who has never written a good line except under the influence of brandy.[49] When Warner's wife discovers that his inspiration depends upon strong drink, she leaves him alone in a room with some liquor. Though Swinburne was an alcoholic up to the time he decided to live at The Pines with Watts-Dunton, there is no evidence that brandy was a poetic stimulus.[50] According to Gosse, a small quantity of liquor could lead to loss of self-control and subsequent obliviousness of events that had happened under its influence.[51] The verses published in 1866 in the *Spectator* (No. 9), signed 'Caliban' but written by Robert Buchanan, portray a drunken Swinburne. In 1876 Buchanan stated that he had merely been dramatizing the effect of *Poems and Ballads*; clearly he was not describing an actual occasion, though apparently some readers and even a recent biographer have assumed otherwise. During his long controversy with Swinburne, F. J. Furnivall, the irascible scholar, once referred to the poet as a 'drunken clown'. Swinburne's drinking was in his early years obviously a source of much gossip.

Legend also coloured the reputation of Swinburne in France, where he was proud to be recognized; in 1872, when he was asked to contribute to a memorial volume in honour of Théophile Gautier, he felt he had 'in Parisian literary circles a recognized position among contemporary French poets'. He corresponded with Stéphane Mallarmé, the leader of the Symbolists, and was invited to contribute to the *République des Lettres*, the first issue of which (20 December 1875) contained a translation of 'The Pilgrims'. Paul Verlaine is said to have learned English before 1873 in order to read his poetry.[52] An earlier influential article in the *Revue des Deux Mondes* (15 May 1867) by Louis Étienne had as its subject '*Le Paganisme Poétique en Angleterre*', in which the author shows how different Swinburne's 'paganism' is from that of Keats and that of ancient times. He contrasts the more temperate poem of Sappho, for example, with Swinburne's expanded paraphrase in 'Anactoria', in which the combination of passion and violence seems alien to Sappho. He describes Swinburne's work as too full of revolt against the gods to be Greek, remarking that the poet's impiety reminds one of fanatical Calvinists of an older era. This intelligent article may well have given Swinburne pause; in 'Matthew Arnold's New Poems' he does refer to 'M. Louis Étienne, who lately laid lance in rest against me unoffending in championship of the higher powers'. Some French men of letters, like Paul Bourget, the novelist, who regarded Swinburne as a great European poet, also dwelt upon Swinburne's 'paganism' but did not limit the application of the term as Étienne did.[53]

In 1891 appeared Gabriel Mourey's prose translation of *Poems and Ballads*, introduced by 'Notes on Algernon Charles Swinburne' by Guy de Maupassant (No. 24). Maupassant knew little of Swinburne's poetry but, as a youth of eighteen, had met George Powell, Swinburne's friend, and later, after the poet's narrow escape from drowning, the poet himself. The undercurrent that swept Swinburne out to sea was destined to affect his image in France, since the incident resulted in Maupassant's being invited to Powell's cottage, where the young man formed the impressions of which he later wrote. He found the poet's appearance startling and described it more fully than did Taine, who during his visit to England in 1871 had noted Swinburne's enthusiasm for modern French literature and also the 'incessant convulsive movement of the members as if he had the delirium tremens. ... His style is that of a sick visionary who, as system, looks for sensation.'[54] Maupassant gave other writers, including his master Flaubert, his impressions of Swinburne. A conversation during which Maupassant told of observing the English poet at Étretat is recorded by Edmond de Goncourt in his *Journal* on 28 February 1875. Goncourt, himself something of a neurotic, was extremely curious about oddities of character and a lover of gossip; he, too, made a slight contribution to the Swinburne legend in France.[55] It is perhaps of more interest that, partly because of Maupassant, in that country Swinburne came to be regarded as '*un Edgar Poe "fin de siècle"* '.

Eileen Souffrin, from whom this phrase is quoted, also points out that in 1891 Pierre Louÿs had asked Swinburne to contribute to the *Conque* and that the poet had responded with his 'Ballad of Melicertes', a ballade honouring Théodore de Banville, who had recently died. A young Symbolist poet, Francis Vielé-Griffin, published during the nineties a translation of 'Laus Veneris'. No doubt Swinburne's vogue in France owed something to his enthusiasm for Hugo, Baudelaire, Gautier, Banville and other French authors, making his work seem more congenial and leading to some correspondence and in a few instances to personal contacts. The most important translation of Swinburne on the Continent was by Mourey, and we should not overlook the effect of Maupassant's 'Notes' for its reflection of Swinburne's image in France.

Mourey's translation of *Poems and Ballads* was important in Italy, too, where Gabriele d'Annunzio and others found it stimulating.[56] Tancredi Galimberti's speech in the Italian Parliament in 1903, recognizing his 'lifelong love of Italy', was a source of pleasure to Swinburne,[57] who would have been pleased by the tributes in the Italian press after his death in 1909.

Swinburne received less recognition in Germany. There was a translation of *Atalanta* into German in 1878. Theodore Opitz translated *Bothwell, Mary Stuart*, and *Marino Faliero*, but apparently none of these translations has been published.[58]

## IV

Memories of *Poems and Ballads* often created a prejudice against Swinburne's new work. Most reviews of *A Song of Italy* (1867) and *Ode on the Proclamation of the French Republic* (1870) were either cold or hostile. The *Saturday Review* denounced both volumes; poverty of thought, excessive verbiage, and subordination of sense to sound were mentioned as recurring faults. The charge of Red Republicanism was also brought forward.[59]

Swinburne's prose essays in the *Fortnightly Review*, then edited by John Morley, the vigorous assailant of *Poems and Ballads* but now his friend (a letter indicates that Swinburne was aware of the identity of that assailant), won a certain recognition, though some reviewers scanned Swinburne's prose for lurking impropriety. Between 1867 and 1870 the *Contemporary Review* was conspicuously hostile, publishing H. A. Page's 'The Morality of Literary Art' in June 1867 and 'The Immoral Theory of Art' by R. St. John Tyrwhitt in August of the same year.[60] Both articles denounced Swinburne. Peter Bayne's 'Mr. Arnold and Mr. Swinburne' in November now charged that 'Mr. Swinburne makes *Atalanta in Calydon* the vehicle of a vociferous atheism, obtrusively blasphemous'.[61]

In 1869 Alfred Austin, a future poet laureate, notorious as the author of some of the most prosaic lines written by a claimant to that title, published in *Temple Bar*[62] a series of magazine articles, collected in the following year as *The Poetry of the Period*, in which he paints a glowing picture of Byron's poetry as a contrast to effeminate contemporary verse, referring to 'those falsetto notes which appear to compose most of Mr. Swinburne's emasculated poetic voice' (No. 13). In 'the Austin creature's literary evacuations' Swinburne could discover 'no varying degrees of imbecility',[63] and in *Under the Microscope* he devoted attention to Austin's attack.

Of all his books, *Songs before Sunrise* (1871) was the one that Swinburne considered most important and that, as he explained in a letter to E. C. Stedman, contained most of himself. 'At an early age, without teaching or example, I became convinced of the truth and justice of the republican principle.'[64] Gosse, while admitting the merits of *Songs before Sunrise*, was unable to appreciate the depth of Swinburne's feelings for Italy and for the ideal republic. Was not Italy a foreign country to Swinburne? Critics like John Bailey and Samuel C. Chew[65] have understood the book much better. Chesterton's cavil that the sunrise did not become factual seems irrelevant to those readers aware of the Republic as a deathless ideal, one which incarnates not merely Swinburne's political faith but his vision of the 'lamplit race' that forms a part of the human story.

The use of *Songs before Sunrise* by Professor W. K. Clifford to illustrate his lecture on 'Cosmic Emotion' (1877) (see No. 22) was a landmark in the appreciation of that volume and a stimulus to later critics.

A slight majority of the reviews of *Songs before Sunrise*, which was issued by F. S. Ellis, was predominantly hostile. On 14 January 1871 the *Saturday Review* again assailed Swinburne vehemently, comparing him to a naughty little boy rolling in a puddle, who, kept out of one puddle, finds another as muddy (No. 15). 'Much as he delights in what used in our younger days to be called blasphemy, he delights still more, if that were possible, in the reddest of Red Republicanism.' To most reviewers the 'Hymn of Man' and 'Before a Crucifix' were the most offensive poems in the volume, supporting allegations of blasphemy and atheism. The *Academy* (No. 17), the *Fortnightly Review*, the *Westminster Review*, and *Tinsley's Magazine* emphasized the merits of *Songs before Sunrise*, especially its sublimity and singing power.[66] The American edition of the book, brought out by Roberts Brothers, was almost completely ignored.

Swinburne's adaptation of the language of the Bible, as in *Songs before Sunrise*, was offensive to many readers. This we see in the controversy over the sonnets headed 'The Saviour of Society', which appeared in the *Examiner* for 17 May 1873. The title was of course ironic, being intended to focus attention on the presumptuous claims on behalf of Napoleon III, called 'the Saviour of Society' by enthusiastic followers. The *Spectator* for 24 May—apparently the editor, Richard Holt Hutton, long kept a disapproving eye on his former contributor—unmindful of the import of the phrase, which referred to Napoleon and not to Christ, described the sonnets as 'a deadly and indecent insult to the faith of the vast majority of Christians'. Swinburne was sincere in confuting the 'imbecile dishonesty'—not 'honest imbecility', he added—that would attribute blasphemy to him, and he addressed a letter to the *Spectator* and two to the *Examiner*.[67] Both D. G. Rossetti and Theodore Watts had misgivings about the likely effect of the sonnets (in a series entitled 'Dirae', but when they were published along with 'A Song of Italy' and the 'Ode on the Proclamation of the French Republic' in *Songs of Two Nations* (1875), the angry attack was not renewed. Swinburne's adaptation of biblical language, natural to a man familiar with the Prayer Book from boyhood and one who greatly admired the beauty of the King James version, aroused opposition throughout his lifetime.

The most important of the articles preceding Swinburne's second formal reply to critics, *Under the Miscroscope*, is 'The Fleshly School of Poetry', signed 'Thomas Maitland', in the *Contemporary Review* for October 1871—really by Robert Buchanan, who expanded his material in a pamphlet, *The Fleshly School of Poetry, and Other Phenomena of the Day* (1872). D. G. Rossetti is the chief target of the article, Swinburne being censured for 'hysteric tone and overloaded style' and other peculiarities he is said to share with Rossetti. *Poems and Ballads* was more blasphemous than anything in Rossetti, Buchanan explains, but 'it was only a little mad boy letting off squibs'. Buchanan's use of a pseudonym and his reference to his own work proved embarrassing to him. He finally published in the *Athenaeum* a letter admitting his authorship and claiming that his name had been suppressed through an 'inadvertence'—a claim inconsistent with his declaration in his preface to the later pamphlet, that his name had been omitted 'in order that the criticism might rest upon its own merits'. This letter was printed along with one from the publishers of the *Contemporary Review* which still sought to disguise Buchanan's authorship. These circumstances, which led D. G. Rossetti to respond with his article on 'the stealthy school of criticism' and which explain some ironical passages in Swinburne's *Under the Microscope*, were discreditable to Buchanan and weakened his position. His article popularized a phrase, 'the fleshly school', but its remarks about Swinburne were no harsher than many attacks preceding it, including Buchanan's anonymous review of 1866 (No. 7). An article in the *Edinburgh Review* for July 1871 had denounced *Poems and Ballads* with all the bitterness of the earliest reviewers, using again such catchwords as obscurity, sensuality, blasphemy. The part dealing with *Songs before Sunrise* comes near to paralleling Buchanan's article in associating Swinburne with 'the sensational school of literature' and finding his work to be derived from the 'corrupted French school' (No. 16).

Buchanan's pamphlet dwells upon the obligations of 'the fleshly school' to French authors, in particular ridiculously overstating Swinburne's indebtedness to Baudelaire: 'All that is worst in Mr. Swinburne belongs to Baudelaire. The offensive choice of subject, the obtrusion of unnatural passion, the blasphemy, the wretched animalism, are all taken intact out of *Les Fleurs de* [*sic*] *Mal.*' Students of Swinburne's early writings will recognize the absurdity of this statement,[68] calculated to appeal to the current prejudice against French literature, which not infrequently led to the banning of French novels from parlours and libraries. But the reviews of Buchanan's pamphlet were not as favourable as he hoped. Even the *Saturday Review* condemned it for flippancy, arrogance, and bad temper, intimating, too, that Buchanan had collected salacious passages in order to increase interest in his book.

Other articles preceding Swinburne's *Under the Microscope*, which was partly concerned with the relative merits of the two English poets, included 'Byron and Tennyson' in the *Quarterly Review*, unsigned but written by Abraham Hayward; this article, like the critique by Alfred Austin, compared Tennyson unfavourably with Byron. Swinburne may well have been incorrect in his assumption that a hostile review of *Songs before Sunrise* in the *Quarterly Review* was also by Hayward,[69] a review censuring him on familiar grounds, emphasizing atheism and remoteness from human interests. It, too, is among the articles of which *Under the Microscope* took account.

Since that work contains Swinburne's most sustained invective, the poet's characteristic way of responding to his critics deserves consideration here. His letter to Theodore Watts on 4 May 1877 sets forth his code for dealing with personal attacks: 'That except in quite exceptional cases a gentleman is equally bound *not* to take notice of an anonymous insult, and to chastise any insult which is *not* anonymous'. He thought Tennyson's sensitivity to critics deplorable and wrote in 'Changes of Aspect':[70] 'And those who quail and wail and wince and spit and sputter when attacked—who do not hit straight back, and whip their insulters openly out on the courses—dishonour the standard with which they must be supposed to wish that their names should be associated.' Since he was the object of many attacks, Swinburne often exercised his own power of invective. Much of it was direct and hard-hitting, as in such phrases as 'the drivelling desperation of venomous or fangless duncery', 'dirty and dwarfish creatures of simian intellect and facetious idiocy', 'the most horny-eyed and beetle-headed of pedants'. Like most of those who engage in flyting or satire, Swinburne draws comparisons from the animal world: 'This stupid piece of obscure and clumsy jargon could have been the work of no man endowed with more faculty of expression than informs or modulates the whine of an average pig.' A more famous example of the device is perhaps Swinburne's reply to Emerson's alleged comments (No. 14, d). Mythological allusions, too, give point to his barbs. A detractor of Byron, Mrs. Stowe, appears as 'a blatant Bassarid of Boston, a rampant Maenad of Massachusetts' and a 'plume-plucked Celaeno'. As a versifier George Eliot offers 'the pitiful and unseemly spectacle of an Amazon thrown sprawling over the crupper of her spavined and spur-galled Pegasus'.

Simple name-calling may be either crude or subtle. Swinburne's name for Carlyle, 'St. Thomas Coprostom, late of Craigenputtock and Chelsea', is appropriate for one who, as Swinburne recalled, held his nose over 'Eternal Cesspools'; Carlyle, who used that phrase, had apparently described Swinburne as a man standing in a cesspool (No. 14, d). 'Coprostom', combining 'copro-' and 'Tom', recalls the analogy of 'St. Chrysostom', the Greek church father. Probably Lowell's criticism of *Atalanta* was in Swinburne's mind when he characterized Clough, whom Lowell praises in that review, as 'the weary and wearisome laureate of Oxonicules and Bostonicules', Lowell qualifying as the latter and perhaps Arnold as the former.

While Swinburne's invective is occasionally powerful and often amusing even when rather obviously rhetorical, his liking for it was costly for the *Examiner* when Buchanan sued that periodical in 1876 for publishing 'The Devil's Due', which Swinburne wrote under the impression that Buchanan was the author of a verse passage derogatory to him, a passage really written by the Earl of Southesk. Nor was the public impression of Swinburne bettered by his embroilment in various controversies which it would be tedious to describe. A comment he wrote during the most prolonged of these, that with the irascible scholar F. J. Furnivall, illustrates Swinburne's zest for the fray: Swinburne acknowledged Furnivall's Chaucerian scholarship but almost breathlessly proclaimed his 'monumental, his pyramidal, his Cyclopean, his Titanic, his superhuman and supernatural nescience of everything and of anything that could give him the faintest shadow of a moment's right to put forth the humblest whisper of a neophyte's suggestion on the simplest and most insignificant subject connected with the text of Shakespeare'.[71] It is not strange that *Punch* poked fun at the language Swinburne used in one of his essays (see No. 28).

Just as Swinburne explained that *Notes on Poems and Reviews* is a set of casual notes on his own poems such as Byron and Coleridge wrote on theirs, he liked to think of *Under the Microscope* as concerned with the relative merits of Byron and Tennyson, as well as with the merits and limitations of Whitman. Some of his chief critics—for example, Alfred Austin and the *Quarterly Review*—had compared the first two poets. Austin and Buchanan, to say nothing of Swinburne's friend W. M. Rossetti, had expressed varying opinions on the American bard. The passage from *Under the Microscope* cited below (No. 18), one of Swinburne's most triumphant bits of invective, shows how successfully he could turn Buchanan's own words against him.

To Buchanan was reserved the final severe scourging. Early in *Under the Microscope* Swinburne had contemptuously dismissed the 'anonyms' and 'coprophagi', probably thinking of personal attacks like that by Buchanan's friend Mortimer Collins, whose novel *Two Plunges for a Pearl* (1871) was issued both anonymously as a serial in *London Society* and as a book of acknowledged authorship. In its fourteenth chapter appears Reginald Swynfen, portrayed as vain, diminutive, eccentric in his manners, alliterative in conversation—a character finally humiliated after his presumptuous wooing of a woman who drops him into a deep hole. The defamatory characterization was approved in some circles, whose stories about Swinburne's personal convictions James Hain Friswell had admitted having in mind when, in *Modern Men of Letters Honestly Criticized* (1870), he described Swinburne as possessed of two devils—'incontinence' and 'an arrogant rebellion against God'.

## V

Reviewers of *Bothwell* (1874), issued by Chatto & Windus, Swinburne's publisher during the rest of his lifetime, tended to be generous, though several of them found the play too long and not suitable for the theatre. The *Saturday Review*, admitting that 'there is nothing here to gratify the prurient or to alarm the prudish', adds, 'His earlier writing, amid much that was rank and noisome, contains also much that was noble and beautiful.'[72] An unsigned article by John Morley in *Macmillan's Magazine* commends Swinburne's power of imagination and respect for historic truth, though, like most reviewers, Morley found the play too long. There was no American edition of *Bothwell*.

Swinburne's other drama of the seventies, *Erechtheus* (1876), won almost unanimous approval.[73] The author may have made this play more like the ancient Greek drama in tone because of the criticism of

*Atalanta* as un-Greek. The *Dedicatory Epistle* to his *Collected Poems* (1904) indicates the poet's conviction that in *Erechtheus* the whole is greater than the parts. In general, critics of his plays have dwelt upon the excellence of parts rather than of the whole. His least successful play, *The Sisters* (1892), attempts realistic portrayal of contemporary life, but most of his plays, as he remarked in reviewing them, were written 'with a view to their being acted at the Globe, the Red Bull, or the Black Friars'. In his *Dedicatory Epistle*, just quoted, Swinburne comments on the 'generally ungracious' reception of *Mary Stuart* (1881), which most reviewers considered undramatic.[74] Some compared *Marino Faliero* (1885) with Byron's play thus entitled, but few considered it dramatic rather than lyrical. *Locrine* (1887) was praised for its poetic beauties. *Rosamund, Queen of the Lombards* (1899), more rapid, concise and restrained than the other dramas, seemed to be an attempt to guard against the diffuseness of which critics often complained. It was hardly successful, though some commended its craftsmanship, and W. C. Brownell, the American critic, called it 'a tragedy of incontestable power'. The last of the tragedies, *The Duke of Gandia* (1908), in spite of some dramatic intensity, was an inconspicuous failure.

A brief consideration of Swinburne's prose also seems appropriate here. The first important prose work, *William Blake* (1868), had been begun five years before its publication. It introduced modern appreciation of Blake, and reviewers unfamiliar or unsympathetic with that writer thought that Swinburne overrated Blake or had paid too much attention to the prophetic books. They also quarrelled with his views on morality and art. Notices in the *Fortnightly Review* (by Moncure D. Conway) and in the *Examiner* were the most friendly.[75]

Most English reviewers of *Essays and Studies* (1875), one of Swinburne's more important critical works, were also friendly. Swinburne marvelled that the *Spectator* and the *Pall Mall Gazette*, 'which never before agreed except in abuse of me now agree in my praises!'[76] The *Quarterly Review* objected to Swinburne's severity regarding an emendation of Shelley and to his excessive praise of Hugo, Rossetti, and Morris. The *North American Review*, whose reviewer could not forget *Poems and Ballads*, mingled personal abuse with comments on the new volume.

A book published during the following year, *A Study of Victor Hugo*, being unrestrained panegyric, has lowered Swinburne's reputation as a critic. The *New York Daily Tribune* of 21 February 1886 commented that Hugo must have been a sacrament, since Swinburne spoke of 'the bread of his deathless word and the wine of his immortal song'. Swinburne's uncritical praise of Hugo in this book adversely influenced the reception of *Miscellanies* (also 1886).

In his appreciation of the Brontës, as in his criticism of Blake, Swinburne was again in advance of his time. While preparing *A Note on Charlotte Brontë* (1877), the poet did not forget remarks by the *Quarterly Review*, probably including those on *Essays and Studies*, for he recalled 'the memorable infamy and imbecility' of the notorious *Quarterly Review* article on *Jane Eyre*, and enlarged on the shortcomings of that article. In deprecating Swinburne's comparison of Charlotte Brontë and George Eliot, Edward Dowden had some misgivings, reflecting that 'possibly it [Dowden's review in the *Academy* of 8 September 1877] may secure me the distinction of being named an anthropoid ape, a polecat, or an aborted ascidian, in the next piece of dithyrambic prose which Swinburne writes'.

*George Chapman* (1875), *A Study of Shakespeare* (1880), and *A Study of Ben Jonson* were Swinburne's most notable books on Elizabethan drama.[77] Contemporary estimates of them mingled praise and detraction. In 1893 William Archer, who considered Swinburne the inheritor of the Charles Lamb tradition of dramatic criticism, emphasized Swinburne's insufficient regard for the dramatic point of view.[78] In the present century T. S. Eliot has paid tribute to what he characterized as Swinburne's almost unerring judgment of Elizabethan drama. The fact is that occasional over-indulgence in 'the noble pleasure of praising' and intemperate invective has tended to obscure Swinburne's merits as critic. Professor Oliver Elton has well stated the case for Swinburne's insight: 'It may seem wild to call him judicial; but if we can suppose a judge tossing up his wig and dancing a Border fling on the bench, while he shouts or flutes or shrieks out a balanced and penetrating summing up, ending perhaps with a lofty high-wrought peroration, we shall have some image of Swinburne's mode of criticism. . . . If he could have recomposed his pages on Byron into the key of his study of Congreve, he would have been more obviously what in fact he is, the acutest judge of drama and of lyrical poetry, and perhaps also of fiction, in his age.'[79] In recent years two books have been devoted to Swinburne's aesthetic theories and criticism—an indication that appreciation of his criticism has grown.[80]

Swinburne's contemporaries took little heed of his novel, *Love's Cross-Currents* (1905), though it was commended for its satire. Among recent critics Edmund Wilson has most warmly praised Swinburne's novels (including the so-called *Lesbia Brandon*, not published during Swinburne's lifetime), for their realistic portrayal of contemporary life and character.[81]

## VI

*Poems and Ballads: Second Series* (1878) met a reception very different from that of its predecessor in 1866. Writing anonymously in the *Athenaeum* (No. 23), Theodore Watts justifiably described it as the most priceless book of English poetry for many years. Conscious of recurring criticisms, he defended Swinburne's poetry as ethical and also sought to explain on technical grounds his abundant use of alliteration (incidentally, not found objectionable by the twentieth century in the work of Swinburne's contemporary, Gerard Manley Hopkins). In the following year, Watts, a shrewd solicitor with some literary talent, who had succeeded in making himself agreeable to Rossetti and other authors and who had already been helpful to Swinburne in his publishing arrangements, rescued him from almost certain death from alcoholism. In the twentieth century, partly because of Gosse's point of view, Watts-Dunton (as he was then called) became for some a scapegoat for whatever they did not like, whether it was Swinburne's poetic decline or some apparent change of opinion. If the examples of Wordsworth, Coleridge, and Arnold do not suggest that growing old may be accompanied by waning poetic power, other entirely satisfactory explanations are lacking. Swinburne's letters indicate that he retained his characteristic independence of judgment, and his writings reveal that his shifts in literary opinion are evolutionary, being mostly shifts of emphasis. Among the sympathetic sketches of Swinburne and Watts-Dunton at The Pines, Max Beerbohm's (No. 31) is the most attractive. Watts-Dunton did what he could for Swinburne's literary standing, as well as his health, and from 1877 to 1899 himself reviewed his friend's books in the *Athenaeum*.

Like Watts's, George Saintsbury's review of *Poems and Ballads: Second Series*, in the *Academy*,[82] was appreciative, extolling poems that have stood the test of time—'At a Month's End', 'Ave atque Vale', 'A Vision of Spring in Winter', 'A Forsaken Garden', and the song 'Love Laid His Sleepless Head'. Following the example of the *Athenaeum* and the *Academy*, most periodicals were cordial. The *Saturday Review*, to be sure, thought the volume a bit disappointing after *Erechtheus*, admitting that Swinburne is an artist in words but asking whether beautiful diction is enough.

Swinburne had gained an influential American champion in Edmund Clarence Stedman, who, in an anonymous article in *Scribner's Monthly* for March 1875, had praised him for *Atalanta*, for miraculous command of rhythm and literary culture. Paul Hamilton Hayne, the Southern poet, had sent a copy of Stedman's article to Swinburne. A correspondence between Stedman and Swinburne ensued, and Swinburne wrote what may well be his most autobiographical letter, with a value beyond its immediate use by its recipient. The estimate of Swinburne in Stedman's *Victorian Poets* (No. 20) speaks more highly of *Songs before Sunrise* and places Swinburne foremost among the new British poets. Aside from reviews, little else that was friendly had appeared in America except a sketch in *Appleton's Journal* for 2 April 1870 by the poet-critic Richard Henry Stoddard, who was to review *Poems and Ballads: Second Series* in the same magazine (October 1878), as well as to publish a volume of *Selections* in 1884. Despite such new evidence of friendliness in the United States, *Poems and Ballads: Second Series* met with more disfavour there than in England. Swinburne was remembered for little besides the *Poems and Ballads* of 1866; few American readers were familiar with *Songs before Sunrise* or *Erechtheus*. The *Nation* sermonized on Swinburne's supposed separation of art and morality. The *North American Review* followed suit, calling Swinburne's treatment of love 'bad morals for the average reader'.[83] The American reviews illustrate the tendency to admit Swinburne's mastery of the resources of language and rhythm but to question his originality, his profundity, and his ethical teaching. Some of the adverse criticism was apparently due to inclusion in the American edition of the Prelude and first canto of *Tristram of Lyonesse*.

As objections to Swinburne's poetry on moral grounds gradually diminished, aesthetic objections increased in vigour, partly because of the quality of later volumes. *Songs of the Springtides* (1880) contained two of his better poems—'Thalassius' and 'On the Cliffs' ('Thalassius', like its fellow, is 'a symbolical quasi-autobiographical poem after the fashion of Shelley or of Hugo').[84] *Songs of the Springtides* was also more highly favoured in England than in America. *Studies in Song* (1880) brought additional complaints of verbosity. Mastery of metre was said to be linked with thinness of substance. According to the *Spectator*,

'The idea is too slender to hold the magnificent tide of poetic expression.'[85] Nor did the *Spectator* relish its political invective. *A Midsummer Holiday and Other Poems* (1884) was obnoxious to some, welcome to others, for a poem aimed at the House of Lords; whereas in 1886 and 1887 and later the poet's conservative views on the Irish Question and on the Boers were offensive to the Liberals. *Poems and Ballads: Third Series* (1889) was more kindly received than *Studies in Song* or *A Midsummer Holiday and Other Poems* or than two later volumes—*Astrophel and Other Poems* (1894) and *A Channel Passage and Other Poems* (1904).

Though it was further evidence of the poet's dexterity, *A Century of Roundels* (1883) has not greatly added to his fame. It is otherwise with his two long narrative poems on Arthurian themes. The impact of *Tristram of Lyonesse and Other Poems* (1882) was probably softened, as Theodore Watts had hoped, by the inclusion of poems on children and Elizabethan dramatists. The story of Tristram had been Swinburne's 'delight (as far as a child could understand it) before I was ten years old,'[86] and his earlier version, *Queen Yseult*, had been begun while he was a student at Oxford. Although *Tristram of Lyonesse* is clearly one of his finer achievements, the *Saturday Review* pronounced the story barbarous and unsuited for modern treatment; while conceding that Swinburne had written many magnificent lines, the reviewer charged that some are rhetorical, some obscure, and some 'effusively erotic'. In similar vein, the *Spectator* complained that Swinburne 'paints the sensual appetite with a redundancy and excess that excite disgust'.[87]

The renaissance of splendour and energy in *The Tale of Balen* (1896), which made it, too, a high achievement, won commendation from English reviewers; the poem was less well received in the United States, where Swinburne had acquired a new champion, William Morton Payne (No. 27). In both *Tristram* and *The Tale of Balen* Swinburne had challenged comparison by using stories dealt with in Tennyson's *Idylls*. Contemporary critics did not recognize, as most modern critics would, the superiority of Swinburne's versions to Tennyson's.

In the eighties, satire of the so-called aesthetic movement in two plays— one of them the Gilbert and Sullivan comic opera *Patience*—as well as in many parodies and several numbers of *Punch*, reminds us that Swinburne's name was sometimes associated with aesthetes like Oscar Wilde, who usually expressed admiration for Swinburne but with whom his personal acquaintance was slight. In the nineties Swinburne's position as the leading English poet was clearly recognized. Articles on the poet-laureateship after the death of Tennyson mention Swinburne as deserving the honour. In a symposium appearing in 1895, twelve of nineteen writers named him as the desirable first choice.[88] *Poems and Ballads* was one of the reasons why Swinburne was not offered the post he would probably have refused; his anti-Russian writings and advocacy of tyrannicide seem also to have been remembered against him.[89] In 1896, thirty years after the appearance of the volume, the *Saturday Review* deplored the fact that Swinburne was still being judged by it, to the neglect of his later work, and explained the few regrettable early poems as the defiance of a youth eager to shock 'the dull respectabilities of the average Philistine'. Another article in the *Review* regarded the accusation of atheism as 'strangely perverse'.[90] 'Before a Crucifix', it affirmed, was aimed at 'the Roman Catholic travesty of the real Jesus of Nazareth'.

Thus though the *Saturday Review* had reversed its criticism, memories of *Poems and Ballads*, as well as of *Songs before Sunrise*, still beclouded judgment. In reviewing *The Tale of Balen*, the *Nation* (of New York) could not forget the earlier poems. In 1894 there appeared Marie Corelli's *The Sorrows of Satan*, which by 1897 (according to a title-page) had reached its thirty-fourth edition. Miss Corelli, the daughter of Charles Mackay and Mrs. Mary Elizabeth Mills and so half-sister of a poetaster named Eric Mackay (incidentally, an imitator of Swinburne unappreciated by him), had made her first public appearance in a programme of improvising musical interpretations, two of them of poems by Swinburne, before she began writing fiction. *The Sorrows of Satan* portrays the downfall of a beautiful woman who had read Swinburne, 'this satyr-songster', from whose 'Before a Crucifix' Miss Corelli introduces a long quotation (slightly inaccurate) in order to illustrate the blasphemous nature of his work. *The Sorrows of Satan* was not widely reviewed, for Miss Corelli's resentment of previous criticism had led her to ask her publisher not to send out review copies; but leading clergymen preached sermons praising the novel, which was read by many unfamiliar with Swinburne's poetry. Some contemporary articles express an equally hostile point of view.[91]

The enduring influence of *Poems and Ballads* is reflected in many other opinions. Lafcadio Hearn, lecturing at the University of Tokyo, ranked Swinburne as the greatest of modern poets in respect of form but as morally and philosophically a lesser figure than Browning or Tennyson, or even Rossetti. He recognized that the poet's fame was still limited by the notoriety of the early volume: 'It is the greatest lyric gift given to English literature, this book; but it is also, in some aspects, the most immoral book yet written by an English poet. . . . It is astonishing that the English public could have allowed the book to exist. Probably it was forgiven on account of its beauty.'[92]

In the early 1900s most criticism of Swinburne lost its sting. His old foes—the *Contemporary Review*, the *Quarterly Review*, and the *Edinburgh Review*—all published friendly articles.[93] The collected edition of his poems, the first volume of which appeared in England in 1904, was welcomed. The *Saturday Review* observed that probably reviewers would not even refer to 'the timid shrieks' of the sixties, and the *Athenaeum* condemned 'ignorant and illiterate persons' who supposed that the poet had attacked Christianity. Only the *Spectator* maintained that the critics of 1866 were right.[94] Among those who reviewed the collected poems was Oliver Elton (No. 30). In 1905 Harper and Brothers brought out the *Collected Poems* in the United States. In 1905, too, William Morton Payne published his *Selected Poems by Algernon Charles Swinburne*, a volume emphasizing the later poems. While recent critics have favoured *Songs before Sunrise* and the second series of *Poems and Ballads* more than the *Poems and Ballads* of 1866, some editors of selections (for instance, Edith Sitwell, an admirer of Swinburne's technique) have continued to choose mostly from the earlier poems.

In his *Dedicatory Epistle* to the *Collected Poems*, which Swinburne was planning as early as July of 1896 and which he had probably finished by 1902, the poet reviewed his writings, supplying, as in *Notes on Poems and Reviews*, comments on certain individual poems. He paid some attention to particular criticisms, such as, for instance, that the philosophic musings in *Tristram of Lyonesse* were anachronistic[95] or that he had idolized Mazzini and Hugo.[96] He trained his guns on two recurring general criticisms. With regard to the charge of bookishness, he affirmed that books are a valid source of inspiration, whatever they may be to 'the half-brained creature to whom books are other than living things'. Of the notion that his poems eclipse or sacrifice thought, he declared that 'except to such ears as should always be closed against poetry, there is no music in verse which has not sufficient fullness and ripeness of meaning, sufficient adequacy of emotion or of thought, to abide the analysis of any other than the blind scrutiny of prepossession or the squint-eyed inspection of malignity'. This, a poet's answer to a generation of critics, must not be too lightly dismissed. As I have written elsewhere,[97] Swinburne believed that the inner harmony of verse is based on the poet's interpretation of nature—a harmony springing from wholeness of vision. The early Swinburne, an admirer of Carlyle, had certainly read this sentence in *Heroes and Hero-Worship*: 'A *musical* thought is one spoken by a mind that has penetrated into the inmost heart of the thing; detected the inmost mystery of it, namely the *melody* that lies hidden in it; the inward harmony of coherence which is its soul.' In the same work is another sentence, one mentioning Swinburne's beloved Coleridge, of whose theories Swinburne had first-hand knowledge: 'Coleridge remarks very profoundly somewhere, that wherever you find a sentence musically worded, of true rhythm and melody in the words, there is something deep and good in the meaning too.'[98]

Apart from the fact that many of the later poems are of inferior quality, however technically skilful, the poet tended to repeat himself, having, as Edward Thomas declared, 'a harem of words to which he was constantly faithful'. Numerous imitators and parodists seldom reproduced more than mannerisms, though not without an enervating effect on the freshness of Swinburnian style. There were many parodies of choruses in *Atalanta* (Bret Harte's 'Plain Language from Truthful James', the 'heathen Chinee' poem, at least follows the stanzaic pattern of a passage in the play). But *Poems and Ballads* has inspired more parodies than other volumes by Swinburne, and 'Dolores' has inspired more than any other poem by its author. By far the most skilful parody of 'Dolores' was A. C. Hilton's 'Octopus' (No. 19).

But many commentators have perhaps oversimplified their separation of Swinburne's form and thought. Oliver Elton suggests the presence of *outline* as the criterion distinguishing Swinburne's good and bad poems: 'Swinburne is an inveterate waster; but then he has more lyric wealth to waste than almost anybody; he has as much as Shelley, more than Herrick, and more than Tennyson.'[99] Indeed T. S. Eliot mentions the poet's 'diffuseness' as sometimes a virtue: 'That so little material as appears to be employed in *The Triumph of Time* should release such an amazing number of words, requires what there is no reason to call anything but genius. . . . What he gives is not images and ideas and music, it is one thing with a curious mixture of suggestions of all three.' In his *Principles of Literary Criticism* (1925) I. A. Richards remarks, 'A dog is not a defective kind of cat, nor is Swinburne a defective kind of Hardy,' and he cites the notion that Swinburne lacks thought as an example of a popular critical fallacy.[100]

Eliot makes the point that Swinburne's 'language, uprooted, has adapted itself to an independent life of atmospheric nourishment'. A recent defender of Swinburne, John D. Rosenberg,[101] agrees—'Words, severed from the soil of things, send out aerial roots of their own'—but more emphatically defends the cumulative effect of Swinburne's metaphors and imagery, as in his comment on Eliot's criticism of the logic of 'time' and 'grief' in a famous chorus in *Atalanta*. The twentieth-century reversal of older points of view is well illustrated by praise of *Tristram of Lyonesse* as one of the most magnificent of 'erotic poems'; to read it merely as narrative or a 'drama of action' would be to make the same mistake as to approach Wagner's opera *Tristan und Isolde* in this way.

Though the vogue of the 'new critics' is passing, those especially intent on finding poetry suitable for analysis of ironies, paradoxes, and ambiguities have sometimes neglected Swinburne for the same reasons that they have undervalued his master Shelley. Swinburne would have appreciated the distinctions made by Elton, Eliot, and Richards as a flank attack on his unfriendly critics. What would he have thought of some other vagaries—of the whimsies, for example, of certain archetypal or psychoanalytic points of view? Would his reference in 'The Triumph of Time' to 'the great sweet mother' (the sea) be explicable by a tiresome Freudian formula or as a symptom of 'death craving'—an explanation less acceptable to the trained psychiatrist than to the literary critic? The man who loved the sea passionately from childhood and who may well have been aware that scientists have thought of the sea as the mother of life might have smiled; it seems more likely that he would have concocted some picturesque phrases about procrustean theorizing and misty befuddlement by scholiasts. Since current interest in eccentricities of personality and abnormal psychology may distort the central image of a writer's work, have some recent commentators repeated the misplaced emphasis of an earlier day? Swinburne's kind of poetic idiom is not now in style, and the anti-Romantic mood of the age has fostered a conception of poetry different from his, but he will abide detraction; for the beauty he created in his best work will not yield to anything so transient as literary fashion.

## NOTES

1. *The Swinburne Letters* (1959–62), ed. Cecil Y. Lang, i, 17, hereafter cited as 'Lang'.
2. Now accessible in *New Writings by Swinburne* (1964), ed. Cecil Y. Lang.
3. Lang, iii, 12.
4. Reviews, as mentioned, *London Review*, 8 April 1865, x, 382–3; *Fortnightly Review*, 15 May 1865, i, 75–80; *Athenaeum*, 1 April 1865, 450–1; *Spectator*, 15 April 1865, xxxviii, 412–14; *Edinburgh Review*, July 1865, cxxii, 202–16. For the statement about Lord de Tabley see Hugh Walker, *John B. Leicester Warren, Lord de Tabley* (1903), 13, 46, 52.
5. Maurice Baring, *The Puppet Show of Memory* (1923), 112.
6. *Nation*, 9 November 1865, i, 590–1.
7. *North American Review*, April 1866, cii, 544–55; reprinted in *My Study Windows* (1871).
8. Sir Edward Cook, *The Life of Florence Nightingale* (1913), ii, 95.
9. 'The Young Men', *Contemporary Review*, February 1894, lxv, 177–88.
10. According to T. J. Wise, *Atalanta* went through two English editions in 1865, one in 1866, 1868, and 1875, and sixteen between 1879 and 1917.
11. Lang, i, 142.
12. William Tinsley, *Random Recollections of an Old Publisher* (1900), i, 232–3.
13. *Letters to Macmillan*, ed. Simon Nowell-Smith (1967), 95–6. The verses mentioning Macmillan are printed in my *Swinburne's Literary Career and Fame* (1933), 44; they previously appeared in T. J. Wise's *Ashley Library*, vi, 187.
14. *Reader*, 2 December 1865, vi, 621–2.
15. *London Review*, 9 December 1865, xi, 621–2; *Spectator*, 2 December 1865, xxxviii, 1342–4; *Athenaeum*, 23 December 1865, 880–1; *Gentleman's Magazine*, March 1866, ccxx, 398 ff.; *Fortnightly Review*, 15 April 1866, iv, 533–43.
16. *Saturday Review*, 26 May 1866, xxi, 623–5.
17. *Nation*, 18 January 1866, 83–4.
18. *Spectator*, 31 March 1866, xxxix, 356–8; *Pall Mall Gazette* (in its review of *Chastelard*), 27 April 1866, 11–12; *Westminster Review*, July 1866, lxxxvi, 277.
19. *Letters of George Meredith* (1913), i, 183.
20. Lang, i, 139–40, note 1.
21. Lang, i, 141.
22. Quoted by Lang, i, 141, note 2.
23. A later favourable article, unsigned but by John Skelton, appeared in *Fraser's Magazine*, November 1866, lxxiv, 635–48.
24. Quoted in George S. Hellman, *The True Stevenson* (1925), 120.
25. Le Gallienne, in his review in the *North American Review*, 19 October 1906, clxxxiii, 793–5; Douglas in an article in *Chambers's Cyclopædia of English Literature* (1903), iii, 672–80.
26. Lang, i, 122.

27. Letter to Hotten, 10 October 1866; Lang, i, 199.

28. *Examiner*, 27 October 1866, 677; *Spectator*, 3 November 1866, xxxix, 1228–9.

29. *Saturday Review*, 17 November 1866, xxii, 600–1; *Spectator*, 24 November 1866, 1311–12; *London Review*, 1 December 1866, xiii, 610–11.

30. Unsigned article in *Hours at Home*, May 1869, ix, 47; reprinted in Porter's *Books and Reading* (1882).

31. *Letters of James Russell Lowell*, ed. Charles Eliot Norton (1894), i, 377.

32. Lang, iii, 16.

33. *Eclectic Magazine*, November 1866, iv, n.s., 556–60; *Littel's Living Age*, 8 September 1866, xc, 633–6.

34. Quoted from a letter in the Duke University Collection of Hayne MSS.

35. For a reference to the defence of Moncure D. Conway, see Lang, i, 205, and note 2.

36. *Some Reminiscences of William Michael Rossetti* (1906), 221.

37. 'The Swinburne Controversy', *National Reformer*, 23 December 1866, 403–4; reprinted in *Satires and Profanities* (1884).

38. According to Evelyn Hardy, *Thomas Hardy* (1954), 60, 'Apart from the Greek tragedians, the two writers who influenced him most in these formative years were Swinburne and Mill.' See also 71, 72.

39. *Life* (1917), 160–1.

40. Lang, ii, 216.

41. The figures come from T. J. Wise's *Bibliography* (the last edition was in the Bonchurch Edition, vol. xx). They are subject to revision.

42. In *Shelburne Essays: Third Series* (1905).

43. S. M. Ellis, *A Mid-Victorian Pepys* (1923), 78–9.

44. Arnold Bennett, *Books and Persons* (1917), 123–9, an article first printed in *New Age*.

45. 'Swinburne's Lost Love', *PMLA*, March 1959, lxxiv, 123–30.

46. Georges Lafourcade, 'Swinburne Vindicated', *London Mercury*, February 1938, xxxvii, 424–9.

47. From an unpublished letter from Adah Menken to Augustin Daly, written 6 December 1865 (shown to me by Mr. Edward B. Hall): 'I only go around with *old men*. They are generally "slow". But all the Bohemians, critics, and authors are old here. However, they are quite jolly. John Oxenford of *The Times* [is] my sole beau.' Swinburne's letter that mentions adding more stanzas to 'Dolores' is dated by Lang 'May or June 1865'.

48. See Wise's *Bibliography* (Bonchurch Edition, xx), 198–9.

49. A letter from Mrs. Atherton, quoted in my *Swinburne's Literary Career and Fame* (1933), 128, makes the association with Swinburne clear.

50. James Pope-Hennessy, *Monckton Milnes: The Flight of Youth* (1951), 134, expresses a contrary view: 'The necessity to Swinburne's work of the twin stimuli of alcohol and a sadistic fancy seems never to have dawned upon

Milnes' kindly mind.' Those who believe poetic inspiration to be necessarily associated with neurosis might with profit consult a book by an experienced psychiatrist, Lawrence S. Kubie's *Neurotic Distortion of the Creative Process* (1958).

51. Gosse's statement in Lang, vi, especially 239 ff.

52. This point is mentioned in Eileen Souffrin's 'Swinburne et sa Légende en France', *Revue de Littérature Comparée* (1951), xxv, 311–37, of which I have made some use. The author seems to be mistaken in (somewhat tentatively) ascribing the translation of 'The Pilgrims' to Mallarmé and in accepting Lafourcade's attribution of an article by 'Herbert Harvey' to Swinburne. Cf. Lang, iii, 295, note 5, and iv, 50, note 1.

53. Souffrin, *ibid.*, 330 ff., which may suggest that Étienne's article was less critical than it really was.

54. Translated from Gosse's quotation in his *Life* (Bonchurch Edition, xix, 185).

55. As has been pointed out, Goncourt used one or two details from Maupassant's oral statement in the characterization of an Englishman in his novel *La Faustin* (1882).

56. Mario Praz, *The Romantic Agony* (1951), 283, note 103. C. S. Brown, Jr., deals with d'Annunzio's borrowings, chiefly from Gabriel Mourey's translation of *Poems and Ballads*, in 'More Swinburne-d'Annunzio Parallels', *Publications of the Modern Languages Association* (1940), lv, 559–67.

57. Lang, vi, 167.

58. Bernhard Fehr, 'Swinburne und Theodor Opitz', *Englische Studien*, 1927, lxii, 243–9, cited in Lang, iii, 230, note 1.

59. Gosse identifies the reviewer as H. N. Oxenham, 'a Catholic journalist'.

60. R. St. John Tyrwhitt, 'Ancilla Domini: Thoughts on Christian Art. The Immoral Theory of Art', *Contemporary Review*, August 1867, v, 418–36; 'H. A. Page' (pseudonym for Alexander Hay Japp), 'The Morality of Literary Art', *Contemporary Review*, June 1867, v, 161–89.

61. Peter Bayne, 'Mr. Arnold and Mr. Swinburne', *Contemporary Review*, November 1867, vi, 337–56.

62. The article on Swinburne appeared in *Temple Bar*, July 1869, 457–74.

63. Lang, ii, 46.

64. Lang, ii, 176.

65. John Bailey, 'Swinburne', *Quarterly Review*, July 1917, ccxxviii, 228–48; Samuel C. Chew, *Swinburne* (1929), chapter III, 'The Risorgimento and the Ideal Republic'.

66. *Fortnightly Review*, 1 February 1871, xv, 281–2; *Westminster Review*, April 1871, xcv, 579–80; *Tinsley's Magazine*, June 1871, viii, 561–8.

67. Lang, ii, 243–50.

68. As Harold Nicolson's 'Swinburne and Baudelaire', in *Essays by Divers Hands Being the Transactions of the Royal Society of Literature of the United Kingdom*, vi (1926), n.s., ed. G. K. Chesterton, pointed out, the resemblances

between the two writers are largely due to their being exposed to similar influences and experiences—a matter not of 'seed' but of 'soil and climate'.

69. The unsigned article by Hayward on 'Byron and Tennyson' appeared in *Quarterly Review*, October 1871, cxxxi, 354–92; the article on Swinburne, Morris, and Rossetti, reviewing *Songs before Sunrise*, written, according to *The Wellesley Index to Victorian Periodicals* (ed. Walter E. Houghton *et al.*, 1966), by William John Courthope, in *Quarterly Review*, January 1872, cxxxii, 59–84.

70. Now accessible in *New Writings by Swinburne*, ed. Cecil Y. Lang (1964); originally published by C. K. Hyder in *PMLA*, March 1943, lviii, 223–44.

71. Lang, iii, 310.

72. *Saturday Review*, 6 June 1874, xxxvii, 719–21.

73. For details see my *Swinburne's Literary Career and Fame* (1933), 161 ff.

74. For details about this and later titles see the book mentioned in the preceding note.

75. *Fortnightly Review*, 1 February 1868, iii, n.s. 216–20; *Examiner*, 8 February 1868, 84–6.

76. Lang, iii, 43.

77. Swinburne's essays on contemporaries of Shakespeare were included in *The Age of Shakespeare* (1908).

78. William Archer, 'Webster, Lamb, and Swinburne', *New Review*, January 1893, viii, 96–106.

79. *A Survey of English Literature 1780–1880* (1920), iv, 81.

80. The latest is Robert L. Peters' *The Crowns of Apollo: Swinburne's Principles of Literature and Art* (1965).

81. In his introduction to *The Novels of A. C. Swinburne* (1962).

82. *Academy*, 13 July 1878, xiv, 25–6.

83. *Nation*, 18 July 1878, xxvii, 45–6; *North American Review*, September–October 1878, cxxvii, 342–4.

84. Lang, iv, 106.

85. *Spectator*, 5 March 1881, liv, 316–17.

86. Lang, iii, 332.

87. *Spectator*, 12 August 1882, lv, 1055–7.

88. *Idler*, 1895, vii, 400–19.

89. P. Knaplund, 'Swinburne and the Poet-Laureateship', *University of Toronto Quarterly*, January 1937, vi, 236–41.

90. 'The Ethics of Mr. Swinburne's Poetry', *Saturday Review*, 25 January 1896, lxxxi, 95–7; 'Mr. Swinburne on Christianity', *Saturday Review*, 21 March 1896, lxxxi, 296–8.

91. For instance, W. L. Courtney's 'Mr. Swinburne's Poetry', *Fortnightly Review*, May 1885, xliii, 597–610; John Charles Earle's 'The Vices of Agnostic Poetry', *Dublin Review*, July 1882, xxxix, n.s., 104–20. Robert Shindler's

'The Theology of Mr. Swinburne's Poems', *Gentleman's Magazine*, November 1891, cclxxi, 459–71, is, however, friendly.

92. Lafcadio Hearn, *A History of English Literature* (1927), ii, 675–86; *Pre-Raphaelite and Other Poets* (1922), 122–79.

93. George Barlow, 'On the Spiritual Side of Mr. Swinburne's Genius', *Contemporary Review*, August 1905, lxxxviii, 231–50; 'The Poetry and Criticism of Mr. Swinburne', *Quarterly Review*, October 1905, cciii, 525–47; 'Characteristics of Mr. Swinburne's Poetry', *Edinburgh Review*, October 1906, cciv, 468–87, reprinted in Sir Alfred C. Lyall's *Studies in Literature and History* (1915).

94. *Saturday Review*, 2 July 1904, xcviii, 17–18; *Athenaeum*, 18 June 1904, 775–6; *Spectator*, 16 July 1904, xciii, 88–9.

95. In *Saturday Review*, 29 July 1882, liv, 156–7.

96. One of the intemperate criticisms made by Alice Meynell, which did not appear, however, till after Swinburne's death, in 'Swinburne's Lyrical Poetry', *Dublin Review*, July 1909, cxlv, 172–83; reprinted in *Hearts of Controversy* (1917).

97. In the introduction to *Swinburne Replies* (1966).

98. *Heroes and Hero-Worship*, Centenary Edition, v (1904), 83, 90.

99. *A Survey of English Literature 1780–1880* (1920), iv, 55.

100. T. S. Eliot, *The Sacred Wood* (1920), 131–6; I. A. Richards, *The Principles of Literary Criticism* (1925), 130.

101. John D. Rosenberg, 'Swinburne', *Victorian Studies*, December 1967, xi, 131–52.

# Acknowledgments

I wish to thank the following for permission to reprint copyright extracts or complete items from the sources listed below:

Edward Arnold (Publishers) Ltd. for Oliver Elton, *Modern Studies*; William Heinemann Ltd. and E. P. Dutton & Co. Inc., for Max Beerbohm, 'No. 2 the Pines' from *And Even Now*; Houghton Mifflin Company for *The Education of Henry Adams*; Longmans Green & Co. Ltd. for J. W. Mackail, *Life of William Morris*; Macmillan & Co. Ltd. for extracts from *Alfred, Lord Tennyson: A Memoire*, *The Letters of Matthew Arnold*, and *The Life of Edward Bulwer First Lord Lytton*; © *Punch*, reprinted by permission, for 'An Imaginary Correspondence'; Syracuse University Press for *Swinburne Replies*; University of Texas Press for *Dearest Isa*; and Yale University Press for *The Swinburne Letters* edited by Cecil Y. Lang.

# NOTE ON THE TEXT

The materials printed in this volume follow the original texts in all important respects. Lengthy extracts from the works of Swinburne have been omitted whenever they are quoted merely to illustrate the work in question. These omissions are clearly indicated in the text. Typographical errors in the originals have been silently corrected.

# THE QUEEN-MOTHER AND ROSAMOND

## 1860

## 1. Unsigned notice, *Spectator*

12 January 1861, xxxiv, 42

The only notices of *The Queen-Mother and Rosamond* during 1861 are apparently this and No. 2. For a note on later reviews, see Introduction, section I.

We cannot say so much of the two dramas entitled, *The Queen Mother and Rosamond*. We have with some difficulty read through them. Mr. Swinburne has chosen two painful subjects, the Massacre of St. Bartholomew and the Murder of Rosamond Clifford by Queen Eleanor. He has some literary talent, but it is decidedly not of a poetical kind. His 'thoughts are combinations of disjointed things'— and the language in which these thoughts are expressed is painfully distorted, vague, elliptical, and bristling with harsh words. Honey and rosewater verses are, we imagine, what Mr. Swinburne holds to be quite wrong in poetry; but he has mistaken reverse of wrong for right. In feeling and in thought, the daring, the disagreeable, and the violent, are in these dramas, substituted for boldness, beauty, and strength. We do not believe any criticism will help to improve Mr. Swinburne. He writes, as we believe, upon a strongly rooted bad principle. He will not, by such dramas, convince the world that it has always been wrong about poetical beauty, and that he has come to set us right. Mr. Swinburne is a man of education,—at least, we infer this from some indications in his dramas. They are fashioned on no conventional model.

## 2. Unsigned notice, *Athenaeum*

4 May 1861, 595

---

To toil through 'The Queen-Mother' will cost the critic

Many a weary step and many a groan.

We should have conceived it hardly possible to make the crimes of
Catherine de' Medici dull, howsoever they were presented. Mr.
Swinburne, however, has done so. There is more of real drama in
Mr. Browning's short poem of the French poisoner in the laboratory
than in the entire hundred and fifty pages here wearily spun off.—
Having had such ill-luck with one wicked Queen, we were unable to
cope with a second one; and thus the Tragedy of Woodstock, once
again told, though shorter as a play, is gladly handed over to others
who are disposed to venture into the labyrinth.

# SOME VIEWS OF THE YOUNG SWINBURNE

## 1860s

3 (a) HENRY ADAMS, a descendant of two Presidents of the United States and son of Charles Francis Adams (in the sixties American Minister to England), describes a dinner party at the home of Richard Monckton Milnes, soon to be known as Lord Houghton. A passage preceding the following extract mentions the three men present besides Swinburne and Adams—Milnes, 'Stirling of Keir', and Laurence Oliphant.

*The Education of Henry Adams* (1918), 139–41, by permission of Houghton Mifflin, the publisher.

The fourth was a boy, or had the look of one, though in fact a year older than Adams himself. He resembled in action—and in this trait, was remotely followed, a generation later, by another famous young man, Robert Louis Stevenson—a tropical bird, high-crested, long-beaked, quick-moving, with rapid utterance and screams of humour, quite unlike any English lark or nightingale. One could hardly call him a crimson macaw among owls, and yet no ordinary contrast availed. Milnes introduced him as Mr. Algernon Swinburne. The name suggested nothing. Milnes was always unearthing new coins and trying to give them currency. He had unearthed Henry Adams who knew himself to be worthless and not current. When Milnes lingered a moment in Adams's room to add that Swinburne had written some poetry, not yet published, of really extraordinary merit, Adams only wondered what more Milnes would discover, and whether by chance he could discover merit in a private secretary. He was capable of it.

In due course this party of five men sat down to dinner with the usual club manners of ladyless dinner-tables, easy and formal at the same time. Conversation ran first to Oliphant who told his dramatic story simply, and from him the talk drifted off into other channels, until Milnes thought it time to bring Swinburne out. Then, at last, if never before, Adams acquired education. What he had sought so long, he found; but he was none the wiser; only the more astonished. For once, too, he felt at ease, for the others were no less astonished than himself, and their astonishment grew apace. For the rest of the evening Swinburne figured alone; the end of dinner made the monologue only freer, for in 1862, even when ladies were not in the house, smoking was forbidden, and guests usually smoked in the stables or the kitchen; but Monckton Milnes was a licensed libertine who let his guests smoke in Adams's bedroom, since Adams was an American–German barbarian ignorant of manners; and there after dinner all sat—or lay—till far into the night, listening to the rush of Swinburne's talk. In a long experience, before or after, no one ever approached it; yet one had heard accounts of the best talking of the time, and read accounts of talkers in all time, among the rest, of Voltaire, who seemed to approach nearest the pattern.

That Swinburne was altogether new to the three types of men-of-the-world before him; that he seemed to them quite original, wildly eccentric, astonishingly gifted, and convulsingly droll, Adams could see; but what more he was, even Milnes hardly dared say. They could not believe his incredible memory and knowledge of literature, classic, mediaeval, and modern; his faculty of reciting a play of Sophocles or a play of Shakespeare, forward or backward, from end to beginning; or Dante, or Villon, or Victor Hugo. They knew not what to make of his rhetorical recitation of his own unpublished ballads—'Faustine'; the 'Four Boards of the Coffin Lid';[1] the 'Ballad of Burdens'—which he declaimed as though they were books of the *Iliad*. It was singular that his most appreciative listener should have been the author only of pretty verses like 'We wandered by the brookside', and 'She seemed to those that saw them meet'; and who never cared to write in any other tone; but Milnes took everything into his sympathies, including Americans like young Adams whose standards were stiffest of all, while Swinburne, though millions of ages far from them, united them by his humour even more than by his poetry. The story of his first day as a member of Professor Stubbs's household was professionally clever farce,[2] if not high comedy, in a young man who could

[1] Entitled 'After Death' in *Poems and Ballads*.

[2] William Stubbs, afterwards Bishop of Oxford and Regius Professor of History at the University, was at the time a clergyman with whom Swinburne's father had arranged for his son to study. For an account of the poet's first day with Stubbs, see Edmund Gosse's *Life* (Bonchurch Edition, xix, 58–9).

write a Greek ode or a Provençal *chanson* as easily as an English quatrain.

Late at night when the symposium broke up, Stirling of Keir wanted to take with him to his chamber a copy of *Queen Rosamund*,[1] the only volume Swinburne had then published, which was on the library table, and Adams offered to light him down with his solitary bedroom candle. All the way, Stirling was ejaculating explosions of wonder, until at length, at the foot of the stairs and at the climax of his imagination, he paused, and burst out: 'He's a cross between the devil and the Duke of Argyll!'

To appreciate the full merit of this description, a judicious critic should have known both, and Henry Adams knew only one—at least in person—but he understood that to a Scotchman the likeness meant something quite portentous, beyond English experience, supernatural, and what the French call *moyen âgeux*, or mediaeval with a grotesque turn. That Stirling as well as Milnes should regard Swinburne as a prodigy greatly comforted Adams, who lost his balance of mind at first in trying to imagine that Swinburne was a natural product of Oxford, as muffins and pork-pies of London, at once the cause and effect of dyspepsia. The idea that one has actually met a real genius dawns slowly on a Boston mind, but it made entry at last.

[1] *The Queen Mother and Rosamond.*

3(b) GEORGIANA BURNE-JONES was wife of Edward (later Sir Edward) Burne-Jones, who met Swinburne at Oxford and became a close friend. Her portrait of the poet was inserted in an account of events in 1862, in *Memorials of Edward Burne-Jones* (1906), I, 215.

---

Swinburne was the next remarkable personality I remember in these days; he had rooms very near us and we saw a great deal of him; sometimes twice or three times in a day he would come in, bringing his poems hot from his heart and certain of welcome and a hearing at any hour. His appearance was very unusual and in some ways beautiful, for his hair was glorious in abundance and colour and his eyes indescribably fine. When repeating poetry he had a perfectly natural way of lifting them in a rapt, unconscious gaze, and their clear green colour softened by thick brown eyelashes was unforgettable: 'Looks commercing with the skies'[1] expresses it without exaggeration. He was restless beyond words, scarcely standing still at all and almost dancing as he walked, while even in sitting he moved continually, seeming to keep time, by a swift movement of the hands at the wrists, and sometimes of the feet also, with some inner rhythm of excitement. He was courteous and affectionate and unsuspicious, and faithful beyond most people to those he really loved. The biting wit which filled his talk so as at times to leave his hearers dumb with amazement always spared one thing, and that was an absent friend.

[1] From Milton's 'Il Penseroso', l. 39.

3 (c) BAYARD TAYLOR discussed Swinburne in his letter of 24 April 1867 to E. C. Stedman, who in a few years was to become Swinburne's most effective champion in America. In his day Taylor was respected as a world traveller, man of letters, and poet; people who remember him now may recall that he was the translator of *Faust*.

By permission of the Yale University Press, the passage is reprinted from *The Swinburne Letters*, ed. Cecil Y. Lang, I, 233-4.

---

In all important respects except one I found him to be very much what I had anticipated. The exception is, instead of being a prematurely blasé young man o' the world, he is rather a wilful, perverse, unreasonable spoiled child. His nature is still that of the *young* Shelley, and my great fear is that it will never be otherwise. He needs the influence of a nature stronger than his in everything but the imaginative faculty—such a nature as Byron's was to Shelley. Again, a clear headed and hearted woman could cure him of his morbid relish for the atrocious forms of passion. He has a weak moral sense, but his offences arise from a colossal unbalanced affectation. This, or something like it, is the disorganizing element in his nature, which quite obscures the organizing (that is artistic) sense. What I admire in him—yet admire with a feeling of pain—is the mad, unrestrained preponderance of the imagination. It is a god-like quality, but he sometimes uses it like a devil. He greatly interests my intellect, but he does not touch me magnetically. He could have no power over me, but on the contrary, I felt that I should be able to influence him in a short time. I had a letter from him the other day, which shows he feels an intellectual relationship between us. Now this is not a question of relative poetic power, but of a certain diversity of qualities, and I don't mean to be egotistic in saying that I might perform somewhat of the same service for him as Byron for Shelley. I feel that (if it is not already too late) I could help him to some degree of poise, of system, of law—in short, art.

In this sense he moves my deepest sympathy, for I see now the matter that might be moulded into a splendid poet relapsing into formless conditions. It is sad, it is tragic—and if this fancy of mine be foolish, there it is nevertheless. Without this sense of giving assistance, a week

7

alone with Swinburne would be intolerable to me, to any other human being. The preponderance of some disorganizing force in him gave me a constant keen sense of pain. I have urged him to join us in Italy next winter, but I doubt whether he will succeed in doing so. If he comes, and I find there is no hope of establishing any germ or central point of order in his nature, I shall really be forced to keep out of his way. He is now, with all his wonderful gifts the most wretched man I ever saw.

I said that he has a weak moral sense, but his English friends say that he has none at all. Here I don't agree with them, and moreover I don't think they quite understand his nature and therefore can't be of much service. One thing is certain—his aberration of ideas is horrible. He told me some things, unspeakably shocking, which he had omitted from his last volume. I very freely expressed my opinion and he took it with a gentle sort of wonder! He is sensitive, hugely ambitious and utterly self-absorbed—which things have wrought disease. If I did not think so, I should never wish to see him again.

# ATALANTA IN CALYDON

## 1865

## 4. Unsigned Review, *Saturday Review*

### 6 May 1865, xix, 540-2

Most reviewers of *Atalanta* concerned themselves with the extent
to which the play was Greek in style and ideas. The *Saturday
Review*, which like other periodicals praised Swinburne's command of language and rhythm, did not recognize his 'anti-theism'
as clearly as did Richard Monckton Milnes, writing anonymously
in the *Edinburgh Review*, though after the scandal of *Poems and
Ballads* this aspect of the play received more attention.

Any one who had tried, whether by way of a school or college exercise
or for his own pleasure, to compose a poem or an essay in one of the
classical languages, must remember how forcibly he was led, in such
an attempt, to realize the unspeakable differences in thought and feeling
which separate the ancient world from ourselves. In reading a Greek
poet or philosopher, we surrender ourselves for the time being to his
influence, appear to breathe the same atmosphere, and to see things in
the colours which they wore to his eyes. But the moment we cease to
be passive, and endeavour either to imagine what a Greek would have
said on a given subject, or, taking our own thoughts upon it, to throw
them into the form which they would have assumed under his hands,
we feel that it is not merely in form, nor even in our actual notions and
beliefs, that we are unlike him, but rather in the habit and method of
our minds. And if the thoughts we ascribe to him are, in truth, not
modern, they are artificial, and all but meaningless to us. If they are
modern and genuine, the ancient dress with which we would clothe

them is found to be stiff and unbecoming. As an exercise of ingenuity, the thing may be worth trying; but for the purposes either of art or of argument, it is almost sure to be a failure. Nevertheless, in spite of this, and indeed because of this, it is always well that the experiment should be made, and those who, like Mr. Swinburne, make it boldly and cleverly deserve no small credit.

*Atalanta in Calydon* is an attempt to reproduce a Greek tragedy in its ideas as well as its form, to some extent even in its metres—an attempt necessarily chargeable with faults and weaknesses, yet still one of the most brilliant that our literature contains. Mr. Swinburne has judged well in his choice of a subject. The legend of Calydon is one of the most beautiful in the whole compass of the Greek mythology; fresh, simple, romantic; solemn and pathetic, yet without any of those horrors which shock us in the stories of Thebes or Argos—no Jocasta, no Thyestes, but figures full of heroic truth and nobleness, standing out in the clear bright light of the early morning of Greece. Then, although very popular among the ancients, as one may see from the frequent representations of its scenes in works of art, it does not form the subject of any extant Greek tragedy, so that a modern may treat of it without being forced into direct comparison with an ancient poet. Mr. Swinburne has been sensible of his advantages, and has used them well. His faculty of imitation is in some respects very surprising. A careful study of the Attic dramatists has enabled him to catch their manner, and to reproduce felicitously many of their terms of expression. The scholar is struck, every few lines, by some phrase which he can fancy a direct translation from the Greek, while yet it is in its place both forcible and unaffected. The matter, although not really Greek in its essence, is thrown with great cleverness into a mould which almost beguiles us into forgetting the author, and imagining that we are listening to one of the contemporaries of Euripides who sought to copy the manner of Æschylus. That moralizing vein of Greek tragedy, which is not free from a dash of platitude, is very well given, and we hear, as is fitting, a great deal about fate, and the elder gods, and the weakness of mortals, and the duty of submission, and fire, and blood, and Até the unconquerable, yet so managed as not to be a parody, but a veritable and tasteful imitation. Nevertheless, while admiring the skill and the sympathy which Mr. Swinburne has shown, we cannot but mark serious deficiencies. Some of these are due, not specially to himself, but to the very nature of his attempt. An imitation must always lack what is the highest charm of poetry and the truest mark of genius—the rare and native flavour of originality. What we really want to hear a man say is that which he alone can say; and this, in copying other people, he cannot say, or must say with contortions and posturings which go far to spoil it altogether. Mr. Swinburne has a lively fancy and a gay profusion of expression which accord ill with the solemn and severe stateliness of Attic tragedy, and, in the effort to acquire what may be called its sacrificial procession step, he is forced to check and lose many of his peculiar excellences. We say 'effort to acquire', for he has not, after all, acquired it. He has an intense sympathy with the Greek dramatists, and a full perception of their grandeur and purity, as well as of the exquisite finish of their workmanship. He has, further, a strong and fine sense of beauty, although, as we conceive, rather the beauty of visible things than of sounds, or feelings, or ideas. But his mind is cast in a mould most unlike the Greek. A Greek poet is never confused, nor are his thoughts obscure, although they may seem so when they hint at something without wishing or being able to follow it out. It is his tendency to dwell upon insoluble problems, not a want of light and force in his own mind, that makes us think Æschylus difficult. Himself, although in an inferior degree to Sophocles, he is definite, precise, subtle; his ideas are single and separate, often delicately interwoven in a complex web of thought, while yet each thread retains its individual colour, and is not blended undistinguishably in the whole. Modern habits of thinking and writing want this clear singleness, and Mr. Swinburne is wholly a modern. His images, metaphors, and allusions are heaped upon one another in a wild prodigal way which reminds us of Shelley or Browning more than of any ancient poet; he lays on stroke after stroke of colour till the last obliterate the first, and we are bewildered among thick-coming sensations. His metaphors are not often incongruous, but they follow so fast as to be confusing, and it is seldom that any distinct and vivid impression is left on the reader's mind. We will take an instance or two where the parts are good, but the effect of the whole is injured by this luxuriance. The chief huntsman, at the beginning of the poem, addresses the rising sun:—

> Let earth
> Laugh and the long sea, fiery from thy feet,
> Through all the roar and ripple of streaming springs,
> And foam in reddening flakes and flying flowers,
> Shaken from hands and blown from lips of nymphs,
> Whose hair or breast divides the wandering wave,

> With salt close tresses cleaving lock to lock,
> All gold, or shuddering and unfurrowed snow.

Half of this would be better than the whole. So, again, Castor and Pollux are called

> Gracious heads,
> Like kindled lights in untempestuous heaven;
> Fair flower-like stars on the iron foam of fight.

Here we seem to see the images absolutely elbowing each other out of the way.

This profusion, a quality least of all to be found in a classical poet, has two unfortunate results. Mr. Swinburne has so many things to compare everything to, that he becomes almost prolix; he runs on dilating upon a theme till, as the proverb says, we cannot see the wood for the trees. He is not content to make a point and be done with it. The instance we will give is far from being a flagrant one, but it is worth taking because it is meant to imitate a passage of Homer which Tennyson also has paraphrased in a piece which every one knows. First let us give Homer's lines from the fourth book of the *Odyssey*:—

[The eight lines quoted from the *Odyssey* are translated as follows by A. T. Murray (Loeb Library edition): 'But for thyself, Menelaus, fostered by Zeus, it is not ordained that thou shouldst die and meet thy fate in horse-pasturing Argos, but to the Elysian plain and the bounds of the earth will the immortals convey thee, where dwells fair-haired Rhadamanthus, and where life is easiest for men. No snow is there, nor heavy storm, nor ever rain, but ever does Ocean send up blasts of the shrill-blowing West Wind that they may give cooling to men. . . .'] Next, Tennyson:—

> I am going a long way
> To the island valley of Avilion,
> Where falls not rain or hail or any snow,
> Nor ever wind blows loudly; but it lies
> Deep-meadowed, happy, fair with orchard lawns,
> And bowery hollows crowned with summer sea.

Last, Mr. Swinburne:—

> Immortal honour is on them, having passed
> Through splendid life and death desirable,
> To the clear seat and remote throne of souls,
> Lands indiscoverable in the unheard-of West,
> Round which the strong stream of a sacred sea

Rolls without wind for ever, and the snow
There shows not her white wings and windy feet,
Nor thunder nor swift rain saith anything,
Nor the sun burns, but all things rest and thrive.

Mr. Swinburne's lines are good, although they do not equal the voluptuous dreamlike ease of the Laureate's version; but how he has amplified upon his model! Πείρατα γαίης is expressed thrice over by 'remote throne', 'lands indiscoverable', 'unheard-of West'. The line beginning Οὐ νιφετὸς is represented by three. Homer's last two lines here are one of the finest instances of that power which only the greatest poets possess, but which all poets should diligently strive after, of creating a picture by a touch. There is more in them than pages of brilliant description like Mr. Swinburne's could convey.

The second error into which Mr. Swinburne's luxuriant fancy leads him is that of too frequently repeating, not perhaps the same images, but at any rate images of the same class. The stock of things in the world which can be made to yield similes is, after all, not inexhaustible, and if every line is to contain a new figure, it needs a wonderfully acute and fertile mind to prevent the same or similar ones from recurring. Thus, through the poem, we have a sense of flowers, stars, sea foam, wine, thunder, and fire, which grows at last a little fatiguing, and blunts the force of each particular image.

We might go on to quote passages where Mr. Swinburne's ideas, as well as his poetical style, are unclassical, examining in particular a fine choral song upon the dealings of the gods with men, the pious and the impious parts of which it would have been equally impossible for a Greek to write. But we prefer to hasten on to say a word or two upon Mr. Swinburne's merits as a poet, apart from those which he may claim as an imitator. The general plan and character of the drama are so largely determined by the desire to follow closely the practice of the Greeks, that it is not fair to censure Mr. Swinburne for defects so caused. Yet we cannot but think that the story might have been made more interesting. It was not with the ancients, as it is now, the tragedian's first business to let his portraits be vividly lifelike; yet to any sort of dramatic success a measure of individualization is necessary, and that measure we scarcely find here. Meleager is described finely, but throws none of his character into his words. Toxeus and Plexippus are lay figures. Atalanta herself—Atalanta, one of the brightest and loveliest creations of Greek legend, and who reminds us less of a Greek maiden than of some heroine of mediaeval romance—is, in Mr. Swinburne's hands, pure indeed and stately, yet at the same time colourless and cold as her own Arcadian snows. Althaea is better, yet even Althaea seems to us, if we may use the expression, insufficiently studied. Mr. Swinburne has not thought hard enough or long enough upon the meaning of the tale, and the forces that moved its personages; else would he, with his cleverness and power of expressing passionate thought, have made us sympathize more with Meleager's love, and made his mother's deed at once more terrible and more pitiable. He would have shown that she relit the fateful torch not merely in wrath at her brothers' death, nor to honour their spirits by a revenge which was their meed, nor under a wild belief that fate willed it so and it must be so, but from the irresistible temptation of having, or seeming to have, her son's life in her hand. She believed, but she did not realize to herself the truth of, the Fates' prophecy; she half reasoned, in her passion, that if his life would end with the torch, such a power over him must have been given her to be exercised now; that, if not, no harm could happen; that at least she might and must put it to the proof. Mr. Swinburne, as we believe, sees all this, but he sees it somewhat dimly, and has not made of it what he might.

When we come to speak of the execution and details of the poem, we may praise him more unhesitatingly. His fancy is lively, his sense of beauty rich and delicate, his thoughts too vague perhaps, yet always ingenious and sometimes full of force. On the whole, however, it is by his command of poetical language and his power of light and harmonious versification that we are chiefly attracted and delighted. Let us quote two passages.

Here is the second song of the Chorus:—

[quotes 'Before the beginning of years. . . .']

The lines that follow are from the κόμμος between Oeneus, Meleager, Atalanta, and the Chorus at the end of the poem:—

### MELEAGER

But thou, O mother,
The dreamer of dreams,
Wilt thou bring forth another
To feel the sun's beams,
When I move among shadows a shadow, and wail by impassable streams?

### OENEUS

Who shall give back
Thy face of old years,

With travail made black,
Grown grey among fears:
Mother of sorrow, mother of cursing, mother of tears?

ATALANTA

I would that as water
My life's blood had thawn,
Or as winter's wan daughter
Leaves lowland and lawn
Spring-stricken, or ever my eyes had beheld thee made dark in thy dawn.

Lyrical passages such as these, where the poet can give free rein to his fancy, please us better than the dialogue parts of the drama, in which we complain of a certain indistinctness of thought, and an occasional languor of expression. There is too little of the nerve and fibre of passion in the words; too much of mere ornament and play of picturesque ideas. Yet even in these less animated parts of the poem many fine passages occur, from among which we select one as an example of Mr. Swinburne's descriptive style. He is, indeed, never more happy than in painting nature, knowing and loving her well, and inspired by her beauty into a vivid force and fulness of expression:—

And chiefliest when hoar beach and herbless cliff
Stood out ahead from Colchis, and we heard
Clefts hoarse with wind, and saw through narrowing reefs
The lightning of the intolerable wave
Flash, and the white wet flame of breakers burn
Far under a kindling south-wind, as a lamp
Burns and bends all its blowing flame one way;
Wild heights untravelled of the wind, and vales
Cloven seaward by their violent streams, and white
With bitter flowers and bright salt scurf of brine;
Heard sweep their sharp swift gales, and bowing birdwise
Shriek with birds' voices, and with furious feet
Tread loose the long skirts of a storm; and saw
The whole white Euxine clash together and fall
Full-mouthed and thunderous from a thousand throats.

In criticizing Mr. Swinburne's work we have cared less to indulge in praise than to point out defects, just because his drama seems to us so full of promise that even present merits ought to be regarded rather as an earnest of the future than dwelt upon as though they were sufficient. Those merits are, however, very considerable, and no one who reads *Atalanta in Calydon* can doubt that its author is a poet—a poet of great grace, flexibility, and power of expression. Our only complaint is that he trusts too much to this power, and allows his command of spirited and melodious language to carry him along faster than his thought can follow. Shelley, too, is brilliant and fanciful, but Shelley can be severe on occasion; his language is always strong and his thought passionate. It is in this sort of strength and passion that the drama before us is somewhat deficient, and without it no first-rate work can ever be done. Facility is the most perilous of gifts, yet we believe that time and labour will, to use one of his own metaphors, give Mr. Swinburne strength of stem and wealth of fruit, as well as the pride of leaves and blossoms; and it is with real pleasure that we welcome him to an honourable place among the younger poets of England.

# CHASTELARD

1865

---

## 5. Unsigned review, *Athenaeum*

### 23 December 1865, 880–1

Some reviews of *Chastelard* were more emphatic than the *Athenaeum* in their opinions that the portrait of Mary Queen of Scots is unhistorical and that the characters and scenes of the play are repugnant. A more friendly review was that of Henry Morley, who reviewed the book with *Poems and Ballads* (No. 10).

---

The power of poetic expression so remarkably displayed in Mr. Swinburne's *Atalanta in Calydon* is not absent from his new work. He still writes with force and beauty of phrase, though not without drawbacks of straining and affectation. In a dramatic point of view, too, he shows, up to a certain point, striking qualities. Passion, at times, obtains from him a startling utterance, and his delineation of Mary Stuart is, in some respects, as vivid as it is morally repulsive on the whole. We seem not only to hear

> The soft and rapid shudder of her breath
> In talking—the rare tender little laugh—
> The pitiful sweet sound like a bird's sigh
> When her voice breaks—

And to see

> —The playing of those eyelashes,
> The lure of amorous looks as sad as love;

but, through the early scenes, we trace, in her speech and manners, the

nature, over-vital at surface, but shallow, empty, and futile, which
Mr. Swinburne ascribes to her. We have of course no intention of
re-discussing the character of Mary Stuart here. So far as we have
already described Mr. Swinburne's estimate of her, it is one of several
which a dramatist might fairly derive from the conflicting evidence
before him. We are aware, too, that no one absolutely depends upon
the incidents or characters exhibited in a drama, or denies the poet's
right to modify facts, within certain limits, for the purposes of art. It
must be remembered, however, that although a drama be not authoritative in the sense that history is, it has great power over the emotions
and prejudices of mankind. A dramatic poet, therefore, dealing with
historical characters, is bound to observe some measure of justice. He
will not hastily convert possibilities or floating rumours into direct
accusations of the dead, however culpable they may have been, nor, for
the sake of a psychological 'study', prefer new indictments against
those who can no longer plead to them. This point, however, we leave
to Mr. Swinburne's sense of fairness and chivalry. It is with his drama
as a work of art that we are directly concerned, and we protest against
his full rendering of Mary, chiefly because in connexion with his other
characters it affords little scope for tragic development. Doubtless conceptions of extreme depravity will at times yield rare scope to the
dramatist. The gradual encroachments of evil on a weak, but not
unscrupulous nature,—like that of Macbeth, for instance,—is fraught
with suggestion. A creation like Iago, again, is admissible for the sake
of the conflict of emotion which it produces in a higher nature, and also
for the light which that nature throws upon the baseness of the
tempter. In a third case, triumphant and impenitent sin may be
properly exhibited when it is at last confronted with a retribution of
its own sowing, as in that renowned scene of Sophocles', where the
adulterous murderer stands appalled, less by the sight of the avenger
than by the mute form of his partner in guilt. In the Mary Stuart here
presented we find none of the elements which give tragic fitness to
crime. Hopelessly bad from the first, exulting at the close, Mary has
no inner conflict, no remorse, no punishment. She excites no pity, and
no terror, for the guilt that causes terror must suggest the wreck of a
nature in which, more or less, the possibility of good had once existed.
Horror is the feeling which she calls forth, but horror is not in itself
poetical. Nor does her alleged wickedness develop or throw into relief
any nobler qualities in others. Chastelard is here as foolish, as inconsistent, and as incapable of love, in any high sense, as Mary is vain,

dastardly and cruel. Discovered in Mary's bedroom, when the return of her husband is imminent (Mr. Swinburne chooses for the purpose of this scene to antedate her marriage with Darnley), Chastelard madly refuses to retire, though of course aware that his stay must fatally compromise the Queen. Yet this is the chevalier who afterwards rejects a pardon lest such a proof of Mary's lenity to him should be construed to her disadvantage. He is, first, selfish and rash enough to stab the fame of his mistress, and then foolish enough to perish in the defence of what he has already slain. His illicit passion for Mary, again, has not even the poor excuse of the glamour which love often casts round a worthless object. Captivated by the beauty and grace of their idols, men have been fain, for love's very sake, to endow them with generosity and truth. The hero of this tragedy nurses no such delusion. He believes Mary from the beginning to be utterly heartless and false. His passion is solely of the senses, and he avows it:—

> I know her ways of loving, all of them:
> A sweet soft way the first is; afterward
> It burns and bites like fire; the end of that,
> Charred dust, and eyelids bitten through with smoke.

And he thus addresses the Queen herself shortly before the death to which she consigns him:—

> Why should one woman have all goodly things?
> You have all beauty; let mean women's lips
> Be pitiful, and speak truth: they will not be
> Such perfect things as yours. Be not ashamed
> That hands not made like these that snare men's souls
> Should do men good, give alms, relieve men's pain;
> You have the better, being more fair than they,
> They are half foul, being rather good than fair;
> You are quite fair: to be quite fair is best.

   Had Chastelard been capable of a higher attachment than that which he himself describes, there would have been fitness and deep pathos in the words so intense, yet nobly simple, which he afterwards utters to Mary:—

> It may be, long time after I am dead,
> For all you are, you may see bitter days;
> God may forget you or be wroth with you:
> Then shall you lack a little help of me,
> And I shall feel your sorrow touching you,

A happy sorrow, though I may not touch:
I that would fain be turned to flesh again,
Fain get back life to give up life for you,
To shed my blood for help, that long ago
You shed and were not holpen; and your heart
Will ache for help and comfort, yea for love,
And find less love than mine—for I do think
You never will be loved thus in your life.

Or if we could once accept the revolting cruelty of Mary here portrayed, we should grant that her treachery was profoundly worked out in the scene where she suggests to Murray the 'taking off' of her lover. With equal art, her momentary resolution to pardon him at the end of the scene is ascribed less to pity than to the vanity which triumphs in the news of his blind devotion to her. Throughout the scene, indeed— which is too long to quote—Mr. Swinburne tracks the evil nature of his heroine through its many windings, almost with the unerring nicety of scent.

An extract or two in proof of the writer's felicity of description is all that our space now admits of. The Queen thus explains the device of her breast-clasp, evidently intended by Mr. Swinburne to symbolize herself:—

A Venus crowned, that eats the hearts of men: . . .

[quotes the next eleven lines of I, ii]

Mary, wishing that she had been a man, proceeds thus:—

No, then I would not fail, . . .

[quotes the next twenty-one lines of II, i]

The picture with which this burst concludes, though too much elaborated, has undeniable grandeur. We could point out passages which, in a dramatic point of view, are yet finer. Those given to Mary Beaton—the only touching character in the play—often reach the height of tragic intensity. Nor is it to be disputed that Mr. Swinburne shows at times a keen insight into the subtleties of human motive, but his chief characters are out of the pale of our sympathy; besides being inherently vicious, their language will offend not only those who have reverence, but those who have taste. We decline to show by quotation how often the Divine Name is sported with in scenes which are essentially voluptuous. The incidents, again, are often so repulsive that we gain a sort of relief by reflecting that they are equally incredible. To those which we have already pointed out we may add the visit of Mary to Chastelard's prison, that she may bribe the poor wretch, with smiles, to return the pardon which she had sent him,—the perjury of the dying man when to use his own words, he prays that he may be cast

> Even to the heaviest place there is in hell

if the Queen be not innocent, though her guilt is assumed as the basis of the play,—and lastly, the hideous levity, of Mary at the death of him whose lips she had kissed half an hour before.

Let us remark, before concluding, that Chastelard's attestation of Mary's innocence is matter of history, though as used here it only serves to blacken her character. Upon such persons and events as those which we now gladly lose sight of, the powers of the highest dramatist would be wasted. If *Chastelard* be remembered at all, it will be solely for its detached beauties of expression. We hope, should we meet Mr. Swinburne again, that he will be able to exhibit Vice without painting a Monster, and to give us a higher type of knightly devotion than an infatuated libertine.

# POEMS AND BALLADS

## 1866

---

## 6. John Morley, *Saturday Review*

### 4 August 1866, xxii, 145–7

Though the unsigned review by John Morley was perhaps the most telling blow against *Poems and Ballads*, Edmund Gosse was badly mistaken in believing that it determined the reception of the volume (the Introduction, section II, discusses this point). Eventually a statesman, biographer and critic, and editor of the English 'Men of Letters' series, in 1866 Morley was already recognized as an able journalist.

---

It is mere waste of time, and shows a curiously mistaken conception of human character, to blame an artist of any kind for working at a certain set of subjects rather than at some other set which the critic may happen to prefer. An artist, at all events an artist of such power and individuality as Mr. Swinburne, works as his character compels him. If the character of his genius drives him pretty exclusively in the direction of libidinous song, we may be very sorry, but it is of no use to advise him and to preach to him. What comes of discoursing to a fiery tropical flower of the pleasant fragrance of the rose or the fruitfulness of the fig-tree? Mr. Swinburne is much too stoutly bent on taking his own course to pay any attention to critical monitions as to the duty of the poet, or any warnings of the worse than barrenness of the field in which he has chosen to labour. He is so firmly and avowedly fixed in an attitude of revolt against the current notions of decency and dignity and social duty that to beg of him to become a little more decent, to fly a little less persistently and gleefully to the animal side of human nature, is simply to beg him to be something different from

22

Mr. Swinburne. It is a kind of protest which his whole position makes it impossible for him to receive with anything but laughter and contempt. A rebel of his calibre is not to be brought to a better mind by solemn little sermons on the loyalty which a man owes to virtue. His warmest prayer to the gods is that they should

> Come down and redeem us from virtue.

His warmest hope for men is that they should change

> The lilies and languors of virtue
> For the raptures and roses of vice.

It is of no use, therefore, to scold Mr. Swinburne for grovelling down among the nameless shameless abominations which inspire him with such frenzied delight. They excite his imagination to its most vigorous efforts, they seem to him the themes most proper for poetic treatment, and they suggest ideas which, in his opinion, it is highly to be wished that English men and women should brood upon and make their own. He finds that these fleshly things are his strong part, so he sticks to them. Is it wonderful that he should? And at all events he deserves credit for the audacious courage with which he has revealed to the world a mind all aflame with the feverish carnality of a schoolboy over the dirtiest passages in Lemprière. It is not every poet who would ask us all to go hear him tuning his lyre in a stye. It is not everybody who would care to let the world know that he found the most delicious food for poetic reflection in the practices of the great island of the Ægean, in the habits of Messalina, of Faustina, of Pasiphaë. Yet these make up Mr. Swinburne's version of the dreams of fair women, and he would scorn to throw any veil over pictures which kindle, as these do, all the fires of his imagination in their intensest heat and glow. It is not merely 'the noble, the nude, the antique'[1] which he strives to reproduce. If he were a rebel against the fat-headed Philistines and poor-blooded Puritans who insist that all poetry should be such as may be wisely placed in the hands of girls of eighteen, and is fit for the use of Sunday schools, he would have all wise and enlarged readers on his side. But there is an enormous difference between an attempt to revivify among us the grand old pagan conceptions of Joy, and an attempt to glorify all the bestial delights that the subtleness of Greek depravity was able to contrive. It is a good thing to vindicate passion, and the strong and

[1] Like the three preceding quoted lines and the later 'Daughter of Death and Priapus', from 'Dolores'.

large and rightful pleasures of sense, against the narrow and inhuman tyranny of shrivelled anchorites. It is a very bad and silly thing to try to set up the pleasures of sense in the seat of the reason they have dethroned. And no language is too strong to condemn the mixed vileness and childishness of depicting the spurious passion of a putrescent imagination, the unnamed lusts of sated wantons, as if they were the crown of character and their enjoyment the great glory of human life. The only comfort about the present volume is that such a piece as 'Anactoria' will be unintelligible to a great many people, and so will the fevered folly of 'Hermaphroditus', as well as much else that is nameless and abominable. Perhaps if Mr. Swinburne can a second and a third time find a respectable publisher willing to issue a volume of the same stamp, crammed with pieces which many a professional vendor of filthy prints might blush to sell if he only knew what they meant, English readers will gradually acquire a truly delightful familiarity with these unspeakable foulnesses; and a lover will be able to present to his mistress a copy of Mr. Swinburne's latest verses with a happy confidence that she will have no difficulty in seeing the point of every allusion to Sappho or the pleasing Hermaphroditus, or the embodiment of anything else that is loathsome and horrible. It will be very charming to hear a drawing-room discussion on such verses as these, for example:—

> Stray breaths of Sapphic song that blew
> Through Mitylene
> Shook the fierce quivering blood in you
> By night, Faustine.

[quotes three more stanzas of 'Faustine']

We should be sorry to be guilty of anything so offensive to Mr. Swinburne as we are quite sure an appeal to the morality of all the wisest and best men would be. The passionate votary of the goddess whom he hails as 'Daughter of Death and Priapus' has got too high for this. But it may be presumed that common sense is not too insulting a standard by which to measure the worth and place of his new volume. Starting from this sufficiently modest point, we may ask him whether there is really nothing in women worth singing about except 'quivering flanks' and 'splendid supple thighs', 'hot sweet throats' and 'hotter hands than fire', and their blood as 'hot wan wine of love'? Is purity to be expunged from the catalogue of desirable qualities? Does a poet show respect to his own genius by gloating, as Mr. Swinburne does, page after page and poem after poem, upon a single subject, and that subject kept steadily in a single light? Are we to believe that having exhausted hot lustfulness, and wearied the reader with a luscious and nauseating iteration of the same fervid scenes and fervid ideas, he has got to the end of his tether? Has he nothing more to say, no further poetic task but to go on again and again about

> The white wealth of thy body made whiter
> By the blushes of amorous blows,
> And seamed with sharp lips and fierce fingers,
> And branded by kisses that bruise.

And to invite new Félises to

> Kiss me once hard, as though a flame
> Lay on my lips and made them fire.

Mr. Swinburne's most fanatical admirers must long for something newer than a thousand times repeated talk of

> Stinging lips wherein the hot sweet brine
> That Love was born of burns and foams like wine.

And

> Hands that sting like fire.

And of all those women,

> Swift and white,
> And subtly warm and half perverse,
> And sweet like sharp soft fruit to bite,
> And like a snake's love lithe and fierce.

This stinging and biting, all these 'lithe lascivious regrets', all this talk of snakes and fire, of blood and wine and brine, of perfumes and poisons and ashes, grows sickly and oppressive on the senses. Every picture is hot and garish with this excess of flaming violent colour. Consider the following two stanzas:—

> From boy's pierced throat and girl's pierced bosom
> Drips reddening round the blood-red blossom,
> The slow delicious bright soft blood;
> Bathing the spices and the pyre,
> Bathing the flowers and fallen fire,
> Bathing the blossom by the bud.

Roses whose lips the flame has deadened
Drink till the lapping leaves are reddened
    And warm wet inner petals weep;
The flower whereof sick sleep gets leisure
Barren of balm and purple pleasure
    Fumes with no native steam of sleep.

Or these, from the verses to Dolores, so admirable for their sustained power and their music, if hateful on other grounds:

Cold eyelids that hide like a jewel
    Hard eyes that grow soft for an hour;
The heavy white limbs and the cruel
    Red mouth like a venomous flower;
When these are gone by with their glories
    What shall rest of thee then, what remain,
O mystic and sombre Dolores,
    Our Lady of Pain?

[quotes two more stanzas and six lines of a third]

It was too rashly said, when *Atalanta in Calydon* appeared, that Mr. Swinburne had drunk deep at the springs of Greek poetry, and had profoundly conceived and assimilated the divine spirit of Greek art. *Chastelard* was enough to show that this had been very premature. But the new volume shows with still greater plainness how far removed Mr. Swinburne's tone of mind is from that of the Greek poets. Their most remarkable distinction is their scrupulous moderation and sobriety in colour. Mr. Swinburne riots in the profusion of colour of the most garish and heated kind. He is like a composer who should fill his orchestra with trumpets, or a painter who should exclude every colour but a blaring red, and a green as of sour fruit. There are not twenty stanzas in the whole book which have the faintest tincture of soberness. We are in the midst of fire and serpents, wine and ashes, blood and foam, and a hundred lurid horrors. Unsparing use of the most violent colours and the most intoxicated ideas and images is Mr. Swinburne's prime characteristic. Fascinated as everybody must be by the music of his verse, it is doubtful whether part of the effect may not be traced to something like a trick of words and letters, to which he resorts in season and out of season with a persistency that any sense of artistic moderation must have stayed. The Greek poets in their most impetuous moods never allowed themselves to be carried on by the swing of words, instead of by the steady, though buoyant, flow of thoughts. Mr. Swinburne's hunting of letters, his hunting of the same word, to death is ceaseless. We shall have occasion by and by to quote a long passage in which several lines will be found to illustrate this. Then, again, there is something of a trick in such turns as these:—

> Came flushed from the full-flushed wave.
> Grows dim in thine ears and deep as the deep dim soul of a star.
> White rose of the rose-white water, a silver spendour and flame.

There are few pages in the volume where we do not find conceits of this stamp doing duty for thoughts. The Greeks did not wholly disdain them, but they never allowed them to count for more than they were worth. Let anybody who compares Mr. Swinburne to the Greeks read his ode to 'Our Lady of Pain', and then read the well-known scene in the *Antigone* between Antigone and the Chorus, beginning ἔρως ἀνίκατε μάχαν,[1] or any of the famous choruses in the *Agamemnon*, or an ode of Pindar. In the height of all their passion there is an infinite soberness of which Mr. Swinburne has not a conception.

Yet, in spite of its atrocities, the present volume gives new examples of Mr. Swinburne's forcible and vigorous imagination. The 'Hymn to Proserpine' on the proclamation of the Christian faith in Rome, full as it is of much that many persons may dislike, contains passages of rare vigour:—

> All delicate days and pleasant, all spirits and sorrows are cast. . . .

[quotes the next seventeen lines]

The variety and rapidity and sustention, the revelling in power, are not more remarkable here than in many other passages, though even here it is not variety and rapidity of thought. The anapaest to which Mr. Swinburne so habitually resorts is the only foot that suffices for his never-staying impetuosity. In the 'Song in Time of Revolution' he employs it appropriately, and with a sweeping force as of the elements:—

> The heart of the rulers is sick, and the high priest covers his head;
> For this is the song of the quick that is heard in the ears of the dead.
> The poor and the halt and the blind are keen and mighty and fleet;
> Like the noise of the blowing of wind is the sound of the noise of their feet.

There are, too, sweet and picturesque lines scattered in the midst of this red fire which the poet tosses to and fro about his verses. Most of the poems, in his wearisomely iterated phrase, are meant 'to sting the senses

[1] Sophocles, *Antigone*, ll. 781 ff., contains the address to 'all-conquering Love'.

like wine', but to some stray pictures one may apply his own exquisite phrases on certain of Victor Hugo's songs, which, he says,

> Fell more soft than dew or snow by night,
> Or wailed as in some flooded cave
> Sobs the strong broken spirit of a wave.

For instance, there is a perfect delicacy and beauty in four lines of the hendecasyllabics—a metre that is familiar in the Latin line often found on clocks and sundials, *Horae nam pereunt et imputantur*:—[1]

> When low light was upon the windy reaches,
> When the flower of foam was blown, a lily
> Dropt among the sonorous fruitless furrows
> And green fields of the sea that make no pasture.

Nothing can be more simple and exquisite than

> For the glass of the years is brittle wherein we gaze for a span.

Or than this:—

> In deep wet ways by grey old gardens
> Fed with sharp spring the sweet fruit hardens;
>   They know not what fruits wane or grow:
> Red summer burns to the utmost ember;
> They know not, neither can remember,
>   The old years and flowers they used to know.

Or again:—

> With stars and sea-winds for her raiment
>   Night sinks on the sea.

Up to a certain point, one of the deepest and most really poetical pieces is that called the 'Sundew'. A couple of verses may be quoted to illustrate the graver side of the poet's mind:—

> The deep scent of the heather burns
> About it; breathless though it be,
> Bow down and worship; more than we
> Is the least flower whose life returns,
> Least weed renascent in the sea.

*　　*　　*　　*　　*

> You call it sundew: how it grows,
> If with its colour it have breath,
> If life taste sweet to it, if death

[1] 'For the hours pass by and are reckoned.'

Pain its soft petal, no man knows:
Man has no sight or sense that saith.

There is no finer effect of poetry than to recall to the minds of men the bounds that have been set to the scope of their sight and sense, to inspire their imaginations with a vivid consciousness of the size and the wonders and the strange remote companionship of the world of force and growth and form outside of man. '*Qui se considérera de la sorte*', said Pascal, '*s'effraiera, sans doute, de se voir comme suspendu dans la masse que la nature lui a donnée entre ces deux abimes de l'infini et du néant.*'[1] And there are two ways in which a man can treat this affright that seizes his fellows as they catch interrupted glimpses of their position. He can transfigure their baseness of fear into true poetic awe, which shall underlie their lives as a lasting record of solemn rapture. Or else he can jeer and mock at them, like an unclean fiery imp from the pit. Mr. Swinburne does not at all events treat the lot of mankind in the former spirit. In his best mood, he can only brood over 'the exceeding weight of God's intolerable scorn, not to be borne'; he can only ask of us, 'O fools and blind, what seek ye there high up in the air,' or 'Will ye beat always at the Gate, Ye fools of fate.' If he is not in his best mood he is in his worst—a mood of schoolboy lustfulness. The bottomless pit encompasses us on one side, and stews and bagnios on the other. He is either the vindictive and scornful apostle of a crushing iron-shod despair, or else he is the libidinous laureate of a pack of satyrs. Not all the fervour of his imagination, the beauty of his melody, the splendour of many phrases and pictures, can blind us to the absence of judgment and reason, the reckless contempt for anything like a balance, and the audacious counterfeiting of strong and noble passion by mad intoxicated sensuality. The lurid clouds of lust or of fiery despair and defiance never lift to let us see the pure and peaceful and bounteous kindly aspects of the great landscape of human life. Of enlarged *meditation*, the note of the highest poetry, there is not a trace, and there are too many signs that Mr. Swinburne is without any faculty in that direction. Never have such bountifulness of imagination, such mastery of the music of verse, been yoked with such thinness of contemplation and such poverty of genuinely impassioned thought.

[1] *Pensées*, 72: 'Whoever regards himself in this way will certainly be frightened to see himself suspended in the body which nature has given him, between the two abysses of the infinite and of nothingness.'

# 7. Robert Buchanan, *Athenaeum*

4 August 1866, 137–8

---

The author of this unsigned review, Robert Buchanan, asks, 'How old is this young gentleman?' Like John Morley, who was more than a year younger than Swinburne, Buchanan was Swinburne's junior. Now almost forgotten except for his attack (later renounced) on Rossetti and 'the fleshly school', Buchanan, in 1866, had already gained recognition as a poet and was to be prolific as versifier, dramatist, and novelist. He became involved in several squabbles, late in life attacking Kipling as vehemently as he had earlier attacked 'the fleshly school'. Published on the same day as Morley's review, Buchanan's differs from Morley's in its allegation of insincerity and its almost unqualified denial of literary merit in *Poems and Ballads*.

---

Mr. Swinburne commenced his literary career with considerable brilliance. His *Atalanta* in *Calydon* evinced noticeable gifts of word-painting and of music; and his *Chastelard*, though written in a monotone, contained several passages of dramatic force and power. In the latter work, however, there was too open a proclivity to that garish land beyond the region of pure thinking, whither so many inferior writers have been lured for their destruction—the land where Atys became a raving and sexless maniac, and where Catullus himself would have perished had he not been drawn back to the shadier border-region by the sincerity of his one grand passion. The glory of our modern poetry is its transcendent purity—no less noticeable in the passionate sweetness of Keats and Shelley than in the cold severity of Wordsworth; a purity owing much to the splendid truth of its sensuous colouring. More or less unavailing have been all the efforts of insincere writers to stain the current of our literature with impure thought; and those who have made the attempt have invariably done so with a view to conceal their own literary inferiority. Very rarely indeed a mighty physical nature has found utterance in warmer, less measured terms than are commonly employed in life or art; but it would be difficult, on fair critical grounds, to decide such utterance to be immoral—it is so genuine. The genuineness of the work as Art, we would suggest, can be the only absolute test of immorality in a story or poem. Truly sincere writing, no matter how forcible, seldom really offends us. When, however, we find a writer like the author of these *Poems and Ballads,* who is deliberately and impertinently insincere as an artist,—who has no splendid individual emotions to reveal and is unclean for the mere sake of uncleanness,—we may safely affirm, in the face of many pages of brilliant writing, that such a man is either no poet at all, or a poet degraded from his high estate, and utterly and miserably lost to the Muses. How old is this young gentleman, whose bosom, it appears, is a flaming fire, whose face is as the fiery foam of flowers, and whose words are as the honeyed kisses of the Shunamite?[1] He is quite the Absalom of modern bards,— long-ringleted, flippant-lipped, down-checked, amorous-lidded. He seems, moreover, to have prematurely attained to the fate of his old prototype; for we now find him fixed very fast indeed up a tree, and it will be a miracle if one breath of poetic life remain in him when he is cut down. Meantime, he tosses to us this charming book of verses, which bears some evidence of having been inspired in Holywell Street, composed on the Parade at Brighton, and touched up in the Jardin Mabile.[2] Very sweet things in puerility, as a literary linen-draper might express it—fine glaring patterns after Alfred de Musset and Georges Sand—grand bits in the manner of Hugo, with here and there a notable piece of insertion from Ovid and Boccaccio. Yet ere we go further, let us at once disappoint Mr. Swinburne, who would doubtless be charmed if we averred that his poems were capable of having an absolutely immoral influence. They are too juvenile and unreal for that. The strong pulse of true passion beats in no one of them. They are unclean, with little power; and mere uncleanness repulses. Here, in fact, we

---

[1] For Shulamite, or Shunamite, a female inhabitant of Shulem or Shunem, see the Song of Solomon, especially 4: 11.

[2] Holywell Street in London, now absorbed in the Strand, was once the site of 'Book-sellers' Row', many of the booksellers dealing in pornographic books. At Brighton, which had long been a fashionable watering-place in the sixties, crowds of pleasure-seekers paraded along the sea-front, among them some hundreds of 'gay women' from London. There was a '*jardin*', as well as a floor show and opportunities to dance, at the Bal Mabille (no longer existing in Paris), under whose auspices the 'can-can' and other daring dances were introduced. Obviously Buchanan mentions all three places because of their unsavoury associations.

have Gito,[1] seated in the tub of Diogenes, conscious of the filth and whining at the stars.

The very first verse in the book, though harmless enough in meaning, is a sample of the utter worthlessness in *form* of most of the poems:—

> I found in dreams a place of wind and flowers,
>     Full of sweet trees and colour of glad grass,
>     In midst whereof there was
> A lady clothed like summer with sweet hours.
> Her beauty, fervent as a fiery moon,
>     Made my blood burn and swoon
>         Like a flame rained upon.
> Sorrow had filled her shaken eyelids' blue,
> And her mouth's sad red heavy rose all through
>     Seemed sad with glad things gone.

Here all the images are false and distracted,—mere dabs of colour distributed carelessly and without art. The following sonnet goes further:—

[quotes 'Love and Sleep']

It would be idle to quote such prurient trash as that,—save for the purpose of observing that Mr. Swinburne's thought is on a fair level with his style of expression:—both are untrue, insincere, and therefore unpoetical. Absolute passion there is none; elaborate attempts at thick colouring supply the place of passion. Now, it may be fairly assumed that a writer so hopelessly blind to the simplest decencies of style, so regardless of the first principles of Art, can scarcely fail to offend if he attempt to discuss topics of importance to his fellow creatures, or deal with themes which demand the slightest exercise of thought properly so called. When, therefore, Mr. Swinburne touches on religious questions, he writes such verses as the subjoined which, though put into the mouth of a Roman, are purely personal, implying precisely the same conditions of thought as we find expressed in the lyrical poems elsewhere:—

> Wilt thou yet take all, Galilean? but these thou shalt not take,
> The laurel, the palms and the pæan, the breasts of the nymphs in the
>     brake; . . .

[quotes twelve more lines of the 'Hymn to Proserpine']

[1] The boy Gito, in Petronius' *Satyricon*, is a homosexual of whom the chief character and narrator, Encolpius, and Ascyltos, his rival, are enamoured.

Here, as in the other poems, we find no token of sincerity. It is quite obvious that Mr. Swinburne has never thought at all on religious questions, but imagines that rank blasphemy will be esteemed very clever. He describes the Almighty as *throwing dice* with the Devil for the soul of Faustine; and in the 'Laus Veneris', inserts the following lines, which he himself, doubtless, considers very grand:—

> Lo, she was thus when her clear limbs enticed
> All lips that now grow sad with kissing Christ,
>     Stained with blood fallen from the feet of God,
> The feet and hands whereat our souls were priced.
>
> Alas, Lord, surely thou art great and fair.
> But lo, her wonderfully woven hair!
>     And thou didst heal us with thy piteous kiss;
> But see now, Lord; her mouth is lovelier.
>
> She is right fair; what hath she done to thee?
> Nay, fair Lord Christ, lift up thine eyes and see;
>     Had now thy mother such a lip—like this?

Impertinence like the above can only be the work either of a misdirected and most disagreeable youth or of a very silly man. It is writing of which no true poet, fairly cultured, could have been guilty.

Gross insincerity in dealing with simple subjects, and rank raving on serious themes, make one suspicious of a writer's quality in all things; and a very little examination enables us to perceive that these poems are essentially imitative. Indeed, Mr. Swinburne's knack of parody is very remarkable, though it weighs heavily against his literary quality. Nothing could be cleverer than his imitation, here printed, of an old miracle-play; or than his numerous copies of the French lyric writers; or than his ingenious parrotings of the way of Mr. Browning. In no single instance does he free himself from the style of the copyist. His skill in transferring an old or modern master would be an enviable gift for any writer but one who hoped to prove himself a poet. Then again, though clever and whimsical to the last degree, he is satisfied with most simple effects. After a little while we find out there is a trick in his very versification, that it owes its music to the most extraordinary style of alliteration:—

> It will grow not again, this fruit of my heart,
>     Smitten with sunbeams, ruined with rain.
> The singing seasons divide and depart,
>     Winter and summer depart in twain.

It will grow not again, it is ruined at root,
The bloodlike blossom, the dull red fruit;
Though the heart yet sickens, the lips yet smart,
    With sullen savour of poisonous pain.

This kind of writing, abounding in adjectives chosen merely because they alliterate, soon cloys and sickens; directly we find out the trick our pleasure departs. We soon perceive also that Mr. Swinburne's pictures are bright and worthless. We detect no real taste for colour; the skies are all Prussian blue, the flesh-tints all vermilion, the sunlights all gamboge. The writer, who has no meditative faculty, evinces total ignorance of nature; his eye rolls like that of a drunkard, whose vision is clouded with fumes.

But we fear we have lingered too long over this book; criticism is thriftless here. We have hinted very slightly at the tone of the poems,—in all of which pure thinking is treated with scorn, and sensuality paraded as the end of life. The impure thought finds its natural expression in insincere verses, without real music, without true colour. One word with Mr. Swinburne before we conclude; perhaps it is not too late for him to turn back from ruin; perhaps, being young, he has evil advisers. Let him, then, seek wisdom, and cast evil advisers aside. Some few years hence he will feel that the only sure hold on the public is the reputation of earnestness in life, and of sincerity in thought; yet, after publishing these poems, he will find it hard, very hard, to convince his readers that he is an earnest man or a sincere thinker. His very parasites will abandon him, and the purer light, pouring in his sick eyes, will agonize and perhaps end him. Let him seek out Nature, let him humble himself, let him try to think seriously on life and art. He it was who, in a recent preface to Byron, described Wordsworth as slicing up Nature for culinary purposes. If that description be true, a sound course of discipline in the kitchen will do Mr. Swinburne a great deal of good; for he will, at least, learn to distinguish the ingredients of things, what will or will not harmonize together, and what kind of dishes form wholesome food for grown-up men.

# 8. Unsigned review, *London Review*

4 August 1866, xiii, 130–1

In his *Notes on Poems and Reviews* Swinburne paid special attention to this review, which he admitted was the work of a gentleman. It appeared on the same day as the reviews by Morley and Buchanan.

From the concluding verses of Mr. Swinburne's new volume, we infer that most, if not all, of these poems were written some years ago, when the author was very young. We hardly know whether or not to hope that this may be so. On the one hand, it would be a relief to think that possibly the diseased state of mind out of which many of them must have issued may have passed away; on the other hand, it would be an additional pain (certainly not wanted) to suppose that such corrupt and acrid thoughts could have proceeded from the very spring and blossoming of youth. For we do not know when we have read a volume so depressing and misbegotten—in many of its con- stituents so utterly revolting. Mr. Swinburne, in his address to Victor Hugo, speaks of having been brought up in France;[1] and it would seem as if he had familiarized himself with the worst circles of Parisian life, and drenched himself in the worst creations of Parisian literature (to the exclusion of the better parts of both), until he can see scarcely anything in the world, or beyond it, but lust, bitterness, and despair. Being a poet, he sees beauty also, of necessity; and this is the one redeeming feature in what would otherwise be a carnival of ugly shapes. But even the beauty of poetic expression, of which he is so great a master, cannot hide the truly horrible substratum of a large part of the present volume. The writer seems to have taken pains to shock in the highest degree, we will not say English conventional morals, but the commonest decencies of all modern lands. For the counterpart

[1] An erroneous interpretation apparently due to a hasty reading of 'To Victor Hugo', in which France is called the 'sweet mother-land'.

of some of his subjects we must go back to the writers of antiquity; and even in them we shall not find the jibing cynicism, the seemingly conscious revelling in the actual sense of evil, which throws such a lurid shadow over many of these pages. Mr. Swinburne deliberately selects the most depraved stories of the ancient world, and the most feculent corruptions of modern civilization, and dwells upon them with a passionate zest and long-drawn elaboration of enjoyment, which is only less shocking than the cold, sarcastic sneer with which (after the fury of sensual passion has vented itself in every form of libidinous metaphor) he assures us that these are not only the best things in the world, but better than anything we can hope for or conceive beyond the world. The strangest and most melancholy fact in these strange and melancholy poems is, not the *absence* of faith, but the presence of a faith which mocks at itself, and takes pleasure in its own degradation. Mr. Swinburne apparently believes in a God, for he makes use of his name with unnecessary frequency; but, quite as often as not, it is to revile him for suffering the merest riot of the senses to end in disappointment and satiety. He seems to have some idea of a heaven; but he tells us in plain language, and in several places, that it is a poor matter compared with a courtesan's caresses. He speaks of a hell, but says he would gladly encounter it for one minute's hot enjoyment.[1] To such faith as this we prefer blank atheism. The atheist may retain his belief in human nature, in goodness, in purity, in self-sacrifice, in the progress and perfection of the world; and may move onward to the grave, in his sad hopeless way, with something of dignity and reverential awe. But a faith that laughs at itself, that insults its own deities and defiles its own temples—this is the wildest and the dreariest aberration of all. There are indeed passages in Shelley (written in his less hopeful moods) which seem to indicate that he believed at times in some malignant persecution of the human race—and these are very much to be regretted; but they are the exceptions. Dominant above them all rises the poet's faith in the natural goodness of things, in the accidental character of evil, in the undying and unquenchable aspirations of the soul after moral beauty and nobility of living. Except as a system of ethics, Shelley rejected Christianity; but he neither lowered humanity nor desecrated the world. Mr. Swinburne will at times talk in the language even of mediaeval faith, and the next moment will turn round with a sort of Mephistophelian laugh, and, in effect, bid us revel like men in plague-time, for there is nothing so good either here or

[1] An allusion to 'Les Noyades'.

hereafter. And then he will fall to cursing, because delight in excess has loathing and despair for its twin brothers. This is literally the spirit of a large part of his volume; and the truly beautiful and tender things he has written in other parts, only make us regret the more the unhappy perversities by which they are accompanied. It is impossible to deny the power of such poems as 'Laus Veneris', 'Phaedra', 'Les Noyades', 'Anactoria', 'Fragoletta', 'Faustine', 'Dolores', etc.; but it is equally impossible to see why they should have been written. 'Anactoria' and 'Dolores' are especially horrible. The first is supposed to be uttered by Sappho, and, beginning with an insane extravagance of passion, it ends in raging blasphemy. The second is a mere deification of incontinence. Both are depraved and morbid in the last degree.

We are unaffectedly sorry to be obliged to write in this manner of Mr. Swinburne's last volume. We were among the first to recognise the extraordinary genius exhibited in *Atalanta in Calydon*, and again in *Chastelard*; and we hoped that whatever excess of purely animal passion they showed would be speedily toned down by deeper thought and larger experience. In both there were evidences of that hopeless mode of looking at life which Mr. Swinburne seems now to have erected into a species of faith; but in the first of those fine dramas the feeling was appropriate to a certain side of the ancient Greek nature, and in the other it harmonized with the gloomy tale which had been selected for illustration. While regretting that it had been so persistently dwelt on, we did not see any reason for concluding that it was an integral and unescapable element of the writer's genius; nor, in *Chastelard*, were we disposed to make too much of the warmth of particular passages, because the tragedy with which they were associated took them out of the region of mere sensuousness, and elevated them into that of awe and wonderment. But when we find the same characteristics repeated in a third volume, and without any excuse of dramatic fitness, we are led to fear that the fault is radical, the evil deliberately chosen. We are unable any longer to refrain from noticing that which is evidently systematic, and which challenges comment by repeated iteration. We do so regretfully, for we see in these baleful extravagances the rock on which a splendid genius will assuredly be wrecked, unless it yet has strength enough to turn aside from the imminent danger. If Mr. Swinburne has any ambition of earning for himself a permanent place in English literature—an ambition which he is certainly entitled to entertain—he is doing his best to destroy all chance of ever realizing such a dream. This kind of writing is so alien to the spirit of our country that it can obtain no root in the national soil. Men may wonder at it for a time; they will cast it out and forget it in the end. The contemporary dramatists of Shakespeare have perished, except in the knowledge of a few, in consequence of the strange fascination they found in forbidden subjects. Byron has suffered from the same cause; yet Byron was a more moderate offender than the author of these *Poems and Ballads*. The fate which has overtaken others must overtake him also if he is determined to pursue this disastrous path; and we shall have to say of him as of them, that he ruined his genius for the sake of an ugly eccentricity, which is no more poetical than it is decent.

Let us turn from the worse to the better aspects of this volume. Nothing can exceed the beauty and lyrical sweetness of some of the poems; and when Mr. Swinburne sings such an exquisite measure as this, called 'Itylus'—in which all the sad old story relives in pulse and passion of music—we forget the heavy reek and mire through which we have been dragged:—

[quotes 'Itylus']

Of a higher mood, and very full of pathos and poignant grief, is the 'Ballad of Burdens':—

[quotes 'A Ballad of Burdens']

In some of the poems—as in 'St. Dorothy', 'The King's Daughter', 'After Death', 'May Janet', 'The Bloody Son', and 'The Sea Swallows' —Mr. Swinburne has imitated with singular felicity the manner and phraseology of Chaucer and the old ballad-writers. Indeed, the ballad of 'The Bloody Son', though here derived from the Finnish, bears a close resemblance to the old Scotch song, 'Edward! Edward!'[1]

Before parting with this volume, we would again beg of Mr. Swinburne to reconsider his course. The region to which we would have him confine himself is no contracted domain. It sufficed for Homer and for Shakespeare, and might surely content him. No land of prudery or simpering mock-virtue, it is alive with passion and character, warm with colour, rich with the senses and the soul. If he will be true to his better genius, he may be one of the crowned singers in that Elysium of beauty, of power, and of ordered grace. If he gives himself to the guidance of his worse promptings, his path is towards chaos, and his bright commencement will set in tumult and disgrace.

[1] 'The Bloody Son' is really a paraphrase of a Finnish ballad of which Swinburne found an English translation of a German translation in F. J. Child's early collection *English and Scottish Ballads* (1857), ii, 350–2.

# 9. Buchanan: 'The Session of the Poets', *Spectator*

15 September 1866, xxxix, 1028

Robert Buchanan, who, soon after their publication, was identified by Swinburne and his friends as the author of the following verses, inserted 'August, 1866' as the month in which *Poems and Ballads* appeared. The epigraph from Catullus (in F. W. Cornish's translation, 'Great gods, what an eloquent manikin!') strikes a satirical note anticipating 'the only event of the evening'. The verses were widely reprinted. Some assumed that they portrayed, not Swinburne's part in a literary sensation, but an actual drunken Swinburne. In choosing his title, Buchanan may have remembered that Sir John Suckling had used the title 'A Session of the Poets'.

THE SESSION OF THE POETS—AUGUST 1866

*Dî magni, salaputium disertum!*—CAT. LIB. LIII

### I.

AT the Session of Poets held lately in London,
    The Bard of Freshwater[1] was voted the chair:
With his tresses unbrush'd, and his shirt-collar undone,
    He loll'd at his ease like a good-humour'd Bear;
'Come, boys!' he exclaimed, 'we'll be merry together!'
    And lit up his pipe with a smile on his cheek;—
While with eye, like a skipper's, cock'd up at the weather,
    Sat the Vice-Chairman Browning, thinking in Greek.

### II.

The company gather'd embraced great and small bards,
    Both strong bards and weak bards, funny and grave,
Fat bards and lean bards, little and tall bards,
    Bards who wear whiskers, and others who shave.

---

[1] Farringford, Tennyson's home on the Isle of Wight, was not far from Freshwater.

39

Of books, men, and things, was the bards' conversation—
Some praised *Ecce Homo*,[1] some deemed it so-so—
And then there was talk of the state of the nation,
And when the Unwash'd would devour Mister Lowe.[2]

### III

Right stately sat Arnold,—his black gown adjusted
Genteelly, his Rhine wine deliciously iced,—
With puddingish England serenely disgusted,
And looking in vain (in the mirror) for 'Geist';[3]
He heark'd to the Chairman, with 'Surely!' and 'Really?'
Aghast at both collar and cutty of clay,—
Then felt in his pocket, and breath'd again freely,
On touching the leaves of his own classic play.

### IV.

Close at hand, lingered Lytton, whose Icarus-winglets
Had often betrayed him in regions of rhyme,—
How glitter'd the eye underneath his grey ringlets,
A hunger within it unlessen'd by time!
Remoter sat Bailey—satirical, surly—
Who studied the language of Goethe too soon,
And sang himself hoarse to the stars very early,
And crack'd a weak voice with too lofty a tune.

### V.

How name all that wonderful company over?—
Prim Patmore, mild Alford,—and Kingsley alsoe?[4]
Among the small sparks, who was realler than Lover?
Among misses, who sweeter than Miss Ingelow?
There sat, looking moony, conceited, and narrow,
Buchanan,—who, finding, when foolish and young,
Apollo asleep on a coster-girl's barrow,
Straight dragged him away to see somebody hung.

---

[1] *Ecce Homo*, published anonymously by Sir John Robert Seeley in 1865, aroused vigorous opposition because of its humanistic interpretation of Christ's life and teachings.

[2] Robert Lowe (1811–1892), whose observations in New South Wales had caused him to distrust democracy, led opposition to the Reform Bill introduced in 1866.

[3] Arnold had published in the *Pall Mall Gazette* letters in which his countrymen are urged to acquire *Geist* ('intelligence')—material later included in *Friendship's Garland*.

[4] *Sic* for more stress on the rhyme? The last two lines of the stanza allude to such poems as 'Liz' and 'Nell' (in Buchanan's *London Poems* of 1866).

### VI.

What was said?   what was done?   was there prosing or rhyming?
  Was nothing noteworthy in deed or in word?—
Why, just as the hour of the supper was chiming,
  The only event of the evening occurred.
Up jumped, with his neck stretching out like a gander,
  Master Swinburne, and squeal'd, glaring out thro' his hair,
'All Virtue is bosh!   Hallelujah for Landor!
  I disbelieve wholly in everything!—There!'

### VII.

With language so awful he dared then to treat 'em,—
  Miss Ingelow fainted in Tennyson's arms,
Poor Arnold rush'd out, crying '*Sæcl' inficetum!*'[1]
  And great bards and small bards were full of alarms;
Till Tennyson, flaming and red as a gipsy,
  Struck his fist on the table and utter'd a shout:
'To the door with the boy!   Call a cab!   He is tipsy!'
  And they carried the naughty young gentleman out.

### VIII.

After that, all the pleasanter talking was done there,—
  Who ever had known such an insult before?
The Chairman tried hard to rekindle the fun there,
  But the Muses were shocked and the pleasure was o'er.
Then 'Ah!' cried the Chairman, 'this teaches me knowledge
  The future shall find me more wise, by the powers!
This comes of assigning to younkers from college
  Too early a place in such meetings as ours!'

CALIBAN

[1] 'O age ill-bred', adapted from Catullus, xliii, 8.

# 10. Henry Morley, *Examiner*

22 September 1866, 597–9

Though he was pleased that the unsigned *Examiner* article on *Chastelard* and *Poems and Ballads* was friendly, Swinburne did not entirely agree with its point of view. But in his own essay on Baudelaire's *Les Fleurs du Mal* he had pointed out that the moral of a poem may be implicit; interestingly enough, Baudelaire mildly demurred at Swinburne's defence of him, just as Swinburne did at the *Examiner*'s of himself.

The author of the unsigned article, Henry Morley, was a professor of English at University College and a biographer, critic, and editor.

Of Mr. Algernon C. Swinburne's *Atalanta* we have said all that we need say, and what he has since published gives us nothing to unsay. He is a young poet with sterling qualities, and the outcry that has been made over his last published volume of *Poems and Ballads* is not very creditable to his critics. The withdrawal of that volume is an act of weakness of which any publisher who does not give himself up to the keeping of a milk-walk for the use of babes has reason to be heartily ashamed. We speak now of Mr. Swinburne's play of *Chastelard*, and of this volume of *Poems and Ballads*. They belong to one another. There is precisely the same tone in both, the same—well, let us say it to the shallow pietists in plain words—the same scriptural lesson. Only Mr. Swinburne, at present, reads his lesson rather out of the Old Testament than out of the New. Old Testament poetry has fastened upon his imagination quite as strongly as the sublime fatalism of the old Greek dramatists. In his volume of *Poems and Ballads* we have whole pages finely paraphrased from Job, and from Ecclesiastes, and from David's Psalms. Say that he declares himself in these two books the Poet of Lust. It is right to say that, it is right also to know what we mean by saying it. He sings of Lust as Sin, its portion Pain and its end Death. He paints

42

its fruit as Sodom apples, very fair without, ashes and dust within. In dwelling on their outward beauty he is sensual. Men see that and say that he is a licentious writer. But again and again when he has dwelt as proper folk object to dwell on the desire of the flesh, the beauty drops away and shows the grinning skeleton beneath with fires of hell below. There is a terrible earnestness about these books. They are in utter contrast to the erotic poetry of the Restoration, which trifled sensually. If the sternest Old Testament wrath of the Puritans could have twisted itself into verse, and made as it were the woof to a warp of Suckling, Sedley, Etheredge, and Aphra Behn, the result would have been some such texture as has been woven out of the young mind of Mr. Swinburne. Some of the pieces in his volume of *Poems and Ballads* were, as we learn from one of the poems, written at school. Here are the passions of youth fearlessly expressed, and stirring depths that have been stirred hitherto by no poet in his youth. He could not, and he should not, stir them in his age. It is the ferment of good wine, and we must think they are no skilled judges of the wine of thought who shake their heads over it.

*Chastelard* and these *Poems and Ballads*, although published after, were, we believe, written before *Atalanta in Calydon*. There are manifest little crudities. Thus Mr. Swinburne seems, at an early period of his life, to have got it into his head that enough hadn't been made of the eyelids in poetical description. He has, therefore, made up arrears on their account for at least the thousand years last past. We have beauty 'tender as the inside of the eyelid is', and 'marriage of the eyelid with the cheek', and seven lines after that, sight of a face 'held fast between the eyelids', and lower down on the same page 'charred dust and eyelids bitten through with smoke', and certain lords glancing 'under the eyelid', and Chastelard with 'half tears under mine eyelids', and the Queen, if she wept much, 'this was blood brake forth and burnt mine eyelids', and souls will cleave to her yet for 'an eyelid's twitch'. When we come to the *Poems*, on the very first page, 'sorrow had filled her shaken eyelid's blue'. My lady makes sin sorrow, and death 'fair as her own eyelids be', and fair love is told 'cover thy lips and eyelids'. Tears fell on the poet through Queen Venus's eyelids, and he has a word of his lady and 'the great curled eyelids that withheld her eyes'. These five sets of eyelids are in the first eight pages of the volume. In the next poem we are at the eyelids again, with Venus's love 'shed between her eyelids through her eyes', and a little afterwards in the same poem,

> Her eyelids on her eyes like flower on flower,
> Mine eyelids on mine eyes like fire on fire.

Also there is in this same poem, 'draining of eyelids' and 'blinded eyelids that expand again'. Presently we have somebody's eyes 'clothed with deep eyelids under and above', and on the same page love with 'clear eyelids lifted toward the north and south'. Love lies presently 'between thine eyelids and thine eyes', and we have 'eyelids folded like a white roseleaf', and in a fine reading from the Old Testament, as a Litany, the delight of the eyes is read into 'the delight of the eyelids'. In Mr. Swinburne's eyelids this is the setting up of a neglected feature in its place of honour, but the effect of the incessant flash of eyelids has to our eyelids the effect of conversation with a man who is perpetually twitching and winking. There is the same indication of crudity in Mr. Swinburne's yet more eager enjoyment of the word bite. Smoke 'biting the eyelids' must have seemed a very fine phrase to him because there he contrived to set his two favourite words in juxtaposition. Of 'sweet'—'sweet'—'sweet', he has the iteration of a canary bird. There are 'sweets' enough in these two little volumes to set up a wholesale grocer for his life-time. No matter. Our eyelids are not blind to the defects of these volumes, and we even recognize in many pages of them an artificial diction that is not poetry, but may be taken for it because it is not prose, a diction that sometimes breeds in Mr. Swinburne's verse obscurity in which there is neither depth of thought nor superficial beauty of expression. But we say that, for all that, there is a music of strength in these books, outspoken honesty, a sturdy love of freedom, earnestness, poetic insight, truth and beauty of expression, beyond anything attained to by other of the young poets of the day.

What is at the core of *Chastelard*, but the thought of the Preacher that falls solemnly at the close of the first scene of the fifth act:—

> The mercy of a harlot is a sword;
> And her mouth sharper than a flame of fire.

and in the words of Mary Beaton on the last page of the book:—

> Then shall I see one day
> When God will smite her lying harlot's mouth—
> Surely I shall.

This being the lesson of the play, the author paints in bold effective contrasts of colour, too sudden, perhaps, in their changes and swift passage between extremes, but with no false proportions and with a rare force, the character of Mary Queen of Scots such as it was—such as Mr. Froude shows it to have been in that history of the reign of Elizabeth which he this week continues. The licentious dalliance, the hard-hearted vanity, the hypocrisy lying to all and even to herself, the cruel selfishness, the shifting moods of a loose nature, and ever again the cruelty, the mercy that is 'as a sword', form the groundwork of a drama in which Queen Mary plays the part of the Fragoletta, the Faustine, the Dolores of the *Poems and Ballads*, and Chastelard that of the brave man who slays his soul for love of the fair deceiver. This idea runs through both *Chastelard* and the *Poems and Ballads*. In *Chastelard* we have the first bold poetical depiction of the truth about Queen Mary. Take, for example, this passage artistically placed in the midst of a scene of hypocritical chamber dalliance with Chastelard when she is about to give herself to Darnley. She has wished to be a man; has asked Chastelard to fasten his sword to her side and change parts with her, but the sword hurts her tender flesh:—

[quotes the Queen's speech in Act 11, scene 1, beginning 'Alas, my side!' and including the next thirty-seven lines]

That is as true as the rest of Mr. Swinburne's picturing to Mary's character. Take for example this passage from the first of Mr. Froude's two new volumes which are published this week. The scene, Carberry hill; and though the extract may be long it has the merit of including in a good historical picture nearly all those features of Mary Stuart's character which Mr. Swinburne has for the first time in literature honestly embodied in a poem:—

[quotes eighteen paragraphs from Froude's *History of England*, chapter 13, dealing with the scene at Carberry Hill]

Can that poem be immoral which paints lust to show that it is set on fire of hell?

In the *Poems and Ballads* there is the same stern blending of pain and wrath with the delight of wantonness. The theme is not one to be sung *virginibus puerisque*,[1] but shall it therefore not be sung? Shall a young poet be praised for the frivolous songs of love and wine that satisfy conventional ideas of decorum, but condemned for fastening upon the inmost life of such themes, painting such uttermost delights as they claim to have in them only to show the rottenness within. 'Laus Veneris' sounds dangerous as title to a poem. It is an old fable of a knight who

---

[1] Horace, *Carm.*, III, i, 4: 'For maidens and youths'.

left the pardon of the church to live with Venus herself 'inside the Horsel', where he 'never feels clear air'. And how sings he of Venus?

> Her little chambers drip with flower-like red,
> Her girdles, and the chaplets of her head,
>    Her armlets and her anklets; with her feet
> She tramples all that winepress of the dead.

[quotes six more stanzas of 'Laus Veneris']

> Sin, is it sin whereby men's souls are thrust
> Into the pit? yet had I a good trust
>    To save my soul before it slipped therein,
> Trod under by the fire-shod feet of lust.

[quotes nine more verses of 'Laus Veneris']

Phaedra, in a fragment finely modelled to the Greek dramatic form, by lust travels the way of murder. The burning Sappho loves and sings defiance of the fate-bound gods in a wild passage that any Bœotian might pick out of its dramatic context and use to support a charge of atheism against Mr. Swinburne.

[quotes 'Me hath love made more bitter toward thee' to 'And mix his immortality with death']

In a poem called 'Satia te Sanguine' the passionate lover cries to her who has eyes and breasts like a dove and kills men's hearts with a breath. In a Litany and a Lamentation he pours a solemn strain of the old Hebrew thought across his verse, as thus:—

[quotes 'Not with fine gold for a payment' to the end of 'A Litany']

He sings of the licentious Faustine; but how? With the significant motto, '*Ave Faustina Imperatrix, morituri te salutant.*'[1] Her praise is such as this:—

> The shameless nameless love that makes
>    Hell's iron gin
> Shut on you like a trap that breaks
>    The soul, Faustine.

---

[1] 'Hail, Faustina the Empress, they who are about to die salute you (adapted from the formula for gladiators' greeting to the Emperor when entering the arena).

He sings of the incarnation of wantonness as Dolores Our Lady of Pain,

> And the lovers whose lips would excite thee
> Are serpents in hell.

He imitates the old miracle play in a masque of Queen Barsabe, with the voice of Nathan the Prophet followed by a vision of lustful women, famous in history, who succeed each other and speak. He imitates the mediaeval style of English narrative verse in a legend of St. Dorothy, who suffered many sharp tortures to resist a tyrant's lust, and, in dying, comforted the doubting Theophile by telling him of God's garden whither she was going.

> And Theophile burnt in the cheek, and said:
> Yea, could one see it, this were marvellous.
> I pray you, at your coming to this house,
> Give me some leaf of all those tree-branches;
> Seeing how so sharp and white our weather is,
> There is no green nor gracious red to see.
> Yea, sir, she said, that shall I certainly.

And he was going sadly home:—

> When they came upon the paven place
> That was called sometime the place amorous,
> There came a child before Theophilus
> Bearing a basket, and said suddenly:
> Fair sir, this is my mistress Dorothy
> That sends you gifts; and with this he was gone.
> In all this earth there is not such an one
> For colour and straight stature made so fair.
> The tender growing gold of his pure hair
> Was as wheat growing, and his mouth as flame.
> God called him Holy after his own name:
> With gold cloth like fire burning he was clad.
> But for the fair green basket that he had,
> It was filled up with heavy white and red, etc.

It is true that Mr. Swinburne's verse seldom touches, as it here does, on the world beyond the grave. At the gate of the Hereafter he makes solemn pause. We do not know that he has doubt. The Old Testament spirit is sometimes caught so completely in his verse that we hardly know whether he may not sometimes have thought that 'there is one end to the just and to the unjust'. But if there be a doubt it is that of an earnest mind, not of a mocker, a questioning to be respected, like all other questionings wherever it is found sincere. These lines professing to describe a cameo, seem to paint a design that is in fact the design of the whole book in which they are included:

[quotes 'A Cameo']

That a book thus dealing with the desire of the flesh should have been denounced as profligate because it does not paint the outside of the Sodom's Apple of like colour with the ashes that it shows within, says little indeed for the thoroughness of current criticism.

# 11. Swinburne defends his poems

## 1866

---

The following selection from *Notes on Poems and Reviews* (for fuller discussion see the Introduction, section II) contains Swinburne's comments on several of the poems that had been attacked, short notes on 'Faustine', 'Hermaphroditus' and 'Laus Veneris' being omitted. The text, that of my critical edition in *Swinburne Replies: Notes on Poems and Reviews, Under the Microscope, Dedicatory Epistle* (Syracuse, New York, 1966), is reproduced by special permission of the Syracuse University Press, owner of the copyright.

---

Certain poems of mine, it appears, have been impugned by judges, with or without a name, as indecent or as blasphemous. To me, as I have intimated, their verdict is a matter of infinite indifference: it is of equally small moment to me whether in such eyes as theirs I appear moral or immoral, Christian or pagan. But, remembering that science must not scorn to investigate animalcules and infusoria, I am ready for once to play the anatomist.

With regard to any opinion implied to expressed throughout my book, I desire that one thing should be remembered: the book is dramatic, many-faced, multifarious; and no utterance of enjoyment or despair, belief or unbelief, can properly be assumed as the assertion of its author's personal feeling or faith. Were each poem to be accepted as the deliberate outcome and result of the writer's conviction, not mine alone but most other men's verses would leave nothing behind them but a sense of cloudy chaos and suicidal contradiction. Byron and Shelley, speaking in their own persons, and with what sublime effect we know, openly and insultingly mocked and reviled what the English of their day held most sacred. I have not done this. I do not say that, if I chose, I would not do so to the best of my power; I do say that hitherto I have seen fit to do nothing of the kind.

It remains then to inquire what in that book can be reasonably offensive to the English reader. In order to resolve this problem, I will not

49

fish up any of the ephemeral scurrilities born only to sting if they can, and sink as they must. I will take the one article that lies before me; the work (I admit) of an enemy, but the work (I acknowledge) of a gentleman. I cannot accept it as accurate; but I readily and gladly allow that it neither contains nor suggests anything false or filthy. To him therefore, rather than to another, I address my reclamation. Two among my poems, it appears, are in his opinion 'especially horrible'.[1] Good. Though the phrase be somewhat 'inexpressive', I am content to meet him on this ground. It is something—nay, it is much—to find an antagonist who has a sufficient sense of honesty and honour to mark out the lists in which he, the challenger, is desirous to encounter the challenged.

The first, it appears, of these especially horrible poems is 'Anactoria'. I am informed, and have not cared to verify the assertion, that this poem has excited, among the chaste and candid critics of the day or hour or minute, a more vehement reprobation, a more virtuous horror, a more passionate appeal, than any other of my writing. Proud and glad as I must be of this distinction, I must yet, however reluctantly, inquire what merit or demerit has incurred such unexpected honour. I was not ambitious of it; I am not ashamed of it; but I am overcome by it. I have never lusted after the praise of reviewers; I have never feared their abuse; but I would fain know why the vultures should gather here of all places; what congenial carrion they smell, who can discern such (it is alleged) in any rose-bed. And after a little reflection I do know, or conjecture. Virtue, as she appears incarnate in British journalism and voluble through that unsavoury organ, is something of a compound creature—

> A lump neither alive nor dead,
> Dog-headed, bosom-eyed, and bird-footed;[2]

nor have any dragon's jaws been known to emit on occasion stronger and stranger sounds and odours. But having, not without astonishment and disgust, inhaled these odours, I find myself at last able to analyse their component parts. What my poem means, if any reader should want that explained, I am ready to explain, though perplexed by the hint that explanation may be required. What certain reviewers have imagined it to imply, I am incompetent to explain, and unwilling to imagine. I am evidently not virtuous enough to understand them. I

[1] Quoted from the *London Review* (No. 8).
[2] Shelley's 'The Witch of Atlas', xi, 7–8.

thank Heaven that I am not. *Ma corruption rougirait de leur pudeur.*[1] I have not studied in those schools whence that full-fledged phœnix, the 'virtue' of professional pressmen, rises chuckling and crowing from the dunghill, its birthplace and its deathbed. But there are birds of alien feather, if not of higher flight; and these I would now recall into no hencoop or preserve of mine, but into the open and general field where all may find pasture and sunshine and fresh air: into places whither the prurient prudery and the virulent virtue of pressmen and prostitutes cannot follow; into an atmosphere where calumny cannot speak, and fatuity cannot breathe; in a word, where backbiters and imbeciles become impossible. I neither hope nor wish to change the unchangeable, to purify the impure. To conciliate them, to vindicate myself in their eyes, is a task which I should not condescend to attempt, even were I sure to accomplish.

In this poem I have simply expressed, or tried to express, that violence of affection between one and another which hardens into rage and deepens into despair. The key-note which I have here touched was struck long since by Sappho. We in England are taught, are compelled under penalties to learn, to construe, and to repeat, as schoolboys, the imperishable and incomparable verses of that supreme poet; and I at least am grateful for the training. I have wished, and I have even ventured to hope, that I might be in time competent to translate into a baser and later language the divine words which even when a boy I could not but recognise as divine. That hope, if indeed I dared ever entertain such a hope, I soon found fallacious. To translate the two odes and the remaining fragments of Sappho is the one impossible task; and as witness of this I will call up one of the greatest among poets. Catullus 'translated'—or as his countrymen would now say 'traduced'—the 'Ode to Anactoria'—*Εἰς Ἐρωμέναν*: a more beautiful translation there never was and will never be; but compared with the Greek, it is colourless and bloodless, puffed out by additions and enfeebled by alterations. Let any one set against each other the two first stanzas, Latin and Greek, and pronounce. (This would be too much to ask of all of my critics; but some among the journalists of England may be capable of achieving the not exorbitant task.) Where Catullus failed I could not hope to succeed; I tried instead to reproduce in a diluted and dilated form the spirit of a poem which could not be reproduced in the body.

Now, the ode *Εἰς Ἐρωμέναν*—the 'Ode to Anactoria' (as it is named

[1] 'My depravity would blush at their modesty.'

by tradition)—the poem which English boys have to get by heart—the poem (and this is more important) which has in the whole world of verse no companion and no rival but the 'Ode to Aphrodite', has been twice at least translated or 'traduced'. I am not aware that Mr. Ambrose Phillips, or M. Nicolas Boileau-Despréaux,[1] was ever impeached before any jury of moralists for his sufficiently grievous offence. By any jury of poets both would assuredly have been convicted. Now, what they did I have not done. To the best (and bad is the best) of their ability, they have 'done into' bad French and bad English the very words of Sappho. Feeling that although I might do it better I could not do it well, I abandoned the idea of translation—ἔκων ἀέκοντί γε θυμῷ.[2] I tried, then, to write some paraphrase of the fragment which the Fates and the Christians have spared us. I have not said, as Boileau and Phillips have, that the speaker sweats and swoons at sight of her favourite by the side of a man. I have abstained from touching on such details, for this reason: that I felt myself incompetent to give adequate expression in English to the literal and absolute words of Sappho; and would not debase and degrade them into a viler form. No one can feel more deeply than I do the inadequacy of my work. 'That is not Sappho,' a friend said once to me. I could only reply, 'It is as near as I can come; and no man can come close to her.' Her remaining verses are the supreme success, the final achievement, of the poetic art.

But this, it may be, is not to the point. I will try to draw thither; though the descent is immeasurable from Sappho's verse to mine, or to any man's. I have striven to cast my spirit into the mould of hers, to express and represent not the poem but the poet. I did not think it requisite to disfigure the page with a foot-note wherever I had fallen back upon the original text. Here and there, I need not say, I have rendered into English the very words of Sappho. I have tried also to work into words of my own some expression of their effect: to bear witness how, more than any other's, her verses strike and sting the memory in lonely places, or at sea, among all loftier sights and sounds— how they seem akin to fire and air, being themselves 'all air and fire';[3]

---

[1] Swinburne refers to Ambrose Philips (as the name is usually written), author of 'A Fragment from Sappho', and Nicolas Boileau-Despréaux, especially to chapter viii of *Traité du Sublime*, a translation of Longinus's treatise.

[2] *Iliad*, iv, 43: 'Of mine own will, yet with reluctant mind' (cited by Swinburne as the equivalent of the Homeric phrase; Lang, iv, 230).

[3] Said of Marlowe by Michael Drayton ('To My Most Dearly-Loved Friend Henry Reynolds, Esquire').

other element there is none in them. As to the angry appeal against the supreme mystery of oppressive heaven, which I have ventured to put into her mouth at that point only where pleasure culminates in pain, affection in anger, and desire in despair—as to the 'blasphemies'[1] against God or Gods of which here and elsewhere I stand accused,— they are to be taken as the first outcome or outburst of foiled and fruitless passion recoiling on itself. After this, the spirit finds time to breathe and repose above all vexed senses of the weary body, all bitter labours of the revolted soul; the poet's pride of place is resumed, the lofty conscience of invincible immortality in the memories and the mouths of men.

What is there now of horrible in this? the expressions of fierce fondness, the ardours of passionate despair? Are these so unnatural as to affright or disgust? Where is there an unclean detail? where an obscene allusion? A writer as impure as my critics might of course have written, on this or on any subject, an impure poem; I have not. And if to translate or paraphrase Sappho be an offence, indict the heavier offenders who have handled and rehandled this matter in their wretched versions of the ode. Is my poem more passionate in detail, more unmistakable in subject? I affirm that it is less; and what I affirm I have proved.

Next on the list of accusation stands the poem of 'Dolores'. The gist and bearing of this I should have thought evident enough, viewed by the light of others which precede and follow it. I have striven here to express that transient state of spirit through which a man may be supposed to pass, foiled in love and weary of loving, but not yet in sight of rest; seeking refuge in those 'violent delights' which 'have violent ends',[2] in fierce and frank sensualities which at least profess to be no more than they are. This poem, like 'Faustine', is so distinctly

[1] As I shall not return to this charge of 'blasphemy', I will here cite a notable instance of what does seem permissible in that line to the English reader. (I need not say that I do not question the right, which hypocrisy and servility would deny, of author and publisher to express and produce what they please. I do not deprecate, but demand for all men freedom to speak and freedom to hear. It is the line of demarcation which admits, if offence there be, the greater offender and rejects the less—it is this that I do not understand.) After many alternate curses and denials of God, a great poet talks of Christ 'veiling his horrible Godhead', of his 'malignant soul', his 'godlike malice'. Shelley outlived all this and much more; but Shelley wrote all this and much more. Will no Society for the Suppression of Common Sense—no Committee for the Propagation of Cant—see to it a little? or have they not already tried their hands at it and broken down? For the poem which contains the words above quoted continues at this day to bring credit and profit to its publishers—Messrs. Moxon and Co. [Swinburne's note.]

[2] *Romeo and Juliet*, II, vi, 9.

symbolic and fanciful that it cannot justly be amenable to judgment as a study in the school of realism. The spirit, bowed and discoloured by suffering and by passion (which are indeed the same thing and the same word), plays for a while with its pleasures and its pains, mixes and distorts them with a sense half-humorous and half-mournful, exults in bitter and doubtful emotions—

Moods of fantastic sadness, nothing worth.[1]

It sports with sorrow, and jests against itself; cries out for freedom and confesses the chain; decorates with the name of goddess, crowns anew as the mystical Cotytto,[2] some woman, real or ideal, in whom the pride of life with its companion lusts is incarnate. In her lover's half-shut eyes, her fierce unchaste beauty is transfigured, her cruel sensual eyes have a meaning and a message; there are memories and secrets in the kisses of her lips. She is the darker Venus, fed with burnt-offering and blood-sacrifice; the veiled image of that pleasure which men impelled by satiety and perverted by power have sought through ways as strange as Nero's before and since his time; the daughter of lust and death, and holding of both her parents; Our Lady of Pain, antagonist alike of trivial sins and virtues; no Virgin, and unblessed of men; no mother of the Gods or God; no Cybele, served by sexless priests or monks, adored of Origen or of Atys;[3] no likeness of her in Dindymus or Loreto.[4]

The next act in this lyrical monodrame of passion represents a new stage and scene. The worship of desire has ceased; the mad commotion of sense has stormed itself out; the spirit, clear of the old regret that drove it upon such violent ways for a respite, healed of the fever that wasted it in the search for relief among fierce fancies and tempestuous pleasures, dreams now of truth discovered and repose attained. Not the martyr's ardour of selfless love, an unprofitable flame that burnt out and did no service—not the rapid rage of pleasure that seemed for a little to make the flesh divine, to clothe the naked senses with the fiery

---

[1] Matthew Arnold, 'To a Gypsy Child by the Seashore', l. 18.

[2] A Thracian goddess whose rites suggest identification with the originally Phrygian Cybele.

[3] The Christian theologian Origen is mentioned as a type of the religious eunuch along with the mythical Atys, who, driven mad by the mother-goddess Cybele, emasculated himself.

[4] An early sanctuary of Cybele stood on Dindymus, a mountain in Phrygia. In Loreto, Italy, was a church reputed to contain the Virgin's house, said to have been brought from Nazareth by angels.

raiment of faith; but a stingless love, an innocuous desire. 'Hesperia', the tenderest type of woman or of dream, born in the westward 'islands of the blest',[1] where the shadows of all happy and holy things live beyond the sunset a sacred and a sleepless life, dawns upon his eyes a western dawn, risen as the fiery day of passion goes down, and risen where it sank. Here, between moonrise and sunset, lives the love that is gentle and faithful, neither giving too much nor asking—a bride rather than a mistress, a sister rather than a bride. But not at once, or not for ever, can the past be killed and buried; hither also the temptress[2] follows her flying prey, wounded and weakened, still fresh from the fangs of passion; the cruel hands, the amorous eyes, still glitter and allure. *Qui a bu boira:*[3] the feet are drawn back towards the ancient ways. Only by lifelong flight, side by side with the goddess that redeems, shall her slave of old escape from the goddess that consumes: if even thus one may be saved, even thus distance the bloodhounds.

This is the myth or fable of my poem; and it is not without design that I have slipped in, between the first and the second part, the verses called 'The Garden of Proserpine', expressive, as I meant they should be, of that brief total pause of passion and of thought, when the spirit, without fear or hope of good things or evil, hungers and thirsts only after the perfect sleep. Now, what there is in all this unfit to be written —what there is here indecent in manner or repulsive in matter—I at least do not yet see; and before I can see it, my eyes must be purged with the euphrasy and rue[4] which keep clear the purer eyes of professional virtue. The insight into evil of chaste and critical pressmen, their sharp scent for possible or impossible impurities, their delicate ear for a sound or a whisper of wrong—all this knowledge 'is too wonderful and excellent for me; I cannot attain unto it.'[5] In one thing, indeed, it seems I have erred: I have forgotten to prefix to my work the timely warning of a great poet and humorist:—

> *J'en préviens les mères des familles,*
> *Ce que j'écris n'est pas pour les petites filles*

---

[1] Byron refers to 'islands of the blest' (*Don Juan*, iii, 700), having in mind ancient Greek references to them. The name Hesperia is of course used for the western land, Italy, by Vergil (*Aeneid*, iii, 163).

[2] The reading of the MS. 'Huntress' in the printed edition was a natural misreading by the printers.

[3] 'Who has drunk will drink,' apparently proverbial.

[4] Cf. *Paradise Lost*, xi, 414.

[5] Psalm 139: 6 in *The Book of Common Prayer*.

*Dont on coupe le pain en tartines; mes vers*
*Sont des vers de jeune homme.*[1]

I have overlooked the evidence which every day makes clearer, that our time has room only for such as are content to write for children and girls. But this oversight is the sum of my offence.

It would seem indeed as though to publish a book were equivalent to thrusting it with violence into the hands of every mother and nurse in the kingdom as fit and necessary food for female infancy. Happily there is no fear that the supply of milk for babes will fall short of the demand for some time yet. There are moral milkmen enough, in all conscience, crying their ware about the streets and by-ways; fresh or stale, sour or sweet, the requisite fluid runs from a sufficiently copious issue. In due time, perhaps, the critical doctors may prescribe a stronger diet for their hypochondriac patient, the reading world; or that gigantic *malade imaginaire* called the public may rebel against the weekly draught or the daily drug of MM. Purgon and Diafoirus.[2] We, meanwhile, who profess to deal neither in poison nor in pap, may not unwillingly stand aside. Let those read who will, and let those who will abstain from reading. *Caveat emptor.* No one wishes to force men's food down the throats of babes and sucklings. The verses last analysed were assuredly written with no moral or immoral design; but the upshot seems to me moral rather than immoral, if it must needs be one or the other, and if (which I cannot be sure of) I construe aright those somewhat misty and changeable terms.

[1] Théophile Gautier, *Albertus*, xcviii: 'I warn the mothers of families that I am not writing for little girls, for whom one makes bread and butter; my verses are a young man's verses.'
[2] Characters in Molière's *Le Malade Imaginaire*.

# 12. W. M. Rossetti, *Swinburne's Poems and Ballads*

## 1866

William Michael Rossetti, less gifted but perhaps more sensible than some other members of the circle of which he was to become an important chronicler, was once known as a critic of art and literature. In the preface to *Swinburne's Poems and Ballads* he explained that he had not been asked, but had volunteered, to undertake his friend's defence. Originally he had planned that defence as an article for the *North American Review*, but J. R. Lowell's harsh judgment of Swinburne's tragedies in that periodical had led him to publish it as a book.

The advent of a new great poet is sure to cause a commotion of one kind or another; and it would be hard were this otherwise in times like ours, when the advent of even so poor and pretentious a poetaster as a Robert Buchanan stirs storms in teapots.[1] It is therefore no wonder that Mr. Swinburne should have been enthusiastically admired and keenly discussed as soon as he hove well in sight of the poetry-reading public, for he is not only a true but even a great poet; still less wonder, under all the particular circumstances of the case, that, with his last volume, admiration and discussion should have ended in a grand crash of the critical orchestra, and that all voices save those of denunciation and repudiation should have been well-nigh drowned. As with many poets of whom our literature is or might be proud—a Shelley, a Byron, a Landor, a Whitman, a Mrs. Browning—the time had to come to Mr. Swinburne when the literary interest in his writings paled before some other feeling excited by them—when the literary gauge was thrown aside by his examiners, and some other one was applied, not to the

---

[1] According to W. M. Rossetti's *Some Reminiscences*, this reference to Buchanan was prompted by Buchanan's 'The Session of the Poets' (No. 9) and led Buchanan to respond with a savage criticism of Rossetti's edition of Shelley.

present advantage of himself or his book. Be it added that Mr. Swinburne has done his very best, or worst, to hasten this time, and to aggravate the crisis. He has courted critics to be—and still more to profess themselves—indignant and horrified; they have responded to his invitation, have exorcised his book with abundant holy water of morals and religion, the salt of literary disquisition being but sparingly used—and the result is, that the book is withdrawn from publication in England. It is practically certain, however, to have reappeared, with no alteration save that of the London publishing-house, long before these remarks are in print. We shall endeavour to look upon this book, along with Mr. Swinburne's other writings, calmly, to appraise them justly in literary and all other respects, and to assign him his due place among poets. We will at once and unreservedly say, we are satisfied that this place will, in the judgment of posterity, be a lofty one, and that Algernon Swinburne is one of that rare and electest class—the writers whom contemporaries, even the well-affected among them, are likely to praise too little rather than too much.

The *Poems and Ballads*, to which we shall have very mainly to confine our attention, is the fourth poetic volume published by Mr. Swinburne. Of prose he has issued scarcely anything except the very independent and remarkable essay upon Byron prefixed to Messrs. Moxon's recent selection from that poet's writings. He is known besides to have in the press an elaborate study upon the poet and painter Blake—a subject than which none requires more delicate or sharp manipulation, more keenness or specialty of sympathy, or more boldness of estimate and statement. To judge from his own powers in the poetic art, and from his essay on Byron, Mr. Swinburne will supply all these requisites in measure hardly to be rivalled. The first of his poetic volumes, issued in 1860, was composed of the two dramas, *The Queen Mother* (Katharine de' Medici[1] at the period of the Massacre of St. Bartholomew) and *Rosamond*. Singular literary power, and scenic eloquence and subtlety of speech, were to be found in this volume to fulness—we might almost say, to repletion. The tragedies show intellectual and poetic, more strictly than dramatic, richness; though the dramatic element also is present, so to speak, 'in solution', needing not so much to be increased or intensified as to be condensed out of the phase of dialogue and mere situation into that of action and crisis. The least that can be said of this volume is that it was

[1] The author's spelling of 'Catherine de' Medici', like that of 'Shakespeare' and words like 'quartet', is unusual.

a most singularly mature one, as well as of the highest promise, from a writer at that time extremely young: it remains to this day almost unknown both to English and American poetic readers, the interest which Mr. Swinburne's subsequent poems have excited seeming not to have reacted to any adequate extent upon these their first precursors and heralds.

Next, in 1865, came the Greek tragedy, *Atalanta in Calydon*. There was no mistake about that volume, and no slothfulness in recognizing its claims. It continues to be the most generally accepted and the most admired of Mr. Swinburne's writings. Greek equally in the ideal according to which it is conceived, and in the model of style and structure to which it conforms, it yet exhibits, in both respects, the independence and remoulding force of an original work. We have to deal, not with a Greek imitation, but with a Greek imagination. Nothing is formal, nothing coerced or vamped up into a trite copyism of externals: the spirit of the drama is Greek, and assumes a Greek shape as its visible semblance; but its art is altogether vital and con-gruous, attesting a master hand of our own day which never seeks to conceal itself under the mere clothes of classicism. The fullest and most ardent poetic expression shows itself compatible with the antique majesty; poetic law and poetic liberty speak out with blended voice. Dramatically considered, the central difficulty, to fail in which would have been to fail in all, is clearly the character of Althaea, Meleager's mother, who horribly slays her heroic son by burning the fated brand to which his life is linked. Even a good dramatic artist might well have failed to conceive the character so firmly and consistently, or to realize it so intensely, as Mr. Swinburne has done. He has presented Althaea as a devoted mother, religiously observant of law and order, full of grave counsel and noble acquiescence; bowed down with grief at the homicide of her brothers, but not more with grief than with horror at the outrage of the deed as coming from her son's hand, the reversal of all order of nature and prescription; brooding with throes of this grief and this horror, till, unmaternal and unsexed, a vindicator of divine law and automaton of divine vengeance, she burns up her son's life in the brand, passionate with exultation and with misery—there-after remaining impenetrably silent, a witness of the ensuing doom. All this is given with a severe outline (to use the draughtsman's phrase), as well as with a sustained and exuberant eloquence, such as offer a very extraordinary study of style. A basis and an issue still wider than any-thing consequent upon the mere personality of Althaea are, however, involved in this legend of Meleager; and these have not been slighted by the poet. The inscrutableness of Fate, the supreme and inappellable ordainer, more than once merged into the term 'God' in the pealing paganism of Mr. Swinburne's choruses, is the ultimate subject of the tragedy. That which Christians have learned to call 'the dispensations of Providence', and to construe by faith in a revealed immortality (as one might read a too unlikely palimpsest of Lucretius or of Petronius with Plato showing through), is here regarded as mere inscrutableness —frightful blows dealt in the darkness by a being from whom there is no appeal whatever, and even to himself none really worth making. This 'God' is, in fact, the arch-enemy and tyrant; and one of the choruses, with faint qualifications (in the interest as much of human dignity of character, or 'self-respect', as of the actual rights of the question), finds most emphatic words in which to say so—the very rapture of protest beneath a hand which is grinding, and will grind, the protester into dust. Agreeing on the whole in the opinion which places *Atalanta* at the head of all Mr. Swinburne's performances, we do not flinch from taking a step beyond, and calling it the most considerable poetic production—scale, subject-matter, form, treatment, artistic completeness, and whatever else, allowed for—that our literature has to show since Shelley's *Prometheus Unbound*, now just about half a century old. Perhaps the only work which could plausibly be pitted against *Atalanta* in such a comparison, is Tennyson's *In Memoriam*; and that, apart from any other questions, can scarcely be regarded as one integral, continuous composition.

In 1865, also, Mr. Swinburne published his *Chastelard*. It might be a moot point of criticism whether such a drama as *Atalanta* or such as *Chastelard* is intrinsically the more difficult attempt: is Sophocles or Shakespear the more exigent, the more unattainable of models? At any rate, it may safely be affirmed that the poet who does supremely succeed in a Greek tragedy on the Greek scheme is not necessarily, perhaps not probably, the one to succeed equally in an Elizabethan tragedy on the Elizabethan or other modern scheme (in the present instance, the analogy is rather to the monarch of living tragedians, Victor Hugo, than to Shakespear and his school, though here also Mr. Swinburne has steered well clear of imitation). Accordingly, *Chastelard* may, we think, be rightly regarded as a less absolute and indisputable achievement than *Atalanta*. Mr. Swinburne could not have come so curiously and splendidly right in *Atalanta* if that had not been a class of work peculiarly fitted to his genius; and, short of having a mind to embrace alike the four points of the compass of tragedy, he could not be expected to find himself, in exactly the same degree, well suited in such an undertaking as *Chastelard*. The round man for the round hole is clearly not destined to snuggle quite so comfortably into the square one. Yet, after making every needful deduction from the claims of the *Chastelard*, after reducing it from the ideal at which it aims to the standard which it actually reaches, we shall still find it to thrill through and through with tragic vibrations and reverberations, to be in most respects an admirable poem, and very nearly a grand drama—the character of Queen Mary, in especial, being at once conceived and realized with an impulse and a subtlety which prove the author's right to attempt this form of tragedy once and again, and probably, before he has done with it, to satisfy both his readers' hopes and his own. Indeed, in this case also, we have to go back to Shelley before we can point out a finer dramatic work or faculty—if even *The Cenci* is finer than *Chastelard*, which we think open to difference of opinion. Of intermediate writers, we know none that can be cited in emulation save Henry Taylor and Browning. For the latter poet we have the acutest sympathy and the most genuine admiration; yet we cannot think but that any competent criticism would show the faults and limitations of such works as *A Blot in the 'Scutcheon*, *Strafford*, *King Victor and King Charles*, to be more damaging and more anti-dramatic than any which can be justly charged against *Chastelard*. Mr. Henry Taylor, it is true, may be rated as having, in *Philip van Artevelde*, achieved a definite success in a certain by no means easy or unimportant class of drama—the drama of public event and grave historic tableau. We are not prepared to say that he has come less near to his ideal than Mr. Swinburne to his; but we must not forget the great difference in the nature of the attempt—how far more closely passion and poetry have to be welded into drama in Swinburne's than in Taylor's work, how much more artfully and hazardously compounded an amalgam they have to form. It is something like the difference between a monumental picture and a cartoon; or between Cellini casting the Perseus in his blazing fiery furnace, and the moulder whose material is plaster of Paris.

Thus much premised as to the books which have preceded the *Poems and Ballads*, and leaving unsaid much more which would claim to be spoken were those earlier books our immediate subject, we proceed to handle—and, if need be, to burn our fingers at—this somewhat scorching and explosive production.

An attentive perusal of the volume will, we think, disclose in it four main currents of influence and feeling—which we set down in descending ratio according to their importance in the work of art; and let us here say once for all that it is as a work of art, mainly if not engrossingly, that we regard these and any other poems which rise above a very restricted aesthetic scope. The currents in question are—

1, the Passionately Sensuous;
2, the Classic, or Antique;
3, the Heterodox, or Religiously Mutinous; and
4, the Assimilative or Reproductive in point of Literary Form.

As just stated, we have ranged these influences 'in descending ratio according to their importance in the work of art', the particular poems before us. We do not, however, consider that the same ratio would hold good if we were analysing the intrinsic, organic importance of these several influences upon the very mind and personality of the poet. For such an analysis, we might be disposed to place our second and fourth influences, the Classic and Assimilative in Literary Form, ahead of all, and to refer them to another influence, larger and more fundamental still—the intensely, the overpoweringly artistic direction of Mr. Swinburne's mind, and the consequent startling predominance of the literary over other modes of thought or writing, and absorption of all other excellences into the literary or verbally plastic excellence, the excellence of poetic result. In like manner, we should place our third influence, the Heterodox or Religiously Mutinous, including (as in our purview it does) the morally mutinous, above our first-ranked influence, the Passionately Sensuous, which it fairly overlaps in the poet's brain, or in essential relation to his mind and his conception of things. In fact, Mr. Swinburne's mind appears to be very like a *tabula rasa* on moral and religious subjects, so occupied is it with instincts, feelings, perceptions, and a sense of natural or artistic fitness and harmony. These are to him the poetic pounds: be they but taken care of, and those other pence may, with the proverb's leave, take care of themselves. On these moral and religious subjects he seems to have no 'innate ideas', no preconceptions, no prejudices. He has no sense of what moral philosophers call a 'sanction'. Dogmas and doctrines come warranted to him from outside; and there is nothing in him which leaps out to meet the warrant half-way. Thus nude of the qualities of mind which send a man forth to seek for some moral or religious foundation, and which dispose him to accept such as he finds ready to his hand, Mr.

Swinburne might have remained neutral enough on such matters, but that others will insist upon knowing all about them, upon proselytizing and evangelizing; and Mr. Swinburne, when he finds he cannot be left alone and unconcerned, flies from neutrality to antagonism, resents what he would naturally leave out of count, and vollies forth 'winged words' of the most audacious aim and the least stinted virus. It is in connexion partly with this attitude of mind, and partly with his literary or expressional intensity just previously noted, that we see reason for contemplating the 'passionately sensuous' aspect of his work in the *Poems and Ballads*. We conceive it to be very closely related to his moral negativeness (by which term we have no intention, as no right, to assume that Mr. Swinburne is a bad man, but only that the facts of the world and of man naturally and primarily appeal to him on other than their moral showing); related also to the antagonistic excitement consequent upon the coercive administration of those moral and religious 'alteratives' of which the British pharmacopœia is so prodigal—and to the fervour of perception and of words which seizes him when fervid subject-matter presents itself to his mental vision, and this because he is so much of an artist, and so little of either a moralist or an immoralist. Thus, strange as it may seem to say so of a book withdrawn from circulation on account of its outrages to decency, and in which 'passionate sensuousness' really is a very leading influence, we believe that that influence is, in fact, one of the *less* genuine constituents of the author's mind: there is even something about it too determinate and prepense, too uneasily iterative—not exceptionally genuine, but near to being actually factitious. It would even ring almost hollow to the ear and the apprehension of the reader, were not the sound transmitted through so intense a medium of artistic perception and harmonic expression. We are certainly far from justifying Mr. Swinburne's course in publishing to a world which was pretty well known not to want them such performances as 'Dolores', 'Fragoletta', and some others[1]—to have done so was both a miscalculation and an

---

[1] Between the time of our writing this passage, and that when our review was completed, symptoms have appeared of a very decided change of public and critical feeling in England regarding the poems for which Mr. Swinburne was most reviled. An article in the London *Examiner* (22d September) deserves the credit of commencing this reaction: it is confidently attributed to no less honourable and responsible a writer than Professor Morley. The reaction even goes so far as to pronounce Mr. Swinburne a severely moral writer, who does indeed proclaim the allurements of sense with exceptional and exceptionable downrightness, but who proclaims these chiefly to show their hollowness, and the Nemesis which dogs them. A pamphlet from Mr. Swinburne's own hand is also notified, and will doubtless have appeared before our review does. For our own part we do not

*inconvenance,*[1] for which he has had to pay the penalty which might have been foreseen; but we are equally far from thinking that any positive stigma attaches to his name or his genius on this account, or that there is any true sense of right or justice in those critics who, stopping their ears at his unseemlinesses, refuse to hear, distinct and predominant above them, the flood of noble and divine music which these only mar with casual and separable though perverse discords. To sum up this part of our subject, Mr. Swinburne is 'passionately sensuous' in his poems chiefly because the passionate and the sensuous are two ultimate and indestructible elements of poetry; and he over-enforces them in expression chiefly because a mighty intoxication of poetic diction mounts to his head, and pours in an unruly torrent through his lips, and he forgets the often still nobler office of self-mastery and reticence.

The 'Classic or Antique' influence is an entirely genuine one with Mr. Swinburne, and cannot be called other than genuine in the part which it plays in his present volume. His mind and his sympathies receive nurture from the antique past. He is a manifest pagan; neither believing in a Christian revelation, nor entering kindly, though he can enter with truth of artistic perception, into a Christian dispensation, and modes of thought and life. This classic influence subserves to some extent his passionate sensuousness; for he can think without intolerance, and write with amazing candour and beauty, about 'Hermaphroditus' or 'Anactoria'. The poem bearing the latter name is, indeed, one of the most glorious exhibitions of fervent imagination and poetic execution in his volume. The reader is not bound to like it: if he does not admire it, he has but a purblind perception of what poetic workmanship means. The statue in the Louvre, and the Lesbian loves of Sappho, are not germane to the modern mind: let them by all means remain un-germane! Yet let not the artificer or the student of poetry be a mark for the mere mud of nineteenth-century highroads if some 'elective affinity' prompts him to penetrate somewhat further than parson or pedagogue into moods of mind and aberrations of passion which were vital enough to some of the great of old, however

exactly subscribe to the opinion expressed in the *Examiner,* as the terms which we use sufficiently show; but we must allow that there is considerable plausibility in that opinion, and a great want of candour in writers who, going into the opposite extreme, entirely ignore those evidences, in their way patent enough, which may be adduced in its support. —[Rossetti's note.]

---

[1] 'Impropriety.'

dead and putrescent they may now most legitimately have become. To these subjects a healthy and open mind stands in the relation expressed by the matron to whom naked men were as so many statues. One might almost say, and not be misunderstood by those whose understanding is worth courting, that everything Greek has become to us as a compound of beauty and of thought, a vestige and an evidence of human soul infused as into Parian marble, marble-like in its purity of appeal to us, and which time has privileged us to love with no gross or abject thought, whatever may be the express image and superscription of the monument. Be it confessed at the same time that Mr. Swinburne receives and transmits the impression without availing himself of this privilege so fully as he might, or, with his exquisite sensibility to beauty of subject-matter and perfection of poetic keeping, ought to, have done. 'Anactoria', impure as is its theme, might conceivably be treated with some nearer approach to comparative purity, and certainly without the feline or tigerish dallyings in which 'the lust of the flesh' passes into a positive lust of blood, equally unknown (if we are not mistaken) to Greek passion, and unknowable, unless as a nightmare of the imagination, to normal sensualists. Why lay hands doubly lawless upon what can be claimed as rightful property only by such a son of Belial and cretinism as the producer, predestined to a madhouse and a hardly utterable name, of some

> scrofulous French novel
> On grey paper with blunt type,

and embellished with a 'woful sixteenth print'?[1] In his other classical poems which touch upon somewhat similarly dangerous ground, 'Phaedra' and 'Hermaphroditus', we see no cause for censuring Mr. Swinburne: he imagines and speaks as a poet has a right to do—the only further requirement being the 'fit audience'.[2]

On the 'Heterodox or Religiously Mutinous' influence we have already commented to some extent: it is closely connected with the Classic influence, and is equally genuine, though hardly so deep-seated. Mr. Swinburne, as we have said, is, in intellectual sympathy and culture, a pagan. This gives a positive direction to his thought on religious subjects, which otherwise seems to amount to little beyond negation,—materialism, and the absence of faith in a beneficent Providence. The negative and the positive currents, encountering and

[1] From Browning's 'Soliloquy of the Spanish Cloister', stanza 8.
[2] *Paradise Lost*, vii, 31.

joining, roll a considerable volume of turbidity, tumult, and spray. In saying this we desire to guard ourselves carefully against any suspicion of levitical or pharisaic intolerance: we make no complaint of Mr. Swinburne's speculative opinions, but, on the contrary, recognise his right to entertain and express them, whatever they may be. They have done us no harm; and we recommend other readers to persuade themselves of the fact that to them also these opinions of a great poetic genius will do no harm. We say 'opinions', feeling that, although Mr. Swinburne very seldom writes otherwise than dramatically, and could not therefore be legally fixed with entertaining as his own the opinions which he puts into the mouths of others, it would nevertheless be affectation to profess serious uncertainty on this point: he, in fact, dramatizes certain opinions, and not their contraries, so continually, because he sympathises with them, and rejoices in giving them words. We would make him welcome to do so. This world, which scandalized readers believe to be regulated by a beneficent Providence, and which Mr. Swinburne (we infer) believes to be regulated by some power of some sort or other which is absolutely inscrutable, unfathomable, and in its operations unamenable to the human reason or sense of right, is big and surprising enough for both opinions: and in the infinite there are possibly infinite disclosures to be made which may prove as astonishing to such readers as to Mr. Swinburne. If readers, only still further scandalized by our summary of the Swinburnian theory, declare that such theory is flat atheism, we shall not concern ourselves to contest the phrase: indeed, our own opinion about the theory is nearly enough the same. There is, as far as we know, only one act of faith, properly so called, possible to be made—namely, the belief in the perfect goodness and justice of the Creative and Disposing Power: all other so-called acts of faith appear, in ultimate analysis, resolvable into persuasion by evidence, which, in the largest sense, includes even that form of belief which consists in the simple acceptance of authority or tradition. Not so this one the supreme act of faith: the whole body of evidence to be brought forward on that most fundamental and vastest of questions, the mysteries and seeming contradictions of it, are so enormous, and so utterly above being cognizable by human intellect or investigation, that no man, it would seem, could ever possibly be convinced of the perfect goodness of the Ruling Power by discovering either the invariableness or the preponderance of its symptoms in the world of nature or of mind. He must take a step from the evidence to the conviction, and that step is faith. The man who has taken that step can alone be rightly said to believe in a God: for to believe in a God who is not all that we can conceive of good and just is to believe not properly in a God, but in a Fate,—or even in a Dæmon, if the sense of shadow, of horror, and of wrong, overpowers that of light, love, and right. Mr. Swinburne, as far as his book shows, never has taken the step in question, never has enacted the act of faith; and, though he seems to believe more or less tentatively and darkly in a supreme Intellect, in a Rule and a Ruler, in something beyond a 'fortuitous concourse of atoms',[1] the idea appears to supply to his mind more fuel for fire of resentment and flashes of protest than for anything like a humble, loving, and filial reliance. In fact, what might have been and was shrewdly surmised from *Atalanta in Calydon*, that the sentiments of the famous and overpoweringly eloquent chorus,

> Yea, with thy hate, O God, thou hast covered us

(minus the submissive close thereof), were the sentiments of Mr. Swinburne himself, is fully confirmed by various passages in the *Poems and Ballads*; passages which either reinforce the same sentiments dramatically, but with a gusto and insistence not to be mistaken, or, as especially in 'Félise', rend the thinnest of dramatic veils, and are manifestly spoken in the author's person. The same is still more clearly the case in the ode 'To Victor Hugo'. Our poet has a singularly acute and terrible conception of the puppet-like condition of man, as acted upon by the forces of Nature and the fiats of her Ruler; and he draws some appalling outlines of it with an equal sense of power and of powerlessness, an equal entireness of despair and of desperation. He jeers and groans in the same act at his and our misery, for the facts appear to him to warrant both moods: 'there are passages in his poem' (as was remarked by one of the best English reviews of the *Atalanta*) 'which seem to wring from the very roots of human experience the sharpest extract of our griefs'. Intellect pitted against a material and moral *pieuvre*[2] appears to be his conception of the state of man: and no wonder that the fight looks to him a most ghastly one, unconvinced as he is (to use the mildest term) of the justice of the Umpire, and convinced, or all but convinced, of the mortality of the soul. His only outlet of comfort is his delight in material beauty, in the fragmentary conquests of intellect, and in the feeling that the fight, once over in this

---

[1] The fortuitous or casual concourse of atoms is ascribed to a sermon by Richard Bentley (1692), though the equivalent may be older than Lucretius or even Epicurus.

[2] French for 'octopus' or 'devil-fish'.

world for each individual, is over altogether; and in these sources of comfort his exquisite artistic organization enables him to revel while the fit is on him, and to ring out such peals of poetry as deserve, we do not fear to say it, to endure while the language lasts.

In illustration of the opinions as to the Creator and Ruler of this world which, on the evidence of his writings, we have seen cause for attributing to Mr. Swinburne, we are tempted to quote a few sentences, faultlessly neat and killingly common-sensible, from Hume's *Enquiry concerning Human Understanding*. The Scotch philosopher has put the words into the mouth of Epicurus, whom he supposes to be arguing against the attempt of his denouncers to 'establish religion upon the principles of reason', though he does not deny that religion may be true notwithstanding. 'Allowing therefore the gods' (says Epicurus) 'to be the authors of the existence or order of the universe, it follows that they possess *that precise degree* of power, intelligence, and benevolence, which appears in their workmanship; but nothing further can be proved, except we call in the assistance of exaggeration and flattery to supply the defects of argument and reasoning. So far as the traces of any attributes at present appear, so far may we conclude these attributes to exist. The supposition of farther attributes is mere hypothesis; much more the supposition that, in distant regions of space or periods of time, there has been or will be a more magnificent display of these attributes, and a scheme of administration more suitable to such imaginary virtues. . . . You persist in imagining that, if we grant that divine existence for which you so earnestly contend, you may safely infer consequences from it, and add something to the experienced order of nature by arguing from the attributes which you ascribe to your gods. You seem not to remember that all your reasonings on this subject can only be drawn from effects to causes, and that every argument deduced from causes to effects must of necessity be a gross sophism; since it is impossible for you to know anything of the cause but what you have antecedently, not inferred, but discovered to the full, in the effect. . . . That the divinity may possibly be endowed with attributes which we have never seen exerted—may be governed by principles of action which we cannot discover to be satisfied—all this will freely be allowed. But still this is mere possibility and hypothesis. We never can have *reason* to infer any attributes or any principles of action in him but so far as we know them to have been exerted and satisfied. Are there any marks of a distributive justice in the world? If you answer in the affirmative, I conclude that, since justice here exerts itself, it is satisfied. If you reply in the negative, I conclude that you have then no reason to ascribe justice, in our sense of it, to the gods. If you hold a medium between affirmation and negation by saying that the justice of the gods at present exerts itself in part, but not in its full extent, I answer that you have no reason to give it any particular extent but only so far as you see it at present exert itself.' Mr. Swinburne appears to be of much the same opinion as Hume's Epicurus. He finds, according to his human experience and intellect, only partial and chequered symptoms of justice, or of wisdom and power along with goodness, in this present world; and, as his mind is very far from an illogical one, and he does not supplement its suggestions by the intuitions of faith, he concludes that partial justice is caused by a partially just cause. The difference is that what Hume thinks and speaks in prose Swinburne thinks and speaks in poetry. He cannot contemplate this conclusion of his reason as a subject for calm acceptance and contented corollary—as a modest but not uncomfortable abiding-place for the spirit: on the contrary, his imagination takes fire, and his heart burns within him, and they vent themselves in clamorous obtestations. Between ideal right and actual fact he sees a great void, and fills it with the deep resonances and echoings of an unsatisfied desire and an unsuccumbing mind.

> *Poscia che il fuoco alquanto ebbe rugghiato*
> *Al modo suo, l'aguta punta mosse*
> *Di quà, di là, e poi diè cotal fiato.*[1]

Of the four main currents of influence and feeling which we noted in the *Poems and Ballads*, we have now discussed all except the one which we termed 'the Assimilative or Reproductive in point of literary form'. This is one of the most curious specialties of Mr. Swinburne's writings, and may be best commented on by a reference to individual poems in his volume. We take them pretty nearly in the order which they hold in the index of contents. The first brace of poems, 'A Ballad of Life' and 'A Ballad of Death', are Italian *canzoni* of the exactest type, such as Dante, Cavalcanti, Petrarca, and the other mediæval, with many modern, poets of Italy have written; and more especially taking the tinge which works of this class have assumed in Mr. Dante G. Rossetti's volume of translations, *The Early Italian Poets*. The 'Laus Veneris', itself sufficiently independent of models, is prefaced by a paragraph in old

---

[1] Dante's *Inferno*, xxvii, 58–60: 'After the fire had roared for a while according to its fashion, the sharp point moved to and fro, and then gave forth this breath' (tr. C. E. Norton).

French purporting to be extracted from a '*Livre des Grandes Merveilles d'Amour, escript en Latin et en Françoys par Maistre Antoine Gaget, 1530*', but which we confidently father upon Mr. Swinburne himself, along with the extract from the *Grandes Chroniques de France, 1505*, appended to 'The Leper', and the Greek lines from *Anth. Sac.* that serve as motto to 'A Litany', which poem is a cross between the antiphonal hymnal form and the ideas and phraseology of the Old Testament. These latter are hardly less prominent in the 'Song in time of Revolution'. 'Phædra' is in the form of a scene from a Greek tragedy, with the interpolated remarks of the Chorus. 'A Ballad of Burdens' is moulded upon some of the old French poems, with an 'envoy'. 'Hendecasyllabics' and 'Sapphics' speak for themselves as regards literary relationship. 'At Eleusis' is an exceptionally long speech spoken by Demeter, as from a Greek tragedy—recalling also such modern work as some of Landor's *Hellenics*, or Browning's so-called 'Artemis Prologizes'. 'A Christmas Carol' presents quaint, cunning analogies to mediæval writings of the same order. 'The Masque of Queen Bersabe' is professedly 'a miracle play', and treated accordingly. 'St. Dorothy' is Chaucerian work, even to the extent of intentional anachronisms in the designations of the personages and otherwise. 'The Two Dreams', from Boccaccio, is almost in equal measure Keatsian. 'Aholibah' brings us back again to the Old Testament. Lastly, we have a quintett of ballads, carefully varied in shade, but mainly conforming to the type of the old ballads of North Britain,—'The King's Daughter', 'After Death', 'May Janet', 'The Bloody Son', and 'The Sea-Swallows'.

Now, there is nothing uncommon or surprising in imitative poetry. It is generally bad in itself, and inefficient in imitation; sometimes clever, without imitative success; sometimes imitative to the point of intentional, and very rarely of realized, illusion. The singular thing about Mr. Swinburne's reproductive poems is that they are exceedingly fine pieces of work, exceedingly like their adopted models, startlingly so from time to time, and yet that they belong strictly and personally to Mr. Swinburne, and stand distinctly on the level of original work, with the privileges, difficulties, and responsibilities thereto belonging. It seems quite clear that this poet could do, if he chose, an imitation, a 'take-off', of almost any style, so close that only the most knowing critics could detect it: but he always stops short of that extreme point, preserving his own poetic individualism and liberty, exhibiting (as we have already said in speaking of the *Atalanta*) 'the independence and remoulding force of an original work'. This state of the case can only, as far as we know, be referred to one cause—the fact that Mr. Swinburne, being truly a poet, a man of imagination, penetrates, by the force of imagination as well as of studentship, into the imaginative identity of poetic models of past time, and thence into their embodying forms. He can create for himself, as he has amply proved; but the determined set of his intellect towards art, and consequently towards literary art, possesses him with so sharp a sympathy for the literary or poetic models of highest style that, as the mood varies, he can pitch his mind into true harmonic concert with Chaucer now, and now with Dante, Sophocles, Keats, or Hugo, and sing, as it were, new vocal music to the accompaniment of these most definite, dominant, and unperishing melodies. In all the roll of poets, we certainly know none who has given such signal proof of his power to enter with re-creative, not imitative, sympathy into so many poetic models of style and form, so diverse and so high; to search their recesses, and extract their essential aroma. A true critic can discern with equal clearness that Mr. Swinburne is a very different sort of writer from a Greek tragedian or a Chaucer, writing things which have a very different ring, and also that his voluntary assimilation to these and other poets is both a genuine and a most singular effort of poetry. Such a critic would find it alike impossible to suppose that he was reading in the 'St. Dorothy' a work really produced by Chaucer, or to miss wondering at the intimate and indwelling Chaucerism of the product.

The foregoing observations, singly and collectively, lead up to the central fact already curtly indicated, that the largest and most fundamental of all the influences acting upon Swinburne is the artistic, or (as one terms it in reference to this particular form of art) the literary, and that his poetry is literary poetry of the intensest kind. It is not only metric eloquence, still less versified rhetoric—something far higher than either: but one hesitates to say whether the primary conception in the poet's mind, the poetic nucleus, or the accretion of images and expressional form which grows and clings to this, the poetic investment, is the more important constituent in the general result. In several instances, however, we would say that the poetic investment is beyond a doubt the more important. Both the great beauties and the faults of Mr. Swinburne's writings are closely connected with this specially artistic or literary turn of his genius, as we shall have occasion to show in the sequel. Shelley has been termed 'the poet for poets': Swinburne might not unaptly be termed 'the poet for poetic students'. His writings exercise a great fascination over qualified readers, and excite a very real enthusiasm in them: but these readers are not of that wide, popular, indiscriminate class who come to a poet to be moved by the subject-matter, the affectingly told story, the sympathetic interpreting words which, in giving voice to the poet's own emotion or perception, find utterance also for those of the universal and inarticulate heart. Mr. Swinburne's readers are of another and a more restricted order. They are persons who, taking delight in the art of poetry, rejoicing when they find a poet master of his materials and the employment of them, kindle to watch so signal a manifestation of poetic gifts and poetic workmanship, and tender him an admiration which, if less than that of an adept, is more than that of a dilettante. It should be added that, while the beauty of execution is the more special attraction to the more special Swinburnian readers, it is by no means the only one: the poet's conceptions are in fact as vivid as his expressions, and he writes with a fire, and even vehemence, which keep his work, elaborate as it often is in verbal or rhythmical subtlety, lifted clear above any such level as that of euphuism or 'word-painting'.

The indecencies in the *Poems and Ballads*, about which more than enough has been said in other quarters, and something in the present review, may here once more be glanced at, to be noted as very much dependent upon this literary direction of mind in the author. Of positive grossness or foulness of expression there is none—nor yet of light-hearted, jocular, jovial libertinism. The offences to decency are in the subjects selected—sometimes too faithfully classic, sometimes more or less modern or semi-abstract—and in the strength of phrase which the writer insists upon using on these as on other topics. He refuses to have his literary liberty abridged; and, as his own indifference or hostility to the common standards of right and wrong, and to the platitudes of their upholders, is necessarily active when he is writing on such subjects, he lashes out with a kind of exasperated and gladiatorial outspokenness which is, after all, as much in the line of literary as of anti-moral licence. We have already expressed our objection to such demonstrations; but we think that these considerations respecting them, being not wiredrawn but simply true, ought in justice to be stated and taken into account.

There are certain advantages and certain disadvantages to a poet in the distinctively artistic or literary direction of genius, such as we have been noting in Mr. Swinburne. It would carry us too far to follow these out with anything like completeness. Suffice it to observe here that one leading advantage is that a writer who has the true poetic faculty, and any adequate share of cultivation, is thus almost entirely saved from the chance of producing really bad work—scrambling, shambling, straggling, or slovenly work; from 'mooning about' in the paths of downright sentimentalism, or of that long-windedness which grows upon a writer who knows that he has something to say more clearly than what it is or how to say it, or of other 'no-man's-land' of the world of song. On the other hand, one leading disadvantage is that the matter written about may have scarcely any *initial force* over the reader's mind, may be such as never to bring the reader face to face with the writer, but only with the written page, may have no hold upon his sympathy, and raise in him no willingness to meet the author's suggestions halfway. In short, the strictly artistic power is a sympathetic power only to artistically constituted minds: to others it is alien, or even antipathetic. Perhaps no instance could be cited of a more nice adjustment of the artistic and the moving or persuasive qualities in poetry than the case of Mr. Tennyson; and even he fails in some wise through the very development of both these capacities. Thus his earlier attempts on the side of art were accounted intangible, and even finikin, and not unjustly in various instances, and the elder generation of readers very commonly refuse to this day to find him substantial and human-hearted—while others vote him almost tame and commonplace in the simplicity, obviousness, and propriety of his affections. The latter is an accusation which has certainly not yet been brought against Mr. Swin-burne, and will not be while he proceeds in his present system of poetic work; but the contrary accusation, of unsympathetic direction of faculty, may without unfairness be preferred, as we shall more parti-cularly note in speaking of his characteristics in detail.

A still larger question arises here—how far artistic excellence can and ought to be pursued to the neglect or disregard of moral truth? We cannot undertake to give this question the full discussion which it would merit *per se*, but will endeavour to state in a few sentences the conclusions which we believe a candid discussion would elicit, to the following effect:—

1st. Minds of the highest order unite moral with artistic energy, and produce work—poetic work when that is in question—which is poetic in so far as it is artistic, but which is also moral because the writer belongs to this highest order of minds. Thus *Macbeth, Othello, Romeo and Juliet,* and the body of Shakespear's Sonnets, are great poems because they are great works of art; but they are also moral because Shakespear was too great a mind to be otherwise than moral essentially.

If even the worst charges which have been hinted against Shakespear on the evidence of some of the Sonnets were established as true, the Sonnets would equally continue to be great poems: the only difference would be that Shakespear's mind or personality, in its total range, would be shown to be of a less grand order than had previously been supposed. Thus again Dante, who professed himself the Poet of Rectitude, is subject to very various constructions on the ground of morals. Some persons believe his ideas on the subject (for instance) of hell to be truly moral; others, at the present date of thought, believe them to be decidedly anti-moral; others believe that the whole external scheme of his poem is a mere veil, or even an introversion, of his real meaning. Whichever of these opinions is adopted, the *Commedia* remains an equally great poem, because it is a great work of art: the only difference is as to the ultimate calibre of Dante's mind. And so again with Milton, who undertook to 'justify the ways of God to men' on grounds which appear to many people to be fallacious, and the opposite of morally true.

2d. It follows that the poet, or artist, can, in so far as he is an artist, and without any express cognizance of morals, write poems whose rank as such will not be thereby lowered; and if he happens to be a man without a strong moral side to his nature, or one who has false or perverse moral tendencies, and even if he exhibits these in his writings, the loss will be to himself in his grade in the intellectual hierarchy, not to his poems, considered as concrete expressions of such intellect and art as were actually in him. His mind will rightly be classed as falling short of those other minds of the grandest order; but his poems will retain their own absolute value, whatever that may be, determinable by the quality and amount of the art which has gone to their production. (We need hardly explain that the term 'Art', as here used, includes imagination, conception, and so on, as well as actual execution.)

3d. A poem which is *founded* upon morals rather than art is likely to be a poem of an inferior class; because the intrinsic constituent of poetry is art, and a thorough artist founds his work of art upon that which is not subsidiary but essential to it—namely, art. At the same time, the very highest morals do, as a matter of fact, pertain to the very highest poems, because, as affirmed from the first, the very highest minds are those which unite morals to art.

4th. A moralist, simply as such, has no title to attempt poetry, because art cannot be approached from the side of morals—the two things are extraneous one to the other, though in no wise conflicting. But an artist may, in a certain semi-paradoxical sense, approach morals from the side of art, because, the more and more he elevates his mind by the gifted practice of art, the nearer and nearer he will come to that highest order of minds which unites morals with art.

5th. Morals do not therefore directly produce, or conduce to the production of poetry. Art does conduce to its production, and does indeed produce it. The very best poems give morals in, over and above the art.

6th. Consequently, in answer to our primary question, we find that artistic excellence can be pursued to the neglect or disregard of moral truth, and even *ought to be* so pursued with a view to the poetic result. But, if it is pursued to the *negation* of morals, that is a symptom that the mind of the author, or the particular poetic work, is not of the very highest class—still more so, if the artistic excellence is pursued with a purpose which can truly, on broad and positive grounds, be pronounced anti-moral. To this—passing from the essence of the work itself to its effect upon the student of it—we may add that it is not the direct function of a poem or other work of art to improve the morals of the reader, or other person addressed, according to the formulated, matter-of-fact sense in which that term 'morals' is ordinarily used. This function is, as we said of morals embodied in the poem itself, 'given in', over and above the direct function of the work, which is to enlarge the mental energy, add delicacy to the perceptions, stimulate and refine the emotions, satisfy the sense of beauty. When this has been done to some purpose, a right moral influence has also been exerted—and not the less substantially because indirectly exerted.

In estimating any poet, one of the most obvious lines of observation is the relation which that poet bears to his compeers and contemporaries —from whom, if any, he derives, to whom he is kin, from whom alien. Mr. Swinburne occupies in this respect a very independent position. There is only one living poet still, or two at most, to whom he is nearly related, and these are not Englishmen. Two other almost contemporary writers may, however, be referred to on the same grounds; and, besides these, we shall briefly pass in review four of the leading living poets of England, without at all implying any invidious exclusion of others not here named—these second four being cited for the purpose rather of contrast than of analogy to Mr. Swinburne.

The four poets to whom he is most nearly related, ranged in order from the nearer to the less near, are Victor Hugo, Landor, Shelley, and Baudelaire.

Of Victor Hugo Mr. Swinburne is a most enthusiastic admirer. He has proved it by the Ode addressed to him in the *Poems and Ballads*, by the dedication of the *Chastelard*, and principally by the vivid traces of a Hugo influence which that tragedy bears. In the sounding march of the verse; in the clenching force and precision of expression and of imagery, verging in both poets on audacity, but less extreme in Swinburne; in the readiness to try special and exceptional feats, whether in subject or in treatment; above all, in the almost convulsive clutch, so to speak, which each poet takes of his theme, and the passionateness of thought and art which he expends upon it, the resemblance may visibly be traced: and this applies not only to *Chastelard*, but to the Swinburnian poems generally. There is, however, one great and fundamental difference between Hugo and Swinburne, which will, no doubt, separate the work of the two men, when completed by both, still more widely than we as yet see the separation. Hugo is one of the most intensely moral natures in the domain of poetry, and the raptures of personal and humanitarian faith form a most important part of his mind, and even too profuse a one of his writings; while Swinburne, as we have seen, is not intensely constituted on the moral or religious side, and indeed, when he is roused at all from neutrality, tends rather towards antagonism than towards expansiveness. To set up his moral back, one has to rub him against the hair; and then one may be sure that his mood is not the blandest. To Landor the analogy borne by Mr. Swinburne is perhaps even more obvious than that which he bears to Hugo; but it is more an analogy of surface in the writings, and of personal notions—of classic sympathies, range of subject determined accordingly, elevation and exactness of literary style. On the negative side, no doubt, the minds of the two men are in very substantial accord: they both tend to disregard other interests, when satisfied on the score of beauty and of intellect; neither of them is much impelled to overstep the magic circle of paganism. But that which burns as a fire in Swinburne was only a genial heat in Landor—there was no such inevitability of poetic expression in that admirable thinker and writer. In terming Swinburne a poet of the literary order, we have only used the word 'literary' as equivalent to 'vividly artistic'; whereas Landor might be almost termed a 'bookish' as rightly as a 'literary' poet, though true poetic rank is not to be denied him. Mr. Swinburne's analogy to Shelley is a kind of cross between his analogies to Hugo and to Landor. Like the first, Shelley had passion, moral intensity, and the most unmeasured sympathies; like the latter, he had an anti-modern and a Greek sphere of thought. In the particular aspect which these qualities wore in

Shelley, he is less closely approached by Swinburne than is either Hugo or Landor. But Shelley (whom, be it said parenthetically, we regard as being, on the whole, decidedly the greatest figure and phenomenon in English poetry since Milton) had a fatal facility, as his contemporaries counted it, for saying the most alarming things on the unsafest subjects, and, along with this, a fusion and shiftingness of ideas perpetually poured forth from a common fountain-head whose taste and tint were dominant in them all, and a certain incompatibility of mind with ordinary minds, such as made the whole of his work somewhat intangible and distant-sounding to them—qualities in all of which Mr. Swinburne presents a clear though diverse-shaded resemblance to this divine poet. Baudelaire, the last of the four authors whom we have named as Mr. Swinburne's congeners, is probably almost unknown to English readers. He is the author of a volume of poems, *Les Fleurs du Mal*, to which the least commendable parts of the *Poems and Ballads* seem to bear a considerable affinity: we must therefore class Baudelaire's influence upon Swinburne as a bad though not an uncongenial one. The French poet is a sort of poetic Mephistopheles: if Göthe's fiend had been more human-natured and imaginative, he would have been not unlike Baudelaire, who sees the facts of the world to much the same effect as Mephistopheles, only with a poetic colouring, and expresses them in terms which are vivid and moving, instead of withering and dry. If he does not quite say, after Milton's Satan, 'Evil, be thou my good,' he does at least say, 'Evil, be thou my inspiration'; and, being a man of powerful mind, and a very real poetic gift, he succeeds in ringing the changes upon this bad tocsin to some purpose. With squeamishness, whether applied to the criticism of a Baudelaire, a Swinburne, or any other man of genius, we have no sympathy; but, as to approval, we must, with Newman Noggs's barber,[1] 'draw the line somewhere', and we draw it before Baudelaire. There is good artistic as well as moral warrant for such a decision. A book like the *Fleurs du Mal* cannot be 'in good keeping' in an enlarged sense: it may be in keeping one part of it with another, but not with a complete, healthy, or true view of actualities; and, being thus both partial and perverse, it must of necessity also be violent.

We now turn to take a glance at our second quartett of poets— English poets contemporary with Swinburne; and the interest of whose works, for our present purpose, is mainly that of diversity. We shall

[1] In chapter 52 of Dickens' *Nicholas Nickleby* the barber refused to shave a coalheaver, drawing the line at bakers.

select Tennyson, Browning, William Morris, and Christina Rossetti. Of these four, the only one who can be pitted against Swinburne in point of executive art is Tennyson. Both are most scholarly poetic aspirants, and most finished poetic artists. Except for this primary likeness, the two are very dissimilar. Tennyson's exquisite descriptive and verbal art is, in his mature writings, singularly measured: one perceives that he is, if possible, still more heedful not to say too much than to say too little or too scantily. He does indeed fill the goblet, but with a chemist's care that not a drop be spilled or excessive. Swinburne pours with a more confident yet not less safe hand, and brims the bowl, barely preventing it from overflowing. Swinburne has a more grasping ambition, Tennyson a more concentrated self-mastery: the first forms a study of noble profusion, and the second of noble discipline. Among artists of great original faculty, Tennyson is remarkable for that which the now almost trivial phrase styles 'a well-regulated mind'; Swinburne's mind may rather be termed unregulated, but instinctively true to the traction of great art, like steel to the lodestone. In Browning we come to contemplate a poet very different from either. We regard Browning's natural wealth of workable poetic perceptions and ideas as the richest entrusted to any English poet of our time, if not even of any time since Shakespear's; marvellously varied and pungent, and thoroughly and essentially human. On this splendid stock he works with luminous flashes of intellect, and strangely captivating though too fleeting felicities of art. Unfortunately, Browning is gifted, along with this lavish fund of poetic material and aptitude, with another endowment which is radically prosaic—ingenuity. We have been informed, as a curious physical fact, that Mr. Browning is a double-sighted man —long-sighted with one eye, and short-sighted with the other: that is the exact analogue of his mental vision, and a singularly appropriate symbol of it, as if mind and feature were literally cast in the same mould. This ingenuity is a heavy drawback to his freedom, consistency, and greatness, as a poet: it is the bar sinister on his poetic shield—it is the false note which menaces several of his astonishing works with final relegation to that category of art which, as some one said of certain ear-battering music, one would wish to be 'not only difficult, but impossible'. For all this, we recognize Browning as so superb and exceptional a poetic genius that no superiority of art, whether displayed by a Tennyson, a Swinburne, or whomsoever else, no obliquity of direction in his own powers, can oust him from a seat second to none in the ranks of our living singers. Between Browning and Swinburne (especially as lyric poets) there is scarcely any point of contact; the former taking an incomparably keener and more varied interest in men and their surroundings, while the latter elicits with a more certain finger the artistic harmonies of the fewer chords he touches. One point of contact may, however, be noted for as much as it is worth. Both Browning and Swinburne are fond (but the former much more so) of out-of-the-way subjects illustrative of character or period: and 'Johannes Agricola', 'Karshish the Arab Physician', 'The Bishop orders his Tomb at St. Praxed's', find a sort of unlike likeness in such poems as 'Les Noyades' or 'The Leper'—though both of these latter compositions exhibit a cross between moral and physical repulsiveness which is more peculiarly Swinburnian.

The poet to whom we next turn, William Morris, author of *The Defence of Guenevere, and other Poems*, published in 1858, has by no means as yet received the recognition he deserves. When he does so, he will be acknowledged as by far the most genially and subtly chivalrous and mediæval of all modern English poets, and even transcending Victor Hugo in this particular department. A page of Morris is as rich as a painted window flooded with afternoon sun, and as dreamily sonorous as the choral chant from the further end of the cathedral. In the pitch and colour of his poems, Mr. Morris is almost unfailingly right; but, as an executive artist, he trusts too much to instinct and the chapter of accidents—very different herein from Mr. Swinburne, some of whose compositions are, however, obviously related to Mr. Morris's style, and even, it might appear, directly influenced by his example, as also by the few original poems of Mr. D. G. Rossetti which have been published. Such are Swinburne's 'Laus Veneris' (founded on the Tannhäuser legend), 'A Christmas Carol', 'Madonna Mia', and one or two others. For what might further be said on this point we must refer back to our observations on the writer's assimilative or reproductive poems. Perhaps we may also find a collateral trace of his interest in Mr. Morris's poetic aims in the dedication of the *Poems and Ballads* to the admirable painter Edward Burne Jones; an artist who expresses in the pictorial art a range of feelings, gifts, and perceptions, very closely and specifically analogous to those of Mr. Morris in verse. The last of our present poetic quartett, Christina Rossetti, is a singer of a different order from all these, reaching true artistic effects with apparently little study and as little of mere chance—rather by an internal sense of fitness, a mental touch as delicate as the finger-tips of the blind. She simply, as it were, pours words into the mould of her idea; and the resultant effigy comes right, because the idea, and the mind of which it is a phase, are beautiful ones, serious, yet feminine and in part almost playful. There is no poet with a more marked instinct for fusing the thought into the image, and the image into the thought: the fact is always to her emotional, not merely positive, and the emotion clothed in a sensible shape, not merely abstract. No treatment can be more artistically womanly in general scope than this, which appears to us the most essential distinction of Miss Rossetti's writings. It might be futile to seek for any points of direct analogy or of memorable divergence between Mr. Swinburne and Miss Rossetti. The prevalent cadence of the poem 'Rococo', and the lyrical structure of 'Madonna Mia', may, however, suggest that the poet is a not unsympathetic reader of the poetess's compositions; nor is 'The Garden of Proserpine' much unlike some of these so far merely as lyrical tone is concerned.

We shall next come to closer quarters with Mr. Swinburne, and endeavour to analyse his particular and characteristic defects and excellences. The former being the less agreeable task, we will get through it the first.

By far the most important defect, and one which infolds most of the others in its sweep, has been already touched upon—the want of broad, common sympathies, of a generous large-hearted humanity; and consequently the want of sympathetic hold upon the mass even of poetic readers. Without raising for the moment any question as to the allowableness of Mr. Swinburne's moral tone and speculative audacities, we must point to them as a strong evidence of this defect in sympathy—this want of a bond to unite him with his fellow-men such as they are, for better or for worse. It is perfectly true that great poets are not bound to be 'hail fellow well met' with all that is most vulgar and incapable among their contemporaries: they are on the contrary (in another than Dante's sense)

*Li cittadin della città partita;* [1]

enrolled not in any municipality fixed in space and time, but in a community which belongs to one age as much as another, and one country as much as another. Still, the ground of a common manhood, feeling strongly and uniformly on the same points on which other unsophisticated men feel the like, is the natural ground for a poet to stand on; and, without this, it seems very problematic whether the most brilliant gifts of mind and of art will avail much for present or

[1] *Inferno*, vi, 61: 'the citizens of the divided city'.

future fame of really wide extension. Milton, whom Wordsworth has finely called

> Soul awful, if the world has ever seen
> An awful soul,[1]

seems to have been the least genially tempered of great English poets, the least likely to engage or win upon his fellows: his austerity might appear to have verged upon rigour, or even pedantry. But at least he commanded a respect amounting to reverence, and he entered heart and soul into the great popular interests of his time, and was a great leader of thought in paths intelligible by the people. Again, Shelley ran directly counter to all the prejudices of the society about him, and roused anger hundredfold in proportion to the hearts he conciliated; but then, as soon as a few mists of preconception and narrowness had cleared aside, people could not help perceiving that their own most ardent affections and aspirations were traceable also in the poet, only in a somewhat altered guise, transfigured in purity and intensity. This cannot be said of Mr. Swinburne. He is radically indifferent, and indeed hostile, to what most persons care for; and he poetizes, for the greater part, from a point of view which they will neither adopt nor understand. This we consider strictly a deficiency, and for practical purposes a defect. It should be added, however, that he is far the reverse of tardy in national or political sympathies and antipathies. On the contrary, he is full of generous ardour and scathing abomination on topics of this nature—an abomination and an ardour which only those who mainly agree with him will rate as stopping short of actual fanaticism. For our part, we would rather be fanatics with Swinburne than prudentialists with Southey.

A second defect is over-doing. Mr. Swinburne conceives, as well as expresses himself, most intensely; and so far all is well, though possibly somewhat in extremes. But this is so much the habit of his mind and pen that, when the subject, or the happy tact of the moment, does not lend itself to such a method, he still not unfrequently writes with what would be intensity under more favourable conditions, but is, as the case stands, only an excess of emphasis. We think no one can doubt that the following lines, which form the opening of 'Laus Veneris', are, apart from any question of seemliness, much overdone. The love-infatuated knight is contemplating Venus in repose:—

> Asleep or waking, is it? for her neck,
> Kissed over close, wears yet a purple speck

[1] *The Prelude*, iii, 286-7.

Wherein the pained blood falters and goes out;
Soft, and stung softly—fairer for a fleck.

But, though my lips shut sucking on the place,
There is no vein at work upon her face:
    Her eyelids are so peaceable, no doubt
Deep sleep has warmed her blood through all its ways.

That is the situation (and there are many such, of one kind or another, throughout Mr. Swinburne's writings) which we would much rather see touched off with the reticence of a Tennyson: he would probably have given one epithet, or at the utmost one line, to it, and it would at least equally have haunted the memory. Nor is it in emphasis only that Mr. Swinburne drifts into overdoing: he sometimes allows his poem to run away with him, and makes it simply too long. We say this with the utmost diffidence, writing as we do of so distinguished a poetic genius and artist, who will no doubt think that he has a right to know best on the point; but such is distinctly our opinion. In the *Poems and Ballads*, 'The Triumph of Time' (fine as is its tissue throughout, and superb its enrichments) is particularly open to this criticism; and the same may be said of 'Dolores'.

The two foregoing defects are partly at the bottom of the third one that we have to specify—a certain degree of monotony in the writer's works, taken as a whole. He does not feel sufficient interest in the multiform phases of human life to write about many different subjects, nor is his mind solicited by many 'occasions' into the frequent inditing of 'occasional poems', such as Göthe and Wordsworth, for instance, were both, in different ways, so prodigal of; and, on the other hand, his habit of potent writing does not undergo very notable modification according as the poetic subject or mood alters. His variations, both in thought and in style, are very mainly artistic variations, not personal. This may explain the consistency of our present remarks with those which have preceded regarding the extraordinary aptitude of Mr. Swinburne for reproductive or assimilative work in a number of styles. That aptitude was truly stated, and it necessarily involves a large amount of differing subject-matter and treatment in the volume; and yet, as this impulse is constantly an artistic or literary one, it does not produce a total effect of variety or relief so great as might on first thoughts be supposed. We must not, however, press this charge of monotony too far. The poet who still a decidedly young man, has done a Greek tragedy, three other dramas, and a volume of narrative and lyrical poems marked by several absolute changes of style and some other not insignificant variations of mood and tint, can only be termed monotonous in a subordinate, though we think it is not an unfair, sense.

A minor form of this monotony is the frequent, and indeed continual, iteration of certain words, phrases, or images. Curious statistics might be compiled, out of Mr. Swinburne's four volumes, of the number of recurrences of the idea of fire, with its correlatives, fiery, flame, flaming, etc.—of kissing, with its correlatives of lips, breasts, breast-flowers, stinging, bruising, biting, etc.—of wine, with spilling, draining, filling, pouring, etc.—of flowers, with flowery, flowering, bud, blossom, etc. (not very frequently the names of *particular* flowers, unless fragrant with some classic reminiscence, or charm of syllables)—of blood, with staining, tingling, bloody, red, crimson, dark, hot, etc.—of the sea, with images and epithets as inexhaustible as itself, and only less noble, for the sea-passion surges through the personal and poetic identity of Mr. Swinburne; and several other of these typical or verbal *revenants* might with ease be picked out for enumeration. This is a matter of detail, which, though by no means strictly insignificant as such, would only deserve a passing glance from us, were not that particular detail, as we have intimated, a symptom of the comparative monotony of poetic excitation acting upon our author—of his being somewhat unduly rapt in his own individual mental world, and not so open in *sympathy* (which lies at the root of most poetic debates) as to be freely and continually receptive, a fresh eye and mind to whatsoever of fresh appeals to either.

We go still further into detail in naming with some degree of blame his great love of alliteration: it is just one more evidence of the specially literary direction of his genius. Nor this alone: it pertains in especial to his powerful rhythmic and lyrical gift. In this connexion, rhythm and rhyme come first; next, assonance, which plays so large a part in Spanish metres; and alliteration is a sort of subordinate assonance, and partly in that character, we have no doubt, natural and dear to Mr. Swinburne. It keeps up and reinforces, to his mind and ear, the lyrical flow and sequence of his metres under conditions in which other expedients are not immediately available. But, leaving this more recondite side of the question, alliteration is a device, a refinement, a dilettantism of literature. Writers who are bent upon saying things with the uttermost relief and pungency, with the '*curiosa felicitas*'[1] of

---

[1] This phrase, originally used of Horace by Petronius, properly refers to a felicity of expression that is the product of careful art—perhaps even of the art which conceals art.

the pen, can scarcely keep out of alliteration now and then—it comes so naturally and temptingly, falls so pat, and so tartly reminds both the writer himself and the reader that it is no bungler at the pothooks and hangers, but an adept, an expert, who is wielding said pen. An alliteration is a sort of beeswing upon the fluent ink. There is no more thorough, more artistic master of this nicety than Mr. Swinburne; but it must be confessed that his use of it runs into abuse, and becomes, if not absolutely a trick, certainly too salient a knack, of style.

The last defect to be named is occasional and partial obscurity. This is a charge brought against most new poets. Shelley and Browning were constantly, and for years together, termed unintelligible: Coleridge, Emerson, Dobell, W. Bell Scott, Edgar Poe, Mrs. Browning, and several others, have been voted at least obscure: even of Tennyson the older-fashioned sort of readers will still tell you 'We can't make him out'. This half-dark stage is therefore one through which most poets in whom there is a good deal have to pass, according to the apprehensions of ordinary readers; such poets—being all, in their degree, creators—come forward with something of a new sphere of ideas and new form of words, and people have to get accustomed to both before they take to them kindly. We should therefore lay little stress upon the mere commonplaces of demur which might be raised against Mr. Swinburne on the like score; and in fact we limit our own objection to *occasional and partial* obscurity. A great deal of what he writes is writing of the heights, not of the depths, and is, if anything, dazzling rather than obscure: the whole of *Atalanta in Calydon*, broadly speaking, may be adduced as an instance. The obscurity, where it can rightly be alleged, flows chiefly from that main source of shortcoming in our poet—the deficiency of broad frank sympathies, or (to use the common and here very apposite term) of 'fellow-feeling'. We will cite the chief examples from the *Poems and Ballads*. The 'Ballad of Life' is about as beautiful a piece of poetic writing as could be found anywhere: but the thing it symbolizes in detail is far from obvious to us; we find various symbolic or allegoric agents afoot, but *why* they in preference to others we rather guess at than perceive, and the introduction of the name 'Borgia' is quite unexplained. 'Fragoletta', again, has to be guessed at, and *is* guessed at with varying degrees of horror and repugnance: it is only readers of De Latouche's novel of the same name who can be certain that they see how much it does, and how much else it does in no wise, mean. In 'A Match' there are expressions to which one can only attach a quasi-significance, and which would seem to derive from that species of sexual enticement towards refinements of pain to which we have already adverted in the 'Anactoria'; a feeling about as germane to healthily constituted men of the ordinary stamp as the propensity of a buck-rabbit for eating up its young ones. 'Dolores' seems, at first, hardly related to anything in one's experience of facts, or scope of speculation: by thinking over it, however, one perceives that it does contain an ample amount of meaning, and even that its loud-rustling attire of immoralities is not so *very* immoral, after all—rather comparable to the seamy, the extra-seamy, side of the moral texture. 'Hesperia' looms dim, intangible, almost vague: we read it through, exulting in its exultant flow of rhythm, and find at the end that we scarcely know what the poem is about; it is only a second perusal, and that an attentive one, which is likely to clear up the vaporous verses, and clear, in the proper sense of the word, they never become. The two ballads of 'The King's Daughter' and 'After Death' have a different sort of obscurity—the abruptness and suppression of facts so characteristic of the old ballad-poetry. One *surmises* the essential point in each of them, which is a repulsive one: not that we mean to blame for this the ballads, which are admirable, and in excellent keeping with the model adopted. We have now pointed out all the poems which strike us most as open to the charge of obscurity (though it would be possible to specify some others also); and we find in each instance that that obscurity, or the obscure phase of the poem, has a close connexion with something unsympathetic in the author's mind.

It does not seem likely that Mr. Swinburne will ever essentially, or in a very great degree, get rid of the defects which we have been analysing: but that he will do so to some fairly appreciable extent we have little doubt. The want of broad sympathies, and of such a canon of moral instincts and perceptions as may place him *en rapport* with his fellow-men, would naturally be diminished by experience of life; and with this the tendency to monotony, and the casual obscurity, would wane. On the other hand, the overdoing, iteration of particular phrases, etc., and alliteration, being so far blemishes in the completeness of art exhibited, would, in the hands of so consummate an artist, be increasingly guarded against. These results may fairly be looked for; though we conceive the impulse which acts upon Mr. Swinburne, and which determines both that he shall be a poet, and what kind of poet he shall turn out, to be of so definite and persistent a kind that the last of his compositions, were he to live a hundred years, would in all probability be no less unmistakably Swinburnian than the first, and recognizable by the same birth-marks. Such exceptionally endowed writers as Shelley, Victor Hugo, and Mrs. Browning, offer a precedent to the like effect.

We have particularised Mr. Swinburne's defects: it remains for us to do the same office for his excellences.

The one which strikes us first is his deep and eager sense of beauty; a sense which, spite of his unjoyous creed and his propensity towards moral repulsiveness, is equally delicate in the selection and the presentation of its objects. To him natural and artistic beauty are in continual communion: and, as soon as he finds a beautiful thing to talk of, he is eliciting its most beautiful aspects in verbal and rhythmical harmonies of the most beautiful. His eye and his speech are always those of a poet —not of a man who enters the portals of poetry nervously muttering a watchword which he only half apprehends, but of one native to the place, and versed in its mazes.

With this sense of beauty he unites fervour and intensity; the three together constituting poetic passion of the most vivid kind. We say '*poetic* passion' because, if we mistake not, it is more through his poetic perceptions than his personal emotions that Mr. Swinburne attains that passion which informs, and sometimes over-informs, his poetic creations—the pulse of their heart and the breath of their nostrils; he himself being possibly rather impressionable and high-strung than passionate in the strictest sense. His fervour pursues the flying thought or the fleeting sentiment or sensation; and his intensity clenches and constrains them. With these qualities we would couple another, for which perhaps no better title can be found than Haughtiness. It is the quality whose formula runs thus, 'Odi profanum vulgus':[1] the quality which dictates to a poet that he shall follow his own proper bent, and none other—that he shall bow to no *ipse dixit*, conciliate no timorousness and no prejudice, subserve no other than poetic ends, acknowledge no other than poetic standards, vail his crest to no master, no enemy, and no friend. It gives authority and sonorousness to the poet's voice, without anxious self-assertion. It depresses or revolts the many— commands or captivates the few—wins over none. A great quality this, and a considerable danger. Dante had it, and Milton, Corneille, Alfieri, Landor, Leopardi; Byron and Schiller frequently; Göthe uniformly, but transmitted through so prismatic a mind and style that one often sees only its diversely-coloured spectra, not itself. We have no doubt that this quality has in some instances betrayed Mr. Swin-

[1] Horace, *Carm.*, III, i, 1: 'I hate the profane crowd.'

burne—that it has some share in his defects, and a large one in his mis-
doings. Still, it remains what the French, with so much tact of insinuated meaning, term '*une qualité*'; a characteristic such as marks its
possessor with superiority, not the reverse.

Among the more closely executive excellences of our poet, the first to
be named is eloquence. Ideas seem to come to him ready-clothed in
words—adapted for, and fitted with, verbal expression. A flood of
verbal appositeness rises at once to his lips—fluent, vehement, persuasive, descriptive, incisive, discriminative, subtilizing. Sustained and
rolling periods, quick turns, sinuous meanderings, undetected shiftings,
succeed and reinforce one another. Eloquence which trenches on
elocution or rhetoric is an essentially prosaic quality: but Mr. Swinburne's is not of this kind. It is free from any 'forensic' twang. His
eloquence is great command of language marshalled forward by ideas,
perceptions, aims, and taste, which are rightly poetic; and in consequence it breaks away at once from the prosaic, and abides within
the poetic, demesne. It is only so far related to eloquence in prose that
one can identify it as, in poetry, the analogue of that gift; a definite
constituent of the poetic whole, not to be confounded with its other
verbal or expressional constituents. Perhaps Sydney Dobell is the only
other living English poet to whom eloquence, in this distinctive sense,
can strictly be attributed; and his approaches much more nearly to the
eloquence of prose.

Extreme choiceness and keenness of phrase are among the components
of Mr. Swinburne's eloquence. His diction is so precise and pointed
that one might call it 'carved'. It exhibits the thing he has to express in
its completest form, with every prominence and every nicety of it
indicated; and this by a rapid process of marking and differentiating
words, not by lengthy set description, though that also is at the author's
command when he applies himself to it. He shoots like Dante's
Centaurs,

*Con archi, ed asticciole prima elette;*[1]

and, having everything ready to his hand, shoots swift and straight,
and full into the mark. In point of style, his diction is about equally
balanced between two of the highest possible models—the classic and
the biblical. Each of these is exceedingly conspicuous in the Swinburnian poems, and the combination of the two forms a valuable
study: even in *Atalanta* a good deal of the phraseology is biblical rather

[1] *Inferno*, xii, 60: 'With bows and darts first selected.'

than directly classic. A third element of style in diction, the romantic, flushes the other two—deepens their colour, and enriches their vibrations and suggestions.

With this force, beauty, and exactitude of diction, is associated a wonderful charm of metric melody, and reverberating volume of music. In this melodic faculty Mr. Swinburne is equally intuitive and cultivated—equally disciplined and daring. Generally conforming to the strictest rules, he often, on the other hand, uses the utmost latitude: but, be he orderly or enfranchised, we doubt whether there is one line in his books which can rightly be accused of inharmoniousness in its context. At any rate, so subtle are his instinct and his art in this respect, we are satisfied that a brother poet would always perceive in Mr. Swinburne's versification some intention which explains every instance of peculiarity; and we could only recognize the *dicta* of a poet as sufficient to suggest that any such peculiarity is unjustified. In blank verse, in the heroic couplet, in every variety, and even (most difficult of attempts) in some novelties, of lyrical flow, Mr. Swinburne is alike a master; a master who can learn little from any contemporary, and who might teach something to each and all. The deliciousness of his single notes, and the sustainment and majesty of his fully uttered roll of song, are most penetrating and rousing, and not to be surpassed.

To add a perfume to the violet[1]

is a notoriously futile task: to explain or illustrate its perfume is hardly less so. Neither shall we attempt, by scraps of quotation or intricacies of comment, to prove what we have been affirming with regard to our poet's versification. We will only refer the reader to such poems as 'Itylus', 'Anactoria', 'Ilicet', 'Fragoletta', 'A Litany', 'A Ballad of Burdens', 'The Masque of Queen Bersabe', 'St. Dorothy', 'A Match', 'A Leave-taking'; and how many another might yet be cited! This power over verse, as it is one of the most primary, so also do we regard it as one of the most final, tests of a true poetic vocation—especially when displayed, which it is by Mr. Swinburne, on a large scale, and with great variety of adaptation. Other powers may be preferred for dignity or value: none is more of the essence of the art of poetry, or so positively discriminates that from all other forms of art. None therefore is more essential to the poet, or more symptomatic of his rank.

The result of these singularly high-pitched executive qualities, taken together, is that Mr. Swinburne is, as a writer, poet, or artist, almost

[1] Cf. Shakespeare's *King John*, *IV*, ii, 12: 'To throw a perfume on the violet.'

entirely free from bathos or blunder. We might perhaps say '*entirely free*'—only further referring our reader to the observations which have preceded upon the author's defects, which, in executive respects, will be perceived to be ascribable to *over-high*, not to deficient, pitch, and as such to be rightly classed under the terms perversion and excess, rather than blunder and bathos. It is obvious, in reading his works, that he has a critical faculty of the acutest, along with his poetic gift; and that his own ear would be the first to feel offence at anything poor or inefficient, if by chance such dropped from his pen. He seems, in one act, to be lavishing and weighing his words; and to have as much of scrupulous nicety for the latter operation as of vehement impulse for the former. Any one can see that he is to the uttermost a self-respecting writer—one who would no more print what he might think inadequate in point of expression or of art than he would shrink from printing what other people consider exceptionable on grounds of morality or faith. One may guess that he often writes with extreme rapidity, and finds very little to revise; but that, be the first draft rapid or leisurely, or the revision slight or copious, the work is equally and strictly tried by the author's lofty standard of art before it greets the public eye.

There is a word which was once familiar to the critic of poetry—the word Sublime; now seldom produced, and still seldomer aright producible, out of the armoury of epithets, to be applied to any contemporary work in our language:

*Ora è diserta, come cosa vieta.*[1]

It is the sum and the crown of Swinburne's great poetic powers that to his work, rather than to that of any of his competitors, this noblest word is apposite and due. We will not walk into the pitfall which inveigles us by attempting a definition of that word Sublime: be it the task of others to say that we are wrong in claiming the title for Swinburne's productions, inasmuch as those productions do not square with some all-inclusive and exclusive definition of the sublime which the objectors may be ready to supply. For ourselves—without at all shutting our eyes to what needs grave demur in his writings, or to such points of minor importance as are still deserving of critical blame—we find in him an impulse, a majesty, a spontaneity, a superiority to common standards of conception, perception, and treatment, an absoluteness (so to speak) of poetic incitement and subject-matter (rendering him perhaps not likely to be ever very widely admired, but certain to

[1] *Inferno*, xiv, 99: 'Now it is deserted, like something outworn.'

be as intimately and as enthusiastically admired at the latest date to which his works may reach as at the present or any intermediate time), and withal a power and splendour in all the media of poetic expression, a wizardry over the auroral brightness and the 'sunless and sonorous gulfs' of song, such as we apprehend to be consistent if not co-extensive with any reasonable definition of the poetic sublime. We conceive *Atalanta in Calydon* to be singly conclusive of Mr. Swinburne's pre-eminence in this attribute of a great poet: and from the *Poems and Ballads* we might quote, in ample confirmation of the same view, the 'Laus Veneris', 'Anactoria', 'Hymn to Proserpine', 'Ilicet', 'A Litany', 'A Lamentation', 'A Ballad of Burdens', 'A Song in Time of Revolution', 'Hesperia', 'Félise', 'To Victor Hugo'.

To that numerous and so far respectable class of readers who, however lively may be the pleasure which they take in a work of art as such, will nevertheless assign its final place among literary productions according as it conforms to or outrages their own standard of spiritual right and wrong, Mr. Swinburne must offer a strange study of perfection of form along with internal disorganization, of disciplined mutiny and cosmic chaos. For our own part, we have already indicated the points in which we find ourselves in contact with, and those wherein we diverge from, such an estimate.

We have endeavoured to make this a tolerably complete review of Mr. Swinburne's genius, both generally and as developed in the *Poems and Ballads*. A really complete review of that volume, however, would of course demand a much closer analysis of the compositions which go to make it up than we either have given or can here give. But we must not finish without offering some slight specimen of what the book contains. Perhaps the fullest representative of the power and the specialty of Mr. Swinburne's work would be 'Anactoria'. That, however, is a poem of not inconsiderable length, and it is one of those to which exception may the most fairly be taken. We shall therefore select three smaller poems, all of which we have had occasion to mention already, showing the writer in different phases, and each first-rate of its order. The first is of mediæval as well as biblical analogies in style, most rich and most mournful in colouring, like a garden left to work out its own decay in autumn. The second is classic in sympathy, and forms a perfect lyrical music of regretful beauty and reluctant desire. (We need hardly remind our readers that, in this poem 'Itylus', the speaker is Philomela the nightingale, whose love, and the perennial pathos of her sorrowing, reproach her sister Procne the swallow, in memory of the horrible fate dealt by that sister's hand to her own son Itylus.) The third of the three subjoined poems is most intense in its seemingly personal passion.

[quotes 'A Ballad of Burdens', 'Itylus', and 'A Leave-taking']

We will not advisedly write anti-climaxes; and therefore, after quotation, we shall have done with criticism. The reader has now before him what we had to say concerning *Poems and Ballads*; a book withdrawn from circulation by Messrs. Moxon & Co., but which the Power that presides over poetic fame has no mind to withdraw.

# 13. Alfred Austin: 'Mr. Swinburne'

## 1870

Austin's critique originally appeared in *Temple Bar*, July 1869, xxvi, 457–74; it was reprinted, with very slight changes, in his *Poetry of the Period* (1870), the text of which is followed here. Austin's leading idea is that the age made great poetry impossible. Most of the poets are compared unfavourably with Byron, a comparison leading Browning to allude to Austin in 'Pacchiarotto' as 'Banjo-Byron'. In *Under the Microscope* Swinburne discusses Austin's views (see Introduction, section IV).

In my essay on Mr. Browning I have shown how dissatisfaction with the poetry of Mr. Tennyson, as an exponent of the age, has driven even his once frantic admirers to hearken for yet another voice, and how, in their ignorance of what it is in Mr. Tennyson that fails to satisfy them, they have pitched upon Mr. Browning of all people to supply the omission. What Mr. Tennyson wanted, I said, was loftiness; what Mr. Browning possessed, I observed, was depth; and I added that, this distinction once made, it was obvious that the one could not possibly supplement the other, having no earthly affinity with it. But there exists another distinction between them, which, though in complete harmony with the one I have already drawn, sets the matter in another, and for my present purpose still more important, light. If I were asked to sum up the characteristics of Mr. Tennyson's compositions in a single word, the word I should employ would be 'feminine', and if I had to do the same for Mr. Browning's genius, the word inevitably selected would be 'studious'. The pen of the latter is essentially the pen of a student; the muse of the former is essentially—I must not say the muse of a woman, for I should be rendering myself liable to misconception, but—a feminine muse. And in these two salient qualities they are unquestionably representative men, and typify two of the prominent tendencies of the time. We have just had, from a much revered source, an essay on the Subjection of Women; but I think it would not be difficult to show that men, and especially in the domain of Art, are, and have for some time been, quite as subject to women, to say the least of it, as is desirable. In the region of morals, women may, in modern times, have had a beneficent influence; though, as we shall see when we come to treat of Mr. Swinburne's particular genius, recent phenomena have somewhat shaken the once favourable opinion on that score. But there can be no question that, in the region of Art, their influence has been unmitigatedly mischievous. They have ruined the stage; they have dwarfed painting till it has become little more than the representative of pretty little sentiment—much of it terribly false—and mawkish commonplace domesticities; and they have helped poetry to become, in the hands of Mr. Tennyson at least, and of his disciples, the mere handmaid of their own limited interests, susceptibilities, and yearnings. I do not say that Mr. Tennyson is never by any chance and on occasion fairly manly, though I think no one can doubt who considers the matter, that he is not even fairly manly very often, and never conspicuously so; and the most unreasonable of his worshippers would not dare for one moment, in describing his supposed merits as a poet, to call him masculine. That feminine is the proper word to apply to his compositions, taken in their entirety, no impartial judge, I feel convinced, would dream of denying.

Between the essentially feminine genius and the genius of the student there is an abyss; and it represents the enormous difference that there is between Mr. Tennyson and Mr. Browning. I am not again going to discuss Mr. Browning's studious quality, for I have already so fully insisted on the 'depth' of his genius in my last paper—and between depth and studiousness there is so obvious a similarity—that I may fairly assume the point as settled. What I now wish to note is, that whilst, as I have said, not altogether satisfied with Mr. Tennyson's feminine, unlofty way of looking at things, the critics, who are so enamoured of their age that they are determined to find in it great poetry somewhere or other, pitched upon the deep and studious Mr. Browning, in the hope that he would afford them the satisfaction they required; they have, in reality, failed, despite all their bravado and assurances to the contrary, to find it in that quarter. It was simply impossible that they should find it there. A studious writer is neither the complement nor the antithesis of a feminine one. When men say, 'This poet is too feminine', what they want, of course, is a poet who shall be masculine. A student, as far as sex is concerned, as far as manly and womanly qualities are involved, is a nondescript. He may be incidentally of a masculine or of a feminine turn, just as it happens. He is a neutral in the matter. It does so happen that Mr. Browning is certainly far more masculine than feminine in his studiousness; but his masculinity is a mere sub-quality to that one great predominating characteristic. He is, over and above all things, an Analyser, and every other attribute is merged and lost, so to speak, in its conspicuous supremacy. Little wonderful, therefore, was it that these same critics, still sadly wanting an adequate poet, for all their copious assurances that they already possessed a couple, warmly welcomed Mr. Swinburne's appearance, and, enrolling him at once with the other two, have exultingly formed for themselves a Trinity of Song. Mr. Swinburne may thank Mr. Tennyson's imperfections and Mr. Browning's shortcomings for the reception he has met with; for let me hasten to say that, had a really great, adequate poet been alive, Mr. Swinburne would have failed to attract much attention, save for those qualities which even his admirers do not admire, but of which I may remark that I shall be found very tolerant. But the existence of Mr. Tennyson and Mr. Browning left ample room for Mr. Swinburne, just as the existence of Mr. Tennyson, Mr. Browning, and Mr. Swinburne still leaves ample room for another, or indeed many another, poetical apparition.

It might be supposed, after what has been said, that, even though Mr. Swinburne should turn out, on examination, to be neither the one great poet we should all be so delighted to hail, nor even a poet bringing precisely those qualities which neither the feminine nor the studious temperament supplies, he would at any rate have contributed something strikingly distinct from what we have seen is contributed by the other two, and be as different from Mr. Tennyson and from Mr. Browning as they are from each other. Different in every respect he unquestionably is from Mr. Browning, as every poet—and Mr. Swinburne *is* a poet—necessarily must be; Mr. Browning not being specifically a poet at all. It is with Mr. Tennyson, therefore, we must compare or contrast him; and thus, once for all, we may dismiss Mr. Browning to his own studious prose territory, having no further need of him in the poetical one.

Now, on the first blush, it would seem as though Mr. Swinburne's poetry were a genuine revolt against that of Mr. Tennyson, and as though he had struck a distinct and even antagonistic note. That Mr. Swinburne himself thinks so is evident from some observations dropped by him in his *Notes on Poems and Reviews*: a defence of his muse against the strictures of those who complained—in my opinion,

94

with absurd extravagance—of its alleged indecency and profanity. 'In one thing', he says, 'it seems I have erred: I have forgotten to prefix to my work the timely warning of a great poet and humorist:—

> "*J'en préviens les mères des familles,*
> *Ce que j'écris n'est pas pour les petites filles*
> *Dont on coupe le pain en tartines; mes vers*
> *Sont des vers de jeune homme.*"[1]

'I have overlooked the evidence which every day makes clear, that our time has room only for such as are content to write for children and girls. . . . Happily, there is no fear that the supply of milk for babes will fall short of the demand for some time yet. There are moral milkmen enough, in all conscience, crying their ware about the streets and byways.'

A few pages farther on Mr. Swinburne adds:—

'The question at issue is, whether or not all that cannot be lisped in the nursery or fingered in the school-room is therefore to be cast out of the library? whether or not the domestic circle is to be for all men and writers the outer limit and extreme horizon of their world of work? . . . Literature, to be worthy of men, must be large, liberal, sincere; and if literature is not to deal with the full life of man and the whole nature of things, let it be cast aside with the rods and rattles of childhood. Against how few really great names has not this small and dirt-encrusted pebble been thrown! A reputation seems imperfect without this tribute also; one jewel is wanting to the crown. . . . With English versifiers now, the idyllic form is alone in fashion. . . . We have idylls good and bad, ugly and pretty; idylls of the farm and the mill; idylls of the dining-room and the deanery. . . . The idyllic form is best for domestic and pastoral poetry. It is naturally on a lower level than that of tragic or lyric verse. Its gentle and maidenly lips are somewhat narrow for the stream, and somewhat cold for the fire of song. It is very fit for the sole diet of girls; not very fit for the sole sustenance of men.'

The point could not be better or more clearly put. Neither could it possibly be made more apparent that Mr. Swinburne here intends to protest against the excessive estimate usually paraded of the Laureate's poetry, both as regards its matter and its manner; and if the above is not an accusation, virtually embodying the distinction I have made, that Mr. Tennyson's muse is essentially a 'feminine' one, and a trumpet-call to critics and the public to demand some more masculine stuff, and

[1] Translated as a footnote to No. 11.

welcome it with open arms if it does appear, language must have lost all its uses. But of course it does embody such a protest against the feminine genius of Mr. Tennyson's verse, and a bold, admirably written plea for what is more 'fit for the sustenance of man'.

The question therefore arises, Has Mr. Swinburne, acting up to his excellent theory, turned his back on the haunts of feminine muses, struck out a masculine strain, and wrung from strenuous chords nervous and extolling hymns worthy of men and gods? Alas! who shall say it? True, he has given us no more idylls of the farm and the mill, of the dining-room and the deanery; nor will any one pretend that his lyrics and ballads are fit for the sole or even for part of the diet of girls. But what have men—to say nothing of gods—men brave, muscular, bold, upright, chivalrous—I will not say chaste, for that is scarcely a masculine quality ('I will find you twenty lascivious turtles ere one chaste man,'[1] says no less an authority than Shakespeare), but at any rate clean—men with 'pride in their port, defiance in their eye',[2] men daring, enduring, short of speech, and terrible in action—what have these to do with Mr. Swinburne's Venuses and Chastelards, his Anactorias and Faustines, his Dolores, his Sapphos, or his Hermaphroditus? If these be his Olympus, we prefer the deanery and the dining-room, or even the drawing-room. I do not say that they are not fair, much less that they are illegitimate, subjects for the poet's pen; but are they masculine? That is the question. Mr. Swinburne need fear no prudish or bigoted criticism from me. Venus or virgin, it is all one to me, provided he can make fine poetry out of either; though, of course, I should always reserve to myself the right of saying which I thought to be the nobler theme. He may take Priapus for his Apollo, if he will, so that he have dexterity and daintiness enough to handle a difficult matter becomingly, and extol a satyr into a Celestial. But it will not do to empty Olympus of its divinities, fill it with tipsy Bacchanals and meretricious Maenads, and then conceive that idylls of the earth, earthy —idylls of the farm and the mill—have been gloriously surpassed. Is this all that his Hellenic culture has taught him? Were 'Kisses that burn and bite' the everlasting theme of Homer, of Pindar, or of the grand tragedians of their country? Who was it but an Athenian that declared that poetry should consist of nothing but hymns to the gods and praises of virtue, and in the severity of his wrath at lascivious strains and Lydian measures banished all bards from his ideal republic? We hear

[1] *The Merry Wives of Windsor*, II, i, 82.
[2] Oliver Goldsmith, *The Traveller*, l. 327.

much of the puritanical spirit of Christianity; and in non-Catholic countries there has been at times considerably too much of this. But what about the occasional puritanism of Greek paganism? It too could revolt against literary excesses, and prove that in that respect, as in many another, it can compete with the creeds that helped to overthrow it. If ever there was a thorough Christian poet, Wordsworth was surely that man. Yet so little did he associate paganism with what he, at least, would have deemed profane and indecent, that, in his despair at the temper of his own times, he cried out:—

> 'Great God! I'd rather be
> A pagan suckled in a creed outworn;
> So might I, standing on this pleasant lea,
> Have glimpses that would make me less forlorn;
> Have sight of Proteus rising from the sea,
> Or hear old Triton blow his wreathèd horn.'

If Mr. Swinburne be really anxious to see the fulfilment of his prophecy in his 'Hymn to Proserpine'—

> 'Though before thee the throned Cytherean be fallen,
> and hidden her head,
> Yet thy kingdom shall pass, Galilean; thy dead
> shall go down to thee dead'—

it were surely desirable that he did not travesty the men and women, the gods and goddesses, of that earlier time. And in what way does he travesty them? By eliminating all that was masculine—and what a masculine epoch it was!—and intensifying and exaggerating what was not masculine by aid of his modern feminine lens. For to this clear charge and distinct conclusion must we come: that far from Mr. Swinburne being more masculine even than Mr. Tennyson, he is positively less so. Where has he given us, to use his own words, 'Literature worthy of men, large, liberal, sincere'? Where the 'literature that deals with the full life of man and the whole nature of things'? I may readily grant that the 'lilies and languors of virtue' do not constitute the full life of man and the whole nature of things; but I must protest that neither do 'the roses and raptures of vice'. Is that the sense in which he reads the magnificent saying of Schiller, when drenched and suffused with the old classical temper he exclaimed, 'Man has lost his dignity, but Art has saved it. Truth still lives in fiction, and from the copy will the original be restored.' What does Mr. Swinburne think is either the copy or the original of man's dignity? Is it represented in such lines as these?—

> 'Ah that my lips were tuneless lips, but pressed
> To the bruised blossom of thy scourged white breast!
> Ah that my mouth for Muses' milk were fed
> On the sweet blood thy sweet small wounds had bled!
> That with my tongue I felt them, and could taste
> The faint flakes from thy bosom to thy waist!'

I do not shrink from quoting anything Mr. Swinburne has written, and treating it with becoming critical fairness; but in quoting the above lines, I should like to know if their author thinks he is using Art to save something man has lost or would otherwise lose? Is this the verse that is peculiarly 'fit for the sole sustenance of man'? Mr. Tennyson, of whose extreme moral propriety some people have made such an absurd parade, has written something very similar, to the full as impassioned, and considerably better balanced:—

> 'My whole soul waiting silently,
> All naked in a sultry sky,
> Droops blinded with his piercing eye:
> I *will* possess him, or will die.
> I will grow round him in his place;
> Grow, live, die looking on his face;
> Die, dying clasp'd in his embrace.'

*Fatima.*

I distinctly remember lending the volume containing this poem to a young lady, and having it returned by her mamma, with the remark —I am indulging in no hackneyed joke, but narrating a simple fact— that she strongly objected to a volume containing such abomination as the foregoing, and preferred that her daughter should restrict her poetical reading to Mr. Tupper. The man who wrote 'Vivien', and the parting scene between Guinevere and Lancelot, has not invariably been a moral milkman. Mr. Tennyson has such immense skill as a craftsman, that he successfully passes off upon proper people what they would call shocking improprieties if proceeding from a less dexterous hand. Therefore, if all that Mr. Swinburne is pleading for in his defence of something 'that cannot be lisped in the nursery or fingered in the school-room', be only the free delineation of sexual passion, I am bound to say that Mr. Tennyson, in his more extreme moods, and the Hon. Robert Lytton, in his ordinary ones, have both anticipated him, and thus blunted the force of his literary complaints. It is true that neither of them has indulged in quite such warm language as Mr. Swinburne; but that is an affair of relative colouring, not a matter of substance, subject, or principle. As far as Mr. Lytton is concerned, one has only to glance at 'The Wanderer', *passim*, for a proof of the assertion; and surely such lines as—

> 'O love! O fire! once he drew
> With one long kiss my whole soul thro'
> My lips, as sunlight drinketh dew,'

from the 'Fatima', from which we have already quoted, or,

> 'And then they were agreed upon a night
> (When the good king should not be there) to meet
> And part for ever. Passion-pale they met
> And greeted: hands in hands, and eye to eye,
> *Low on the border of her couch they sat*
> *Stammering and staring,'*

from the *Idylls of the King*, are sufficient to exonerate Mr. Tennyson from the imputation of writing only for children and girls, and to prove that he can compete—and in my opinion beat—Mr. Swinburne on his own special ground.

But we must grapple still more closely with the relations existing between the muse of Mr. Tennyson and the muse of Mr. Swinburne, inasmuch as in giving a serious account of the 'Poetry of the Period', almost everything turns upon it. I regard each muse alike as essentially feminine, and will proceed at once to illustrate what I mean.

Let us for a moment step aside from the province of poetry proper, and direct our attention to one in which imagination, however, plays a leading part—the province of prose romance. Is there, or is there not, a palpable difference in the tone, and—if I may be permitted the phrase —the atmosphere, of the novels which for twenty years Sir Walter Scott poured forth with such unexampled vigour for the delectation of the public, and the novels with which, since the hand of the great wizard waxed cold, we have been so copiously favoured? Who can deny that the difference is not only palpable, but strikingly palpable? And wherein lies the difference? There is but one answer to the question. Scott was manly and masculine; his successors are just as distinctively feminine. During the last twenty or thirty years, and more decidedly during the last ten than the last twenty, and during the last twenty than during the last thirty, the heroines of novels have been more important than the heroes; and when they were not actually intended to be such by their author or authoress, they have been determinedly invested with more interest by the general public. Let us take one single instance, fairly typical of the tones and tendencies to which I am alluding. Let us compare Sir Walter Scott and Mr. Anthony Trollope. There we have the whole matter in a nutshell—the representative novelists of their time brought face to face and contrasted. It were sheer waste of time to demonstrate the self-evident; that, though Scott can of course be relished by women, girls, and children too, he is pre-eminently a masculine novelist, writing for men in a manly spirit, and from a man's point of view; whilst Mr. Trollope, though he can be relished by men, scarcely by boys, and much less by children, is a feminine novelist, writing for women in a womanly spirit and from a woman's point of view. It would be easy to point out how, during the same period, painting and the stage—matters so distinct from each other as never necessarily influencing one the other—have experienced, as I have already hinted, a like change. On the stage, adventure, heroic courage, variety of passion—Shakespeareanism, in a word—have had to give way to plays in which domestic sentiment and all that is expressed by the phrase 'the female element' have predominated. The walls of the Royal Academy, too, have annually told a similar tale. Mothers, wives, daughters, babies, dolls, in every conceivable touching condition; soft, sentimental canvases, made still more alluring by pathetic, not to say mawkish, titles, have year after year asserted their supremacy over the grand, the heroic, and the manly. When did Scott die? Almost to a year when Mr. Tennyson began to write. And had there, meanwhile, whilst Scott was writing his novels, been no manly poets? Scott himself is the manliest of bards, though he writes of women with all that delicate grace of which the truly manly pen alone is capable. And what of Byron? We well may say, 'he was a man.' Some people think he was more, and regard him as a devil. A critic by no means extravagantly favourable to him talks of his 'demoniac sublimity'. At any rate, he was no moral milkman, and never shirked dealing with sexual passion or sentiment. But he was not for ever harping upon it.

> 'For Love is in man's life a thing apart;
> 'Tis woman's whole existence,'

he sings; and he proved the truth of the first line, as far as he was himself concerned, by his *Cain*, his *Manfred*, his *Childe Harold*, and most of

his dramas. And Wordsworth? 'The worthiest objects,' Wordsworth
writes, 'of the exertion of the faculty of imagination are man's natural
affections, his acquired passions'—an untenable distinction, of course,
between natural and acquired; but let that pass—'his moral and
religious sentiments, and the external universe'. But why pursue the
subject? Even if any should challenge the assertion that there were
giants in those days, they surely will not deny that at least there were
men. In these, as far as the faculty of the imagination and the objects on
which it is exerted are concerned, we have, as novelists and poets, only
women or men with womanly deficiencies, steeped in the feminine
temper of the times, subdued to what they work in, and ringing such
changes as can be rung on what—I mean no disrespect or depreciation
of the sex, that is both fair, devout, dear, and indispensable—has well
been called 'everlasting woman'. Open Mr. Tennyson's first volume,
and read the table of contents straight off: 'Claribel', 'Lilian', 'Isabel',
'Mariana', 'Madeline', 'Adelmine', and so on. What are 'The Lady of
Shalott', 'Oriana', 'Fatima', 'Eleanore', 'Oenone', 'The May Queen',
'The Miller's Daughter', 'The Gardener's Daughter', 'Lady Clara Vere
de Vere', 'Love and Duty', 'Locksley Hall', and the rest, all about? All
about woman. What is *Maud* about? Woman. What is *The Princess*
about? Woman, woman. What are the four *Idylls of the King* about?
Woman, woman, woman, woman. I wonder what the *Flos Regum
Arthurus*[1] and all the Table Round would have thought had they known
that their names and deeds would have served this one small purpose
in the nineteenth century. I think they would have somewhat grimly
smiled as they clanked their spurs and rattled their spears.

But what has Mr. Swinburne got to do with all this? Surely a great
deal. He has tried hard, I grant, and very meritoriously, to shake off
'love's fits and fevers', and to sing something more 'worthy of men,
large, liberal, sincere'. He must have an inkling, at least, of what I am
urging, since he thus makes Althaea address Meleager:—

'For with time
Blind love burns out; but if one feed it full,
Till some discolouring stain dyes all his life,
He shall keep nothing praiseworthy, nor die
The sweet wise death of old men honourable,
Who have lived out all the length of all their years
Blameless, and seen well-pleased the face of God,
And without shame and without fear have wrought

[1] 'Arthur the flower of kings.

> Things memorable; and while their days held out,
> In sight of all men and the sun's great light
> Have gat them glory.'

Accordingly, in *Atalanta in Calydon*, from which the above is taken, and in some shorter poems, Mr. Swinburne has striven to get away from 'Laus Veneris' and 'Our Lady of Pain', and give the world assurance of a man. But with the exception of the lyrical portions—of which more anon—I cannot think, despite the copiousness of his language and the intensely classical air of these compositions, that he has here been really successful as an original poet. They are too obviously, literally, and slavishly Greek, to reap the meed due to spontaneous song. Anybody fairly, but not exhaustively, acquainted with such Greek dramas as have come down to us, would, in reading the foregoing passage, of a certainty conclude, if he were told nothing about it, that it was a translation from some Greek play. Turn to whatever page we will in *Atalanta in Calydon*, the same thing strikes us, even though we know we are reading not even a paraphrase but a presumedly original poem:—

> 'Child, if a man serve law through all his life,
> And with his whole heart worship, him all gods
> Praise; but who loves it only with his lips,
> And not in heart and deed desiring it,
> Hides a perverse will with obsequious words,
> Him Heaven infatuates, and his twin-born fate
> Tracks, and gains on him, scenting sins far off,
> And the swift hounds of violent death devour.'

Here it is Althaea that speaks; but the utterance of Meleager is pitched in precisely the same key:—

> 'O mother, I am not fain to strive in speech,
> Nor set my mouth against thee, who art wise
> Even as they say, and full of sacred words.
> But one thing I know surely, and cleave to this:
> That though I be not subtle of wit as thou,
> Nor womanlike to weave sweet words, and melt
> Mutable minds of wise men as with fire,
> I too, doing justly and reverencing the gods,
> Shall not want wit to see what things be right.
> For whom they love and whom reject, being gods,
> There is no man but seeth, and in good time
> Submits himself, refraining all his heart.'

Could anything more resemble the substance and language of a
Greek drama than these cold, statuesque, stately passages? But that is
their very vice, if we are to consider Mr. Swinburne's claims as an
original poet. All this is sheer and mere imitation—imitation of the
very best kind, no doubt, but still nothing more; and in producing it
Mr. Swinburne is only the slave of his school days, and that selfsame
spirit of the age which, vexed and mortified at having nothing grand
and heroic of its own to say, turns its poetic eyes to the past, and has
compelled so many of its men of letters to 'do' translations of the great
bards of Hellas. Mr. Tennyson, in his 'Œnone', has done something
more than this, infusing a modern flavour into an ancient and classic
theme, and, in my opinion, has by that one short fragment surpassed
all that Mr. Swinburne has written of the avowedly classical kind. For,
as we shall see later, Mr. Swinburne's own real genius is of anything
but a classic, and, least of all of a Greek turn. For the present, however,
I wished only to note what it is he has done outside the sexual region
in which his genius most loves to disport, and in which it has had its
most conspicuous successes; and we arrive at the conclusion that he has
not done much there worth speaking of as original poetry. For the real
truth is, his muse is like that of Anacreon: he wants it to sing of the sons
of Atreus, and to discourse of Cadmus, but it will discourse only of
Love. There at once is its weakness. It is a feminine muse.

But surely, it will be said, Mr. Swinburne's muse is not a feminine
muse in the same sense that Mr. Tennyson's is; and surely he does not
sing of love, woman, and all that is concerned with and gathers about
woman, in the same way Mr. Tennyson does? Certainly not. But there
is such a thing as the 'one step farther', and Mr. Swinburne has taken it.
Again, we must have recourse to our writers of prose romance, to
those who exert the faculty of imagination in novels. I have spoken of
Mr. Anthony Trollope, and have called him a feminine novelist,[1] at
the same time pointing him out as the fair analogue, in prose novels,
of Mr. Tennyson. Now, Mr. Trollope is a very 'proper' writer, as no
doubt in manner and usually in matter Mr. Tennyson also is. But is Mr.
Trollope the only feminine novelist of the time? And are all the
feminine novelists of the time as 'proper' as himself? More than that:
are not the most 'improper' of them—we are obliged to use the word

---

[1] I am well aware that Mr. Trollope would himself stoutly deny the correctness of this
view; and anybody acquainted with him would doubtless pronounce him to be man-
liness personified. But the world is stronger than any one man; and it has compelled him
to write according to its humour. [Austin's note.]

in vogue, in order to be understood, though we wish to convey no
ethical opinion of our own in doing so—are not the most 'improper' of
them not only feminine, but actually women? Mr. Trollope writes of
love, still love; but it is the sentimental love of youths and maidens, of
coy widows and clumsy, middle-aged men, beginning in flirtation and
ending in marriage. In a word, it is pretty, pious, half-comical,
domestic love—love within the bounds of social law. But what is the
love of which many of our men-novelists—men, at least, as far as
nominal sex is concerned, though certainly not men as authors or in any
literary sense—and nearly all our women-novelists, so freely discourse?
It is the love—had we not better call it the lust—which begins with
seduction and ends in desertion, or whose agreeable variations are
bigamy, adultery, and, in fact, illicit passion of every conceivable sort
under every conceivable set of circumstances. Nor have I yet given to
the matter its full proportions. In the novels to which I refer, and they
may be counted by hundreds, it is not men so much as women who
are represented as the leading tempters. The heroines are more animal
and impassioned than the heroes. We take up the last number of a
well-known weekly review, and we turn to its notices of recent novels.
*Trials of an Heiress.* By the Hon. Mrs. G. R. Gifford. I have not read
this particular novel myself, but what do we find the critic saying of it?
'If there is any marked characteristic in the book, it is the strong
tendency of the women to make love to the men.' In one respect, at
least, the criticism is carelessly beside the mark. The strong tendency of
the women to make love to the men cannot possibly be the marked
characteristic nowadays of any individual novel, since it is the marked
characteristic of most of them. Within the last few years three or four
novels, if not more, all by ladies, have been withdrawn from circulation
almost as soon as they were published, on account of this 'feminine'
propensity having been thought by the circulating libraries to be in
their case a trifle too warmly done. But the result was that what few
copies could be got hold of were in immense demand; and the very
fact of their being written proves the condition of our imaginative
atmosphere. What is it that we are seeing simultaneously in a sister art?
The nude—we ought rather to say the undressed, for there is a vast
difference between the two—rapidly threatening to displace the purely
domestic in the painting of the period; and whoever has not lately
noticed the disposition in the illustrations of our serial literature to slide
from the sentimental into the sensuous, must either be without eyes or
strangely unobservant. I have already spoken of the expulsion of the

heroic or Shakespearean from the stage in favour of dramas of domestic pathos; and I have now to add the incontrovertible fact that domestic pathos is being ousted by plays expressly composed with the purpose of bringing as many women on the stage as possible, and of arraying them when there in as scant garments and displaying as much of their physical proportions as is consistent with continued suggestiveness and sustained interest. At the same moment *La Grande Duchesse de Gerolstein* is the great theatrical attraction of the day, since Madlle. Schneider has contrived to unite in herself both of the two phenomena of which we have spoken—a liberal parade of female limbs and the 'tendency of women to make love to men' carried to its crowning point. Surely in this scientific age no one will doubt that all these things are related, and that the Schneiderism of the studio, the stage, and the circulating library are all traceable to the same cause. It is the feminine element at work when it has ceased to be domestic; when it has quitted the modest precincts of home, and courted the garish light of an intense and warm publicity. It is the feminine element, no longer in the nursery, the drawing-room, or the conjugal chamber, but unrestrainedly rioting in any and every arena of life in which an indiscriminating imagination chooses to place it. It is the 'one step farther' of which I have already spoken, but a step that was inevitable and sure to be taken, when the first wrong step—that of making women too conspicuous in life and literature—had once been fatally indulged in. Our 'proper' feminine novelists have but led the way for our 'improper' feminine novelists; and the, on the whole, 'proper' feminine muse of Mr. Tennyson was only the precursor of the 'improper' feminine muse of Mr. Swinburne. There is nothing masculine about the one any more than about the other; or what advantage there is on either side in that particular lies, as I have said, with the muse of the former. Both, however, are substantially feminine muses; only one is the feminine muse of the Hearth, whilst the other is the feminine muse of the Hetairae.

As such, then—for in assigning Mr. Swinburne his precise position I have only been pursuing an indispensable inquiry, and by no means intending to object to his filling it if he found it vacant, or to read him a moral lecture for doing so—what are Mr. Swinburne's literary and poetical merits? I have already expressed my opinion of the value of his statelier and avowedly classical productions. They are the wonderfully faithful echo of a grand poetical literature that flourished more than two thousand years ago; but they are an echo, and nothing more. They are not the poetry of today, though they may be, in a sense, part of the

'Poetry of the Period'. As we may say, they are 'Greece, but living Greece no more'; and poetry that is not alive is not poetry at all. Turn we then to those of Mr. Swinburne's compositions which have a more modern flavour; for in spite of a few—very few—plausible facts that might be adduced in support of such a theory, it was from no dead tongues that Mr. Swinburne caught his two main and essentially modern characteristics, lyrical fluency and erotic ardour. The latter half of the nineteenth century has given him these; and in all that constitutes his original genius he is unmistakably its child:—

> 'Why, two nights hence I dreamed that I could see
> In through your bosom under the left flower,
> And there was a round hollow, and at heart
> A little red snake sitting, without spot,
> That bit—like this, and sucked up sweet—like this,
> And curled its lithe light body right and left,
> And quivered like a woman in act to love.
> Then there was some low fluttered talk i' the lips,
> Faint sound of fierce soft words caressing them—
> Like a fair woman's when her love gets way.
> Ah! your old kiss—I know the ways of it:
> Let the lips cling a little; take them off,
> And speak some word, or I go mad with love.'
>
> *Chastelard.*

Here there is nothing classical, any more than there is anything masculine. But it is a capital specimen of one of Mr. Swinburne's two individual manners, and is as thoroughly modern and as completely feminine—of the 'one step farther' stage—as anything well could be. It is essentially the product of the same age that has given us M. Michelet's *L'Amour* and *La Femme*, and to collate small things with great, the everlasting and wearisome articles about women—the most notable of them by the way, written by a woman—in the *Saturday Review*.[1] It is true that the above is spoken by Chastelard, a man—a man! I scarcely like to own sex with him;—but for all that, it is intrinsically feminine (again, be it always understood, when I am applying this word to Mr. Swinburne's compositions, of the 'one step farther' stage). In fact, it is Schneiderism rampant in blank verse.

When I turn from his blank verse to his lyrical, I feel a little puzzled. In order to prove satisfactorily what I am going to say of it, I should

[1] Probably 'The Girl of the Period', *Saturday Review*, 14 March 1868, xxv, 339-40, an article attributed to Mrs. Lynn Linton.

have to quote almost every line of lyrical poetry Mr. Swinburne has ever written. This, obviously, I cannot do, nor indeed shall I quote more than a few fragments. Those, however, who are well acquainted with his works will, I fancy, feel the truth of my observations; and I must ask those who are not to believe that, as far as *manner* is concerned, with which we are now mainly dealing, the following stanzas are typical, and almost exhaustive, of Mr. Swinburne's genius when it is most lyrical, most original—in a word, at its best. They are from 'Dolores':—

> 'O lips full of lust and of laughter, . . .
[quotes three stanzas of 'Dolores']

It is unnecessary to point out that here, again, it is essentially a feminine muse that is sweeping the chords. But what I wish now to note as characteristic of this and all Mr. Swinburne's lyrical poetry is, that it consists of voluble variations on one small theme. There are no less than fifty-five stanzas like the foregoing in this one poem of 'Dolores', and these are all so thoroughly alike, save for the shuffle, so to speak, of the words, that any three would have served my purpose just as well as any other three, and the whole fifty-five best of all; for it would then be seen that no distinct impression is left by any one of them as opposed to any other. When we have once read the opening lines:

> 'Cold eyelids that hide like a jewel
>   Hard eyes that grow soft for an hour;
> The heavy white limbs, and the cruel
>   Red mouth, like a venomous flower:
> When these are gone by with their glories,
>   What shall rest of thee, then—what remain,
> O mystic and sombre Dolores,
>   Our Lady of Pain?'

we already know all about it. The remaining fifty-four stanzas are mere *fioriture*;[1] shakes and quavers, runnings up and down the scales, displaying wonderful facility and flexibility, but giving us no new air, nor even any genuine modification of the air. Indeed, anybody reading 'Dolores' through must feel puzzled to know, when he reaches the end, why it is the end; why, in fact, Mr. Swinburne did not go on for ever in that strain. There is no question but that, short of physical exhaustion, he could do so, as he proves that he could when he sets to work

---

[1] 'Embellishment.'

to write some fresh lyric, precisely like the one we have quoted from. I may go farther, and safely assert that, with a little practice, Mr. Swinburne might become an improvisatore, and extemporise any quantity of verse like the foregoing. For it is *vox, et præterea nihil*—a voice and nothing more; a most melodious, surprising voice, no doubt, but so recklessly exercised and employed that it reminds us of the noise made by a prepared quill blown in a glass of water rather than of the song of a bird, much less of a human throat. Paganini was before my time, but I believe one of his most popular performances was to fiddle on one string. I never heard, however, that he always fiddled on one string. That was a feat left for Mr. Swinburne to perform, and in a most marvellous manner does he perform it.

If we turn to a 'Song of Italy', precisely the same effect is produced on the mind of the reader, and precisely the same criticism provoked. It is sheer poetical babble; wondrously good poetical babble, but still only babble. To use a colloquial phrase, there is nothing in it. Take away its music and its plash and flutter of words, and it is utterly unworthy of the subject, and miserably inadequate. What we call sparkling wine the Italians call *vino spumante*, and this is what they would call his 'Song' if they read it. It is *spumante*, sparkling and frothy, but with no body in it. It abounds in foam, but we look in vain for the breakers. I may say of it what Mr. Tennyson says with such abominable extravagance of the Pleiads—that the words glitter through the strain 'like a swarm of fire-flies tangled in a silver braid'. But though fire-flies, as any one knows who has seen them in perfection on a southern summer night, are bewitchingly beautiful, they yield no light to speak of; and no light to speak of is to be had from Mr. Swinburne's 'Song of Italy'. Should anybody be inclined to reply, that froth, glitter, and fire-flies are best suited to a Song of Italy, let him remember Dante, Tasso, Ariosto, and Alfieri, to say nothing of the grand heroic, masculine deeds recorded in Italian history, and discreetly hold his peace. Or should that fail to silence him, let him turn to Byron's 'Prophecy of Dante' and Mrs. Barrett Browning's *Casa Guidi Windows*, and there see how Italy can be sung. Neither will it avail Mr. Swinburne to plead that the essence and spirit of lyrical poetry reside rather in its manner than its matter, and that the accusation of there being 'nothing in it' is irrelevant. Mr. Swinburne himself would be scarcely likely, on reflection, to employ or accept any such plea. His classical knowledge would save him from so foolish an apology. Moreover, the shade of Shelley, whom he very properly calls divine whilst improperly arrogating that epithet to him exclusively, would rise in judgment against him. What more perfect specimen of lyrical poetry exists in any language than the 'Ode to a Skylark'? Yet there is stuff enough, thought, matter enough in it, to furnish forth more poets, if it only happened to be their own, than have been born into this world since Shelley wrote it.

Mr. Swinburne is very wroth with Mr. Matthew Arnold for making the admirable distinction—all Mr. Arnold's criticisms are admirable, being at once profound and pellucid—that Shelley too often only tries to render what he has got to say, whereas Byron invariably renders it. The remark is obviously true, when once made; and here we find a corroboration of the distinction between the masculine and feminine elements in poetry. For 'I know what I mean, but I cannot say it,' is essentially a feminine argument and habit; and Shelley, whom probably I admire within the bounds of reason quite as much as Mr. Swinburne does, was infected with this feminine fault. I am ready to fall down and prostrate myself in worship before the genius of Shelley; but, for all that, it was he who first began to mean what he could not say, and in that respect set a pernicious example since too amply followed. But Mr. Swinburne, instinctively aware that he must, in his lyrical manner at least, shelter himself under the wings of Shelley if anywhere, is angry at being told that Shelley too often only 'tried to render' his thoughts, and retorts that Byron was half a Philistine and 'a singer who could not sing'. He means a singer who did not and would not screech, as poor Shelley now and then unfortunately did; and who positively *could not* indulge in those falsetto notes which appear to compose most of Mr. Swinburne's emasculated poetical voice.

This, then, is the summary of the 'Poetry of the Period' as far as Mr. Tennyson, Mr. Browning, and Mr. Swinburne are concerned. No man, despite all the nonsense that has been written to the contrary, and therefore no poet, can, as far as *work done* is concerned, be greater than the age in which he happens to live. It might as well be supposed that a man, by the use of his muscles, could throw a stone farther than the law of gravitation under the circumstances permitted, or by dint of shouting be heard a longer way off than was consistent under the circumstances with the law of acoustics. Every individual that comes into the world, no matter how great his natural gifts, is just as much affected and limited by the atmosphere of his time as is a shrub by the climate or season in which it flourishes. To suppose the contrary is not to have thought about the matter at all. Mr. Tennyson, Mr. Browning, and Mr. Swinburne are mental phenomena of the period—a period which, however distinguished for smaller characteristics, is incapable of doing really great deeds or producing really great poetry. The age plunges into its domestic concerns, its maidens, its undergraduates, its gardens, its pretty little streams, its husbands and wives, their quarrels, reconciliations, and bereavements, its love-making, and semi-mystical attempts at what it thinks religion; and forthwith it finds a voice in Mr. Tennyson. Anon it waxes discontented with itself and rebellious against the pettiness of its narrow circle and its pious domestic interests, puts the latch-key of home into its pocket, sallies forth with a determination to be a free man again, and plunges into a course of naughty dissipation. Mr. Swinburne now is its spokesman. Disgusted with itself even more perhaps for its brief indulgence in the second mood than for its long submission to the first, it then thinks it would like to betake itself to books, study, deep thought, and analysing—analysis of itself mostly, for it is a terrible egotist and a very sickly one. Then Mr. Browning comes to the front, and he, too is equally welcome. Student, domestic character, and sensualist—behold the three *rôles* our age is capable of playing. A really great part is beyond it. Really great song is therefore, and inevitably, equally so. Studious moments are not poetical ones, and Mr. Browning, the representative of the studious moments of the age, is, as we have seen, not specifically a poet at all. Domestic proclivities are quite pretty and pathetic enough to be poetical; and Mr. Tennyson, their representative, is the Poet of the Hearth. Poetical, too, may be the insurrectionary temper which, flinging hotly aside the restrictions so sweetly expressed in the last of the *Idylls of the King*, when Arthur addresses Guinevere—

'For I was ever virgin save for thee'—

or represents his knights as swearing

'To lead sweet lives in purest chastity;
To love one maiden only, cleave to her'—

resolves to fly to those whom it can address in the following very different fashion:—

'Hast thou told all thy secrets the last time,
    And bared all thy beauties to one?
Ah, where shall we go then for pastime,
    If the worst that can be has been done?
But sweet as the rind was the core is;

> We are fain of thee still, we are fain,
> O sanguine and subtle Dolores,
> Our Lady of Pain!'

Poetical, I say, may be this tendency likewise, and the age has strongly exhibited it. In this frame of mind, Mr. Swinburne is its poetical oracle. Higher and grander frames of mind than the foregoing the period has not, or it would have higher and grander poetry. Mr. Tennyson and Mr. Swinburne are such as their age makes them, or at least permits them to be. It is not their fault, but only their misfortune—and ours.

# OBITER DICTA *BY CONTEM-PORARY MEN OF LETTERS*

## 14(a). Alfred Tennyson

Swinburne admired much of Tennyson's work, but as a representative of the new poetry he challenged comparison with the older poet, particularly in the treatment of Arthurian themes. Though some of Tennyson's comments on Swinburne were admiring, D. G. Rossetti's letter to him, cited below, indicates his reservations about *Poems and Ballads*. He resented Swinburne's criticism of his work, too. Finally, 'Birthday Ode' and 'Threnody' were pleasant tributes by the younger to the elder poet. The selections from the *Memoir* are used by special permission of Macmillan & Co. Ltd.

---

(i) From *Alfred Lord Tennyson: A Memoir by His Son*, i, 425 (under '1858'): I must tell you however that young Swinburne called here the other day with a college friend of his, and we asked him to dinner, and I thought him a very modest and intelligent young fellow. Moreover I read him what you indicated [*Maud*], but what I particularly admired in him was that he did not press upon me any verses of his own.

(ii) *Memoir*, i, 496: Accept my congratulations on the success of your Greek play [*Atalanta in Calydon*]. I had some strong objections to parts of it, but these I think have been modified by a re-perusal, and at any rate I daresay you would not care to hear them; here however is one. Is it *fair* for a Greek chorus to abuse the Deity something in the *style* of the Hebrew prophets?

Altogether it is many a long day since I have read anything so fine; for it is not only carefully written, but it has both strength and splendour, and shows moreover that you have a fine metrical invention which I envy you.

(iii) From D. G. Rossetti's letter to Alfred Tennyson, 6 October 1866 (Lang, i, 192; quoted by permission of the Yale University Press): Edward Jones told me today that when he lately saw you, you were speaking of the qualities which displease you in Swinburne's poetry, and after attributing their origin in one respect correctly, you added that you supposed they might be also owing to his intimacy with me.

As no one delights more keenly in his genius than I do, I also have a right to say that no one has more strenuously combatted its wayward exercise in certain instances, to the extent of having repeatedly begged him not to read me such portions of his writings when in MS. I remember that in a conversation I had with you when returning from Mr. Procter's some months ago, I stated this; though not then in denial to reports of which I then knew nothing, and which seem to have more weight with you than my statement. So let me now say distinctly that any assertion to the contrary is either ignorant gossip or lying slander.

The attacks on Swinburne in the press have been for the most part coarse and stupid; and it is only to a very few, such as yourself, that I should at this moment say anything which could by any possibility be misconstrued as taking part against him. I trust to your not so construing it; but having made such efforts as I could before his book appeared, in what I thought his interest, I cannot now myself submit to misrepresentation in a quarter where I should much regret it.

(iv) From *More Letters of Edward FitzGerald* (1901), 186 (written in 1876): He [Tennyson] keeps true to his old Loves, even Bailey's Festus, for some passages. He still admires Browning, for a great, though unshapen, Spirit; and acknowledges Morris, Swinburne, and Co., though not displeased, I think, that I do not.

(v) *Memoir*, ii, 285: 'He is a reed through which all things blow into music.'

# 14(b). Robert Browning

The first passage quoted below indicates that Browning had expressed misgivings about some of Swinburne's early poems, though one may doubt whether he thus discouraged Chapman & Hall from publishing Swinburne's work. Apparently the incident prompted Swinburne to write his essay on 'The Chaotic School' (in *New Writings by Swinburne*, ed. Cecil Y. Lang, who, on 198 ff., discusses the reasons for the essay), which exaggerates Browning's weaknesses and neglects merits of which Swinburne later showed himself aware, as in his digression on Browning in *George Chapman*. The two men were occasionally friendly correspondents, and Browning, like Tennyson, became the subject of a kindly poetic tribute ('A Sequence of Sonnets on the Death of Robert Browning').

---

(i) From Browning's letter to Richard Monckton Milnes, 7 July 1863 (Lang, i, 84, quoted by permission of the Yale University Press): I know next to nothing of Swinburne, and like him much: I have received courtesy from him, and been told he feels kindly to me—I believe it, indeed. Of his works, since his first volume, I know not a line, except a poem which I looked over a long while ago at Rossetti's, and the pieces he recited the other night: I could only have an opinion, therefore, on these. I thought them moral mistakes, redeemed by much intellectual ability. They may be a sample of the forthcoming book,—or just the exceptional instances—I hope so.

When I was abruptly appealed to, some days after, for my estimate of Mr. Swinburne's powers,—I don't know what I could do but say 'that he had genius, and wrote verses in which to my mind there was no good at all'.

If I referred,—as I probably did,—to a similarity of opinion on the part of others present, it was from the reluctance I had to stand forward and throw even this cherry-stone at a young poet.

(ii) From a letter to Isa Blagden, 22 March 1870 (*Dearest Isa: Robert*

*Browning's Letters to Isabella Blagden*, ed. Edward C. McAleer [1951], 332–3, quoted by permission of the University of Texas Press): As to Swinburne's verses, I agree with you—they are 'florid impotence', to my taste, the *minimum* of thought and idea in the *maximum* of words and phraseology. Nothing said and nothing done with, left to stand alone and trust for its effect in its own worth.

(iii) From a letter to Miss Blagden, 19 June 1870 (*Dearest Isa*, 336): Yes,—I have read Rossetti's poems—and poetical they are,—*scented* with poetry, as it were. . . . You know I hate the effeminacy of his school,—the men that dress up like women,—that use obsolete forms, too, and archaic accentuations to seem soft—fancy calling it a lilý,— liliés, and so on: Swinburne started this with other like Belialisms— witness his 'harp-playér' etc.

# 14(c). Matthew Arnold

Personal relations between Arnold and Swinburne were friendly. Arnold was grateful for Swinburne's praise in *Essays and Studies*. Arnold's comments on his contemporaries testify to his lofty standards rather than to his critical acumen. Swinburne's later comments on Arnold, unduly harsh, were partly prompted by Arnold's, especially by his phrase 'a sort of pseudo-Shelley' and his depreciatory estimate of the real Shelley. Arnold's *Letters* are quoted by permission of Macmillan & Co. Ltd.

---

(i) From Arnold's letter to his mother, 16 June 1863 (*Letters*, ed. G. W. E. Russell, 1896, i, 227–8): On Sunday night I dined with Monckton Milnes, and met all the advanced liberals in religion and politics. . . . But the philosophers were fearful! G. Lewes, Herbert Spencer, a sort of pseudo-Shelley called Swinburne, and so on.

[In *Charles Dickens*, after referring to several Dickens characters, Swinburne observed: 'The incredible immensity, measurable by no critic ever born, of such a creative power as was needed to call all these into immortal life would surely, had Dickens never done any work on a larger scale of invention and construction, have sufficed for a fame great enough to deserve the applause and the thanksgiving of all men worthy to acclaim it, and the contempt of such a Triton of the minnows as Matthew Arnold. A man whose main achievement in creative literature was to make himself by painful painstaking into a sort of pseudo-Wordsworth could pay no other tribute than that of stolid scorn to a genius of such inexhaustible force and such indisputable originality as that of Charles Dickens.' In 'Changes of Aspect' and 'Short Notes', first published by the editor of this volume in *PMLA* for March 1943 but now available in *New Writings by Swinburne*, ed. Lang, Swinburne also judged Arnold severely.]

(ii) From Arnold's letter to his mother 16 November 1867 (*Letters* . . ., ed. Russell, i, 436): I am to meet Swinburne at dinner on Monday, at the Lockers'. . . . He expresses a great desire to meet me, and I should like to do him some good, but I am afraid he has taken some bent. His praise has, as was natural, inclined the religious world to look out in my writings for a crusade against religion. . . .

(iii) From Arnold's letter to his mother, November 1870 (Russell, ii, 50–1): With Swinburne the favourite poet of the young men at Oxford and Cambridge, Huxley pounding away at the intelligent working man, and Newdigate applauding the German Education Minister for his reactionary introduction of the narrowest Protestantism into the schools, and for thus sending psalm-singing soldiers into the field who win battles—between all these there is indeed much necessity for methods of insight and moderation.

(iv) From Arnold's letter of 29 July 1882 to Sir Mountstuart Grant Duff (Russell, ii, 232): I was glad to hear from you direct, and I wish all happiness to your little Iseult. She coincides with Swinburne's poem on the subject, which is just published, and which he has sent me with a pretty letter. He has taken the story, answering to the old Theseus story, of the black and white sails [G. W. E. Russell mistakenly read this as 'souls'], and a very fine story it is for poetical purposes. Swinburne's fatal habit of using one hundred words where one would suffice always offends me, and I have not yet faced his poem, but I must try it soon.

# 14(d). Thomas Carlyle and Ralph Waldo Emerson

For many years Swinburne admired Carlyle, but Carlyle's opinion of Swinburne was more unfavourable than Arnold's. William Allingham reported his saying, 'There is not the least intellectual value in anything he writes' (*A Diary*, p. 258). Since more than one person has hinted that Carlyle made harsher remarks than this, the phrasing attributed to him in an interview (first described by the editor of this volume in 'Emerson on Swinburne: A Sensational Interview', *Modern Language Notes*, March 1933, xlviii, 180–2), outrageous as it is, may be less inaccurate than one would prefer to believe. We cannot be sure that the interviewer quoted Emerson accurately, but, since he did not disavow the interview, Swinburne assumed that Emerson was responsible for what he was reported to have said.

---

From an interview appearing in *Frank Leslie's Illustrated Newspaper*, 3 January 1874, 275: He [Emerson] condemned Swinburne severely as a perfect leper and a mere sodomite, which criticism recalls Carlyle's scathing description of that poet—as a man standing up to his neck in a cesspool, and adding to its contents. Morris, the author of *The Earthly Paradise*, is just the opposite of Swinburne, and will help to neutralize his bad influence on the public.

[Swinburne's letter to the *New York Daily Tribune* is given in Lang, ii, 274–5. One sentence will indicate the tone: 'A foul mouth is so ill matched with a white beard that I would gladly believe the newspaper scribes alone responsible for the bestial utterances which they declare to have dropped from a teacher whom such disciples as these exhibit to our disgust and compassion as performing on their obscene platform the last tricks of tongue now possible to a gap-toothed and hoary-headed ape, carried at first into notice on the shoulder of Carlyle, and who now in his dotage spits and chatters from a dirtier perch of his own finding and fouling; Coryphaeus or choragus of his Bulgarian tribe of autocoprophagous baboons who make the filth they feed on.' In the original text of *A Study of Shakespeare* Swinburne alluded to Emerson as 'an impudent and foul-mouthed Yankee philosophaster' (not 'pseudosopher' as in the Bonchurch Edition). In a letter to the Southern poet Paul Hamilton Hayne, he admitted that one or two poems by Emerson ('a foul-minded and foul-mouthed old driveller') are 'exceptionally beautiful and powerful'. Swinburne elsewhere noted that Carlyle's fancy liked to play on 'Eternal Cesspools.' See, for instance, the letter written to Thomas Purnell on 3 January 1877 (Lang, iii, 252–3).]

# 14(e). John Ruskin

John Ruskin did not approve of all of Swinburne's poems but consistently showed himself to be friendly and generously recognized his genius.

---

(i) From a letter to C. E. Norton, 28 January 1866 (*Letters of John Ruskin to Charles Eliot Norton* [1904, i, 157]): Have you read Swinburne's *Atalanta*? The grandest thing ever yet done by a youth—though he is a Demoniac youth. Whether ever he will be clothed and in his right mind, heaven only knows. His foam at the mouth is fine, meantime.

(ii) Letter to Swinburne, 9 September 1866 (Lang, i, 182; this and the following letter are quoted by permission of the Yale University Press): I did not like to thank you for the Poems before I had read them, and their power is so great, and their influence so depressing, that I can read but very little at a time. I have been ill, besides, and unable to read anything.

It is of no use to tell you what you, like all good artists, know perfectly well of your work; and from my own manner of later work you know also very well that I can understand yours, and think of it as I ought, which is all that needs to be said between us, it seems to me, as to the art of the book.

For the matter of it—I consent to much—I regret much—I blame, or reject nothing. I should as soon think of finding fault with you as with a thundercloud or a nightshade blossom. All I can say of you, or them—is that God made you, and that you are very wonderful and beautiful. To me it may be dreadful or deadly—it may be in a deeper sense, or in certain relations, helpful and medicinal. There is assuredly something wrong with you—awful in proportion to the great power it affects, and renders (nationally) at present useless. So it was with Turner, so with Byron. It seems to be the peculiar judgment-curse of modern days that all their greatest men shall be plague-struck. But the truth and majesty which is in their greatest, causes the plague which is underneath, in the hearts of meaner people, smooth outwardly, to be in them visible outside while there is purity within. The rest are like graves which appear not—and you are rose graftings set in dung.

I'm glad to have the book at any rate. I cannot help you, nor understand you, or I would come to see you. But I shall always rejoice in hearing that you are at work, and shall hope some day to see a change in the method and spirit of what you do.

(iii) Letter to Edward Coleridge, 12 September 1866 (Lang, i, 183-4): I am glad you wrote to me about Swinburne: and glad that you think I may do him good. But he is so boundlessly beyond me in all power and knowledge that the only good I *can* do him is to soothe him by giving him a more faithful—though not a less sorrowful, admiration than others do.

I went abroad this year with two old friends—Sir Walter and Lady Trevelyan of Wallington in Northumberland. Lady Trevelyan died at Neuchatel on the 13th May; and I sate all that Sunday by her deathbed; she talking a little now and then, though the rattle in the throat had come on early in the day. She was an entirely pure and noble woman, and had nothing to think of that day but other people's interests. About one o'clock—nine hours before her death, she asked me very anxiously what I thought of Swinburne—and what he was likely to do and to be. (She had been very kind to him in trying to lead him to better thoughts.) And I answered—that she need not be in pain about him—the abuse she heard of him was dreadful—but not—in the deep sense, *moral* evil at all, but mentally-physical and ungovernable by his will,—and that finally, God never made such good fruit of human work to grow on an evil tree. So she was content: and that was the last thing she said—except to her husband—and a little word or two to me —to make me understand how they both cared for me.

I tell you this because I doubt not his mother and sisters will be thankful to know it. The *one* thing that those who love him have to do for him is to soothe him and trust in him;—his whole being is crude and mis-create at present—the divinity in the heat of it sputtering in the wet clay—yet unconquered.

But *his* clay is porcelain—jasper—I am bitterly anxious about him, not for the tone of his life—but for its endurance. I am afraid only of his dying. It is the judgment upon this modern race of ours easily traceable to the punishable causes that their greatest men shall have flawed or cancerous spots in them—and that most of them shall die early—Burns—Keats—Byron—(and Shelley would not have lived.)—

Turner dying in many senses early enough—though the half of him lived on decaying slowly—Beranger, Victor Hugo—have longer life—not less corrupt. There are conceptions of *purity* in Swinburne—(*Atalanta*, and the opening speech of Althea to wit) beyond anything that so strong a man ever wrote—as far as I remember—(for Wordsworth's purity is half weakness) what you tell me of his family accounts for this.

As for criticising the poems—that is a wholly unnecessary piece of business—and would only irritate him. I don't see anything to criticise in *Atalanta*—and if there be—he will find it out himself—he will not listen to me or anyone; and *ought* not, except to know what we enjoy and what we don't. (I've got the original MS of the Hymn to Proserpine, and wouldn't part with it for much more than leaf gold. Say to his people that there are many who much more want praying for than he. We all want it alike I fancy—but he's worth a good many sparrows[1] and won't be lost sight of.

[1] Cf. Luke 12: 6–7; Matt. 10: 31.

## 14(f). William Morris

Swinburne and Morris were always on good terms, though the passage given below may have led Swinburne to note in his 'Changes of Aspect' (as Cecil Y. Lang truly remarks, 'the work of a disgruntled, *old* man') that 'Morris could hardly swim a stroke without support from Chaucer'—hardly a fair statement. Indeed *The Earthly Paradise* is partly inspired by a variety of literary sources, not particularly by Chaucer.

---

From J. W. Mackail's *Life of William Morris* (1899), ii, 74: As to the poem [*Tristram of Lyonesse*], I have made two or three attempts to read it, but have failed, not being in the mood, I suppose: nothing would lay hold of me at all. This is doubtless my own fault, since it certainly did seem very fine. But, to confess and be hanged, you know I never could really sympathize with Swinburne's work; it always seemed to me to be founded on literature, not on nature. In saying this I really cannot accuse myself of any jealousy on the subject, as I think also you will not. Now I believe that Swinburne's sympathy with literature is most genuine and complete; and it is a pleasure to hear him talk about it, which he does in the best vein possible; he is most steadily enthusiastic about it. . . . In these days . . . nothing can take serious hold of people, or should do so, but that which is rooted deepest in reality and is quite at first hand.

# 14(g). George Meredith

Meredith's remark about Swinburne's 'internal centre', concerned with an early work of fiction (now accessible in *New Writings by Swinburne*), has often been quoted in disregard of chronology and Meredith's other statements. His novel *Emilia in England* (later entitled *Sandra Belloni*) introduced a Tracy Runningbrook, whose last name may be equated with the second syllable of 'Swinburne' and who has several Swinburnian characteristics. Though the fictional portrait was by no means offensive, the hypothesis that Swinburne did not relish it may be supported by textual changes in the revision of the early version.

---

(i) From a letter written to a friend in 1861 (*Letters of George Meredith* [1912], p. 55): Swinburne read me the other day his French novel *La Fille du Policeman*: the funniest rampingest satire on French novelists dealing with English themes that you can imagine. One chapter, '*Ce qui peut se passer dans un Cab Safety*,' where Lord Whitestick, Bishop of Londres, ravishes the heroine, is quite marvellous. But he is not subtle; and I don't see any internal centre from which springs anything that he does. He will make a great name, but whether he is to distinguish himself solidly as an Artist, I would not willingly prognosticate.

(ii) From a letter to Frederick Greenwood, 1 January 1873 (*Letters of George Meredith*, 240): I hope when Swinburne publishes his 'Tristram' you will review him. Take him at his best he is by far the best—finest poet; truest artist—of the young lot—when he refrains from pointing a hand at the genitals.

(iii) From a letter to Theodore Watts-Dunton, 13 April 1909 (*Letters*, ii, 634): That brain of the vivid illumination is extinct. I can hardly realize it when I revolve the many times when at the starting of an idea the whole town was instantly ablaze with electric light. Song was his natural voice. He was the greatest of our lyrical poets—of the world, I could say, considering what a language he had to wield.

# 14(h). Edward Lytton Bulwer-Lytton

Having read *Atalanta in Calydon*, which he thought 'promising and vigorous', Bulwer-Lytton came to Swinburne's aid with advice and moral support after Moxon withdrew *Poems and Ballads*. The poet gratefully accepted an invitation to spend a few days at Knebworth. Bulwer-Lytton's later remarks show some misgivings about Swinburne's future. His son Robert expressed depreciatory opinions of Swinburne, as in letters to John Morley and in a note which he published in his father's novel *The Parisians*. Swinburne always remembered Bulwer-Lytton with gratitude but responded to what he referred to as the son's 'scribblings' by composing epigrams and a merciless parody for his *Heptalogia*, 'Last Words of a Seventh-Rate Poet'.

---

(i) Letter of 20 August 1866 to his son Robert (quoted in *The Life of Edward Bulwer First Lord Lytton by his Grandson* [1913], ii, 437–8, by permission of Macmillan & Co. Ltd.): Staying here also is A. Swinburne, whose poems at this moment are rousing a storm of moral censure. I hope he may be induced not to brave and defy that storm, but to purge his volume of certain pruriences into which it amazes me any poet could fall. If he does not, he will have an unhappy life and a sinister career. It is impossible not to feel an interest in him. He says he is 26; he looks 16—a pale, sickly boy, with some nervous complaint like St. Vitus' dance. But in him is great power, natural and acquired. He has read more than most reading men twice his age, brooded and theorised over what he has read, and has an artist's critical perceptions. I think he must have read and studied and thought and felt much more than Tennyson; perhaps he has over-informed his tenement of clay.[1] But there is plenty of stuff in him. His volume of poems is infested with sensualities, often disagreeable in themselves, as well as offensive to all pure and manly taste. But the beauty of diction and mastership of craft in melodies really at first so dazzled me, that I did not see the naughtiness till pointed out. He certainly ought to become a considerable poet

[1] Cf. Dryden's *Absalom and Achitophel*, l. 158.

of the artistic order, meaning by that a poet who writes with a preconceived notion of art, and not, as I fancy the highest do, with unconsciousness of the art in them, till the thing itself is written. On the other hand, he may end prematurely both in repute and in life. The first is nearly wrecked now, and the second seems very shaky. He inspires one with sadness; but he is not so sad himself, and his self-esteem is solid as a rock. He reminds me a little of what Lewes was in youth, except that he has no quackery and has genius. I thought it would interest you to dot down these ideas of a man likely to come across your way, and may serve to warn you first against his mistakes, and also against much intimacy with him personally. I suspect he would be a dangerous companion to another poet. And he seems to me as wholly without the moral sense as a mind crammed full with aesthetic culture can be.

(ii) A later note endorsing some letters (*ibid.*, ii, 439): A. Swinburne, of very doubtful chance of real fame at this date, 1869. He has in him much material as a Poet—great reading and much study of art. But his self-conceit is enormous—his taste in all ways impure. In his passions he is not masculine, in his reasoning not sound. Still he is young, has true stuff in him, and may mellow into excellence in later life if he be spared.

# SONGS BEFORE SUNRISE

## 1871

## 15. Unsigned review, *Saturday Review*

14 January 1871, xxxi, 54–5

Notable for captiousness and unfairness, the following review
begins with a comparison which Swinburne referred to in *Under
the Microscope*.

It was once our fortune, in one of our walks, to come upon a naughty
little boy who was challenging the admiration of a small knot of his
playfellows. He stood by the side of a large puddle and announced
his attention to walk boldly into it. It was in vain that the little girls
of the company reminded him of the precepts of virtue, and held the
wrath of his nurse and mother over his head. In contempt of all such
exhortations and threats he dashed in, scattered the muddy water
about, and splashed himself and all the rest from top to toe. Finding
that this daring action, even if it was regarded with disapproval, yet
met with no small amount of admiration, he went to still further
lengths. He danced about in the puddle, he then stooped down and
dipped his head into it, and at last, rising (or sinking) to a pitch of
heroic defiance of all law and custom, he lay down and had a good roll
in it. Greatness could go no further than this. He was like Alexander
when he had no lands left to conquer, and he saw that there was
nothing remaining for him to do but to have a second and a third
roll. The reproofs which he received from the more timid and proper
among his playfellows, and the applause which he received from the
more daring and turbulent spirits, produced the same effect. They
only urged him on to revel more than ever in his muddy puddle. He
evidently delighted in the thought that he was the naughtiest of the

naughty. At the time we knew of no one to whom we could compare him but Mirabeau, for our young friend too, in Mr. Carlyle's language, had evidently 'swallowed all formulas'. As, however, Mr. Swinburne's poems appeared one after the other, we began to question whether we need go so far back as Mirabeau to find in the great world a worthy rival of our little hero. Mr. Swinburne's acquaintance with classical literature allowed him the choice of one of the muddiest—we might rightly say, one of the foulest—of puddles in which to display his contempt for everything that is decent. He also went gradually to work, and with every fresh poem outdid his previous exploit. Whether he and his prototype of the actual puddle acted on any deliberate plan we can hardly say. It may be the case that they both from the beginning had their whole course marked out clearly before them, and meant with each display to rise to a greater effort. It may also be the case that when they began they had no intention of going to such great lengths, but were carried away by the discovery that the naughtier they were, the more notice did they excite. Whether they acted from design or not, they each went on in the same course. For Mr. Swinburne, too, at first only went in ankle-deep, and merely danced about, though with a surprising vigour and enjoyment. It was later when, finding that the literary world was regarding him with some astonishment, and we may add disgust, he proceeded, so to say, to dip his head. It was not, however, till he published his miscellaneous poems, some year or two ago, that he went the full length, and had his roll in the mire. We felt that he had then gone as far as he could go. A very few years ago those who were ignorant of classical literature might remain in a most blessed state of ignorance of some of the most loathsome things in human nature. It was left for Mr. Swinburne's poetry to make known much of which it is a shame even to speak. We may perhaps excuse little boys and girls who have felt admiration rather than disgust as they have watched a comrade roll himself in his miry puddle. But when educated men, and we may add women too, read with admiration the love poetry of Mr. Swinburne— the most unnatural perhaps of all writers on love since Swift—we cannot repress our indignation. We might almost despair of a generation which looks up to Mr. Swinburne as its poet of poets did we not remember that, however exclusive may be the worship of a young man for the poet of his own age, a time soon comes when he begins to weary of him and to fall back on the greatest poets of all ages.

As we opened Mr. Swinburne's latest poem, we were prepared

to find merely a second or third repetition of the old performance. We must do him the justice at once to admit that he is not indecent. Offensive, indeed, he is, as he always is; and silly, as he often is. We have such phrases as 'beating with odorous blood', 'lips hot with the blood-beats of song', 'sleepy lips blood-suckled and satiate of thy breast', and the rest. We are glad to find that for the more disagreeable word he occasionally substitutes the innocent *sanguine*, as, 'the sanguine shadows and hoary', whatever they may be. We shall not, we believe, be wide of the mark if we ascribe the comparative purity of *Songs before Sunrise*, not to any change in Mr. Swinburne's mind, but to the fact that they are dedicated to M. Mazzini, and have been written, as we gather from the dedication, at his request. Whatever opinion we may hold of the old Republican, there can be little doubt that a collection of lascivious poems would with him have met with nothing but contempt. But if Mr. Swinburne has been kept in on one side, on another he has found liberty to push out to his heart's content. Kept out from one muddy pool, he has gone into another almost as muddy; and he shows himself as alive as ever to the pleasure which is to be derived from the most public display of an excess of naughtiness. We shall not gratify him nor shock our readers by quoting any of his poems on sacred things. If any, however, think that our words are too severe, let them turn to the poem 'Before a Crucifix', and judge for themselves. Much as he delights in what used in our younger days to be called blasphemy, he delights still more, if that were possible, in the reddest of Red Republicanism. He urges France to

> Make manifest the red,
> Tempestuous resurrection
> Of thy most sacred head!

And then, in language almost worthy of Mr. George F. Train's[1] poet —if perchance that worthy gentleman can afford to keep one—he thus turns on England and England's Royal family:—

> And thou, whom sea-walls sever. . . .

[quotes four stanzas of 'A Marching Song']

However much Mr. Swinburne may long for further liberty, he exercises one liberty to its fullest extent—the liberty, namely, of

---

[1] George F. Train (1829-1904), American promoter and author, who had lived during part of the fifties and sixties in England, was known there for his influence on British street railways and his speeches in behalf of the Union cause, as well as for the spectacular happenings of 1870—his siding with the French Communists and expulsion from France and his journey around the world in eighty days.

throwing dirt. To our mind it is much the same whether a man stands above and throws dirt on those below him, or stands below and throws dirt on those above him. We feel equal contempt for the democrat who bespatters those above him as for the aristocrat who bespatters those below him. Let Mr. Swinburne remember the words of a Republican whose republicanism was as noble as his is base: 'I am ready to give up my right to throw dirt on other people if they will give up their right to throw dirt on me.'

Mr. Swinburne perhaps acts wisely in scattering through his writings passages so utterly devoid of sense as to force his readers to believe that they must spring from a disordered brain. Should he ever find himself in a position to claim the benefit of the plea of insanity, what jury could resist the evidence of such lines as the following taken from the 'Hymn of Man'?—

> Men are the heart-beats of man, the plumes that feather his wings,
> Storm-worn, since being began, with the wind and thunder of things.

Or as the following taken from the same hymn?—

> Past the wall unsurmounted that bars out our vision with iron and fire
> He hath sent forth his soul for the stars to comply with and suns to conspire.

Then too we have such wonderful expressions as 'the rhythmic anguish of growth', Love '*hatched* and hidden as *seed* in the furrow', 'white-lipped sightless memories', 'the hinges shrieking spin', &c. &c. But it is not till we take the verses in which Mr. Swinburne indulges in his favourite alliteration that we come to the grossest of all absurdities. We should imagine that in childhood he must have delighted in 'Peter Piper picked a peck', &c. above all poetical compositions. At all events the ring of it never leaves his ears, or, we may add, those of his readers. Take, for instance, such lines as

> The morning-coloured mountains
> That burn into the noon,
> The mist's mild veil on valleys muffled from the moon.

Or

> Blow their dead bale-fires bright,
> And on their broken anvils beat out bolts for fight.

Or

> The hours that fighting fly
> Through flight and fight and all the fluctuant fear.

Or, to give one more instance, when we might give hundreds—

> A ripple of the refluence of day.

In all Mr. Swinburne's poetry we have noticed how like a child he gets hold of pet words which he constantly drags in. Thus, not only have we 'fluctuant fear', but 'fluctuant hours', 'fluctuant heaven', and not only 'the refluence of day', but 'the extreme wave's refluence', 'refluent antiphones', and 'fluent sunrise', which last sounds to us somewhat like fluent nonsense. Not only, however, are detached lines nonsensical, but even whole stanzas; nay, we might add, whole poems. And yet among all this extravagance, this fustian worthy of a second Ancient Pistol, there are lines, stanzas, and poems which are in every way admirable. Indeed there is, we believe, more real poetic power shown in this volume than in any of the poet's earlier works. Take, for instance, such detached lines as—

> Flights of dim tribes of kings.

> The lioness chafes in her hair,
> Shakes the storm of her hair.

> By the surf of spears one shieldless bosom breasted
> And was my shield.

> By the helm that keeps us still to sunwards driving,
> Still eastward bound,
> Till as night-watch ends, day burn on eyes reviving,
> And land be found.

How beautiful, too, are these lines describing Italy when still 'subdued with spears and crushed with shame':—

> By the rivers of Italy, by the sacred streams,
> By town, by tower,
> There was feasting with revelling, there was sleep with dreams,
> Until thine hour.

> And they slept and they rioted on their rose-hung beds,
> With mouths on flame,
> And with love-locks vine-chapleted, and with rose-crowned heads
> And robes of shame.

> And they knew not their fore-fathers, nor the hills and streams
> And words of power,

> Nor the gods that were good to them, but with songs and dreams
> Filled up their hour.

If Mr. Swinburne had always written like this, he would have been justified perhaps in his passionate invocations to the nations. He might then have 'set the trumpet to his lips' and blown to the four quarters of the heaven till he could 'make a rallying music in the void night's ear'. He might then have spoken his wild appeal to Italy and his yet wilder appeal to England. But who is he to say to Italy, 'Have we not worn thee at heart whom none would bear?' Who is he to warn England against those 'who have robbed thee of thy trust and given thee of their shame'? Who is he to tell France that her breast is 'a harlot's now', and that she is 'a ruin where satyrs dance'? While men, in these last few years since Mr. Swinburne left school, have been toiling for the right in Italy, in England, and in France, what has he been doing? He has been wasting his splendid gifts in singing of a hateful love, and has gained the chief rank among those who have given their country 'of their shame'. To him, and not to his great country, should be addressed his passionate question—

> How should the soul that lit you for a space
> Fall through sick weakness of a broken will
> To the dead cold damnation of disgrace?

# 16. Unsigned review, *Edinburgh Review*

July 1871, cxxxiv, 94-9

'Swinburne's Poems' in the *Edinburgh Review* (cxxxiv, 71-99) begins with unfavourable consideration of all Swinburne's earlier volumes except *Atalanta in Calydon* before discussing *Songs before Sunrise*. It anticipated Robert Buchanan's 'fleshly school' by identifying Swinburne as belonging to 'the sensational school' and 'the corrupted school of French art and French poetry'. According to *The Wellesley Index to Victorian Periodicals*, the article was the work of Thomas Spencer Baynes. In 1864 Baynes had been elected to the chair of logic, metaphysics, and literature at the University of St. Andrews. As editor of the ninth edition of the *Encyclopædia Britannica* he enlisted Swinburne as a contributor, and between 1875 and 1883 the two men were occasional correspondents.

It is true that in all periods of art, both ancient and modern, there have been some who, in violation of its higher requirements, have given an extreme and exaggerated prominence to the physical details of human suffering. But it was reserved for the modern sensational school to reverse the great and pervading law which holds alike in nature and in art—to make, that is, bodily suffering an end to itself, instead of employing it as a means for the attainment of higher and nobler ends. The writers of this school appear to delight in extreme physical experiences—ecstasies and horrors—for their own sake, or rather for the sake of the morbid appetite they create and help for the moment to gratify. One of the worst but most inevitable results of this sensational literature is, indeed, to be found in the diseased appetite for artificial mental stimulants it produces, and which takes away the relish for wholesome and nourishing literary food. All coarse and violent stimulants deaden the finer sensibilities on which they act, and thus not only destroy the natural capacity for enjoyment of a more refined and satisfying kind, but produce a restless and intensely selfish craving for the coarser stimulant. Hence the rage for sensational novels and sensational literature, and hence too, we fear, the appearance of a sensational poet.

In all the main features of his poetry Mr. Swinburne is faithful to the school. As a natural result of his poetical temperament, he may be said, indeed, to represent its special characteristics in a more intense and concentrated form than even the most eminent of its prose writers. In many of his more audacious pieces, indeed, Mr. Swinburne fairly out-Herods Herod. Much of his poetry is sensationalism run mad, foaming at the mouth, snapping rabidly at everything in its way, especially at the sanctities and sanities of life, avoiding all natural food, and seizing with morbid avidity on what is loathsome and repulsive, mere orts and offal. But there is still a method in the madness, with all its apparent blindness and fury. Sensationalism, at least in its extremest developments, rests on a speculative basis. It has a philosophy of its own. It springs from the assumption that the senses and their impulses are our highest sources of light and guidance, that reason and conscience are of no authority, that the moral and rational principles they supply—the highest regulative elements of our nature—may not only be disregarded with impunity, but are to be denounced as delusions, and rejected as mere hindrances to the life of nature. On such a theory reason is, of course, subordinated to sense, will to desire, while appetite and impulse are enthroned as lords of all.

In this point of view, as an exposition of what may be called the theory or creed of the extreme sensationalist school, Mr. Swinburne's last volume, *Songs before Sunrise*, is of special interest. Here the writer evidently attempts to meet the objection urged against his poetry even by his best friends, that it embodies no great vital conceptions, has no animating and fructifying spirit, no inspiring impulse of faith, or hope, or effort, that in its moral aspects it is utterly dark, cold, and repulsive, with a background of cheerless impenetrable gloom; in a word, that it recognises no moral element in life or action, no real or ultimate ground for any belief in duty, liberty, or virtue. It will be clear from what we have already said that this complaint is perfectly just, but that it should be made at all, only shows how imperfectly Mr. Swinburne's admirers comprehend the real drift of his poetry, and the kind of philosophy it embodies. Mr. Swinburne's latest volume is, however, in part a kind of reply to this complaint; and it offers an exposition of what may be called the speculative groundwork, or creed of his poetry. This creed, when carefully examined, is found to consist of two points or articles, the first being the ultimate authority of appetite and impulse, and the second the deification of humanity. But these two points may obviously be resolved into one,—the deification of appetite and impulse. The practical recognition of this doctrine is called by Mr. Swinburne liberty, freedom, and he expresses his admiration of it, after his fashion, in a dazzling coruscation of verbal and metrical effects. After all, the conception thus glorified is a negative not a positive one, and ought to be called licence, lawlessness, not liberty. Such as it is, however, he lauds and magnifies it in shrill-toned hymns and hallelujahs of the most surprising kind. The poetical utterance of his creed contained in the volume may indeed be described, as Mr. Disraeli once described a speech delivered by Mr. Bernal Osborne when newly emancipated from the trammels of office, as 'a wild shriek of freedom'. In the same way Mr. Swinburne, having cut himself adrift from all moorings, driven off the pilots with strong language, and thrown the helm and compass and chart overboard, pipes his shrillest to the storm gathering on the horizon, and abandons himself with intoxicated delight to the fury of the coming tempest. At last he is free, clear of all established havens and moorings, emancipated from the degrading thraldom of rudder and chart, lodestar and needle, his frail barque left to welter as a waif, in obedience to the natural laws of wave and storm, on the seething hissing bosom of the angry sea. That exactly represents Mr. Swinburne's idea of freedom and independence. Rejecting all the means which intelligence and foresight provide for controlling the elements or escaping their fury, he blindly abandons himself to their power, or as in such circumstances we justly say, 'to his fate'. That is precisely the case. Extremes meet, and Mr. Swinburne's so-called freedom is absolute fate.

His conception of freedom is, as we have said, wholly negative, and as such it is necessarily delusive and false. True liberty has its root in law, in the higher principles of our nature, is indeed the moral reflex of the responsibility thence arising. If we had no higher light, no authoritative moral perceptions superior to sense, we should have no claim to freedom, and could make no use of it. The right to the enjoyment of liberty is founded on the duty of every man to improve his powers to the utmost, to attain the highest possible degree of moral and spiritual perfection. The true conception of freedom is thus that of means to an end, the end being progress in virtue and knowledge, truth and goodness. Mr. Swinburne, however, cuts away the living root, and utterly destroys the rational basis of freedom. With him it simply means the abolition of all existing restraints, in the last resort the overthrow of all law and order, of all existing moral rules and established government. It is thus a purely anarchical and destructive principle, which would soon make wild work of human life and human society. Enlightened reason and conscience are the highest human sources of guidance for the individual. The principles we reach under the guidance of these powers are often, it is true, narrow and mistaken. But the gradual correction of these defects constitutes, with good and wise men, the very discipline of life. They strive to enlarge and purify their knowledge, and make their principles of judgment and action more enlightened, liberal and true. But because they do not at once illuminate everything, Mr. Swinburne would extinguish these supreme guiding lights in the pathway of life. The impulses of appetite and desire, if blind are at least definite, and with the heat and impatience of a weak and passionate nature, he virtually says, 'Let us follow these impulses as supreme.' Again, positive institutions, political and religious, are the reflex in society of reason and conscience in the individual. These institutions partake no doubt of human imperfection, and are often grievously defective. But the great aim of enlightened patriotism and true statesmanship is to improve them, and make them more and more fitted to secure their great end, the welfare of society. But Mr. Swinburne and his friends seek to destroy them altogether, and substitute in their place the aggregate of ungoverned impulse and passion known as the Red Republic. Not the nobly organised Commonwealth, the vision of which kindled Milton's disciplined imagination, and roused all the austere enthusiasm of his nature, but a mere fortuitous concourse of impulsive and fiery atoms. This, if established on Mr. Swinburne's principles, would simply be anarchy organised, made operative, and systematically employed for destructive purposes. In fact the condition of France, and especially of Paris, during the last three months and at the present time, is the best possible commentary on the political principles more obscurely enunciated in *Songs before Sunrise*.

The spirit of the book is in harmony with its weak, passionate, and negative philosophy. Many of the poems are narrow, violent, and bitter beyond anything that has proceeded from Mr. Swinburne's pen. In this respect much of the volume appears to us justly exposed to unqualified reprobation: not on the mere ground of opinion, for honest opinions can be legitimately held, and be opposed and defended in the proper way. If Mr. Swinburne, as the result of his speculative efforts, has arrived at pantheistic views, he is of course at perfect liberty to hold them. If he chooses to deny the reality of moral distinctions, he can in like manner do this, so long as he confines himself to the speculative side of the question—to the calm and philosophical statement of his theoretical opinions. But that he should indulge in coarse and bigoted denunciations of the central religious doctrines held by the great majority of his fellow-countrymen is, to say the least of it, an unpardonable offence against good taste and good feeling. And that he should revile in blasphemous language the object of their worship is an offence of a far deeper dye. This, however, he repeatedly does in his last volume. In the opening poem, the 'Prelude', one of the best in the volume, he adopts, it is true, a comparatively calm and philosophical tone; and though the philosophy of the poem would suggest suicide as the only consistent course to be pursued by rational beings, our complaint would have been comparatively groundless if its higher philosophical tone had been kept up in the poems that follow. But this is far enough from being the case; the calmer tone is soon abandoned for that of harsh and violent denunciation. The truth is, Mr. Swinburne is not a philosopher at all; he is not even a thinker; he merely sets other people's thoughts—the floating conceptions that he finds most genial—to his own peculiar music, and in doing so the shriller and harsher tones of his lyre are sure to be heard. We have no space for quotations, and if we had, the most pertinent illustrations could not be quoted. But nowhere in his writings has Mr. Swinburne shown an animus so envenomed, a spirit so weak and essentially sectarian, or used language so intemperate and profane, as in this volume. Such poems, for example, as 'Before a Crucifix' and the 'Hymn of Man', are thoroughly fanatical in their wild, blasphemous, and intolerant atheism.

Mr. Swinburne has, it is true, attempted to justify this feature of his writings by referring to Shelley. We are willing to believe, however, that this reference was made not deliberately, but in a moment of excitement. Notwithstanding all we have said of Mr. Swinburne, we feel persuaded he would not venture to challenge a comparison with Shelley, even in this particular. However this may be, the phrases Mr. Swinburne quotes from Shelley all occur in his earliest poem, written when he was still almost a boy—a poem never published by himself, and the publication of which by others called forth his express and indignant censure. In his later writings no such expressions occur, while his latest show a very considerable change of tone on the whole subject. Mr. Swinburne has been before the world as an author for a much longer time than the whole period of Shelley's public life, yet his last productions are in spirit and temper the worst. For the rest, any attempt at a serious comparison of Swinburne to Shelley would oblige one to exclaim, not as a figure of speech but in sober truth, 'Hyperion to a Satyr'.[1] Shelley had wild and perverted views; but his mind was pure, and his poetry, the reflex of his mind, has upon it the very bloom of purity. Had he taken up even Mr. Swinburne's unsavoury subjects, their grossness would have been almost purged away by the exquisite grace and delicacy of his touch. On the other hand, Mr. Swinburne's method of treatment would almost inevitably defile even the most sacred relationships and experiences of life. It is comparatively easy to imitate Shelley's imperfections without sharing the higher qualities of his mind, or approaching the peerless perfection of his noblest work. A writer of verse may produce imperfect lines, indulge in repetitions and plagiarised passages, and even in intemperate denunciations of existing institutions, without having much in common with Shelley. We are glad, indeed, to think that Mr. Swinburne has not derived his inspiration from Shelley, or from any English author or English school of poetry. He is rather an Alfred de Musset without his finesse and grace. What is most distinctive in Mr. Swinburne's work is derived from the corrupted school of French art and French poetry, which, with other influences traceable to a common root, has contributed to the temporary ruin of the finest country and most gifted people in Europe. The principles of the school which Mr. Swinburne represents would, indeed, if successful, not only overturn all existing order, but in the end prove fatal to art, literature, and civilisation itself.

[1] *Hamlet*, I, ii, 140. The earlier 'out-Herods Herod' is also from *Hamlet* (III, ii, 15).

# 17. Franz Hüffer, *Academy*

15 January 1871, ii, 87–9

Franz Hüffer, also known as Francis Hueffer, a musical critic who had studied in Germany for a doctorate in philology, married the daughter of Ford Madox Brown, the painter, and became the father of Ford Madox Hueffer, better known as the novelist Ford Madox Ford. According to the *D.N.B.*, his review of *Songs before Sunrise* attracted much attention.

If the *Songs before Sunrise* had been published anonymously, it would not have required a great amount of penetration in the reader to discover their author. There is indeed but one man in England who could and perhaps would have written them. They will probably meet with the same admiration from the one side and certainly with the same indiscriminate abhorrence from the other as their predecessors, the *Poems and Ballads*. These *Songs before Sunrise* are, in fact, nothing else than the continuation of those eruptions of hot and unfettered passion with which they share the same fundamental idea, applied in this case to the great political and religious questions of our age, and modified only so far as this more serious and elevated subject required. This idea is, in one word, that of Liberty, not so much the liberty which develops and constructs as that which lays low all conceivable limits which may surround the human spirit. All of us know how this Titanic volition led in the *Poems and Ballads* to exaggerations which ought to have been judged from an æsthetical rather than from a moral point of view, and the same might in many cases be said of this new production, although we gladly acknowledge that the *Songs* show a remarkable advance in the way of self-criticism and, in a certain sense, of moderation.

This abstract idea of freedom blossoms under the hand of the poet into a variety of forms, often of extreme beauty. About the morality or immorality of this idea in itself we shall have nothing to say. It seems to us that a poet has to be judged according to moral principles only so far as these are identical with the lines of beauty, and Swinburne before all men may rightly claim this privilege, because in him the purely artistic quality predominates over every other.

Unlimited freedom of human thought and action is Swinburne's first principle of philosophy, and he therefore attacks with the utmost ferocity every belief or institution which seems to restrain this supreme *droit de l'homme*.[1] The Christian revelation, its Divine Author, and its human interpreters, the priests of all confessions, excite his intensest indignation. The Christian God with all His anthropomorphic qualities is, according to our poet, only an impure imagination, which the frightened and servile human mind created for its own thraldom, and which the same human mind purified must abolish:

> Thought made Him, and breaks Him.

This phantom itself is stained with the vices of its creators, and has become their most cruel enemy and bane. In a poem called 'Hymn of Man', which perhaps has never been reached, certainly not surpassed, in its sublime lyrical pathos, the Judge Himself, in whose name generations were slaughtered, is arraigned before the bar of man and condemned to death and utter oblivion. A deity in whose name so many crimes have been committed, cannot be the help of man—

> What for us hath done
> Man beneath the sun?
> What for us hath God?

ask the miserable outcasts of society in 'Outside Church', while their happier brethren sing in pious contentedness their 'Christmas Antiphones'. For the priests have degraded the pure original socialism of Christian doctrine into a religion of the rich; they have made the cross

> Shadowing the sheltered heads of kings.

These are in brief, and so far as it is possible to quote them, the reasons for which Swinburne breaks, and breaks fiercely, with the idea of a personal God. The true and sufficing object, on the other hand, of the religious emotions of man is his own ideal being, the

> Pure spirit of man that men call God.

His idea of this *Être Suprème*[2] our poet has defined in two poems, which

---

[1] 'Human right.'
[2] 'Supreme Being.'

for beauty of poetical expression may fairly be called masterpieces of the highest order: 'The Litany of Nations' and 'Hertha'. The former is a prayer of all the children of the earth, however parted by diversity of customs and nationalities, to their common mother Hertha, 'the earth-soul Freedom', the power of progress and liberty in Nature, as it is manifested by the everlasting struggle of light against darkness, of form against chaos. This power is eternal and universal. Hertha says:—

> Before God was, I am.

> .    .    .    .    .

> The deed and the doer, the seed and the sower, the dust which is God;

her head is crowned by the terrors and hopes of generations; her song is 'hoarse and hollow and shrill with strife', till at last she attains her perfect stature in liberated mankind. The pantheism of these poems, and indeed of every line of this volume, is of a sort quite unrestrained and uncompromising; in this quality markedly distinguished from that of Tennyson.

The following sublime passage, in which Hertha answers the prayers of her children, is in its grandeur like the oracle of some unknown goddess:—

> I am that which began;
>   Out of me the years roll;
>   Out of me God and man;
>   I am equal and whole.
> God changes, and man, and the form of them bodily: I am the soul.

> Before ever land was,
>   Before ever the sea,
>   Or soft hair of the grass,
>   Or fair limbs of the tree,
> Or the flesh-coloured fruit of my branches—I was; and thy soul was
>   in me.

Swinburne's political radicalism is of the same order as his religious. To define his position in relation to this great question, it may be sufficient to say that the book is dedicated to Joseph Mazzini, in a little poem which, by the bye, is the simplest and therefore perhaps the most charming of all. His chief aim throughout is to introduce into this country the principles of the European revolution which this name represents. Since the Restoration, England has stood aloof from the main stream of continental life, but now the poet implores her, 'by the star that Milton's soul for Shelley lighted', to arise and join the cry, and struggle for the universal republic—the sunrise meant to be heralded, as with larks' voices, in these songs. But not to his own country alone does the poet limit his sympathies for the democratic movement. Wherever a sign of this new life is visible, be it in Poland or Greece, in France or Italy, he watches it with loving solicitude, while he sends his song over the ocean to 'Walt Whitman in America', his fellow-sufferer and fellow-singer. But foremost in this struggle he regards France and Italy, and for these two countries his lyre resounds in the most enthusiastic strain. France, 'liberty's sign and standard bearer', and 'Italia, the world's wonder, the world's care', must be united with England and Spain by the link of universal freedom. This ideal and purely humanitarian conception is all the more remarkable and precious for Englishmen, whose most advanced notions of political emancipation have been till quite lately almost, if not entirely, historical and insular. The unsympathetic exclusion of Germany, 'by whose forest-hidden fountains freedom slept armed' (whatever that means), from partaking in the emancipation of man is a proof that our poet knows but little of the country of Heine and Schopenhauer, and but little of the infinite depth in the conception of human freedom which has been sounded by its greatest thinkers. The freedom of Swinburne is the flaming sword 'to destroy the sins of the earth with divine devastation'; it is the principle of '*fiat justitia pereat mundus*'—[1]

> It is better that war spare but one or two
> Than that many live and liberty be slain;

it is the *fraternité ou la mort*[2] of the men of 1793, which in the person of Robespierre erected the guillotine whilst voting for the abolition of capital punishment.

Nearly the same might be said about Swinburne's veneration for the republic, the mere sound of whose name seems to possess for him a magic charm. This is objectionable from an æsthetical point of view. For a republic, like a monarchy, is even, if the best, only a certain form of government, which is in itself no poetical object.

---

[1] 'Let justice be done though the world perish'—said to have been the motto of Ferdinand I (1503–1564), Emperor of Germany.
[2] 'Fraternity or death.'

Swinburne's great qualities appear in a much better light where he abstains from all these accidental forms, and symbolizes the pure idea of liberty, as he has done under the beautiful image of the *Mater dolorosa*, who—

> Sits by the way, by the wild wayside,
> In a rent stained raiment, the robe of a cast-off bride,
> In the dust, in the rainfall sitting with soiled feet bare,
> With the night for a garment upon her torn wet hair.

In fact it seems that the grander the idea is he has to deal with, the higher grows Swinburne's power and felicity, while on the other hand, as soon as he introduces any distinct system or person, the violence of his attacks exceeds by far the limits of artistic propriety. The abuse of Pius IX, in the 'Halt before Rome', or of the Emperor Napoleon, the 'son of a harlot', in 'Quia Multum Amavit', scarcely stops short of the *banale*.[1] At the same time these energetic diatribes are something quite alien in character from the *Weltschmerz*, that hopeless and helpless apathy which paralyses the highest aspiration of the modern spirit. Swinburne's active nature happily preserves him from that malady; his desire is never to leave off struggling and toiling, even without the faintest ray of hope, as his 'Pilgrims' beautifully express it—

> Nay, though our life were blind, our death were fruitless,
> Not therefore were the whole world's high hope rootless.

This is, in the main, what under various forms Swinburne has to say in the *Songs before Sunrise*. It now remains to make a few remarks on his manner of saying it. In the artistic form lies decidedly one of the greatest charms of his poetry. The flow of his rhythm, the composition of his stanzas, the correctness and music of his rhymes are inimitable. At the same time, he has the finest feeling for all the *nuances* of poetical expression; the richness and variety of his epithets is astonishing, and he succeeds even in presenting the most abstract ideas under symbols the most lifelike and picturesque. But in this boundless power over all the treasures of formal beauty lies our poet's greatest danger. Sometimes this grace of form engrosses his mind so entirely that the meaning of the words dwindles away as it were under his hands. We almost venture to say that not a few of his beautiful tirades convey no distinct meaning at all. In other places this meaning is extremely difficult to make out, owing to the great number of the

[1] 'Vulgar.'

different symbolic personifications, which makes it almost impossible to bring home to each the personal pronoun belonging to it.

The same may to some extent be said of several stanzas of the 'Prelude', a fault, however, which is not incompatible with much charming 'præ-Raphaelite' *chiaro oscuro* in the image of youth sitting on the hollow stream of Time, and rising to cast away the shallow joys of Pleasure and Passion which might prevent him on his long and toilsome journey to his own ideal self. Swinburne has also certain formulated expressions whose effect depends mainly upon their unexpectedness, and therefore loses much by their constant repetition. The chief of these is a sort of antithesis (by the way, neither peculiar nor original), as found in sentences like 'we mad *blind* men that *see*', 'these honours without honour', etc. The alliteration, too, appears sometimes overdone, and even tiresome, in these songs. Everyone who knows with how much moderation this was used in old Teutonic poetry, in which the other great modern principle of sound, rhyme, was wanting, must be shocked by a line like the following, 'Hiding her high as her head', for which it is difficult to discover any onomatopoetic reason. But the greatest fault in Swinburne's poems is the immoderate length of almost all of them, which distracts the attention from the delights which lie concealed in single passages. This is the more inappropriate in poetry the pathos of which is chiefly lyrical, intense, and therefore transitory, in the production as much as in the enjoyment of it. This drawback is again traceable to an overmastering richness of gift and idea, but also to a certain want of plastic power which should model the forms of a poem with a necessity akin to nature. Many of these poems might be several stanzas longer or shorter without any great difference in their general impression, and only a very few, like the 'Watch in the Night', have an organic and inevitable conclusion. This fault, once more, might have found its correction in a greater familiarity on the part of our poet with German literature. Had he recalled the range and variety of poetic feeling which is included within the narrow limits of one of Goethe's, Heine's, or Möricke's *Lieder*, he would scarcely have written a marching song of forty and some stanzas. This lengthy exuberance characterizes in different degrees all the modern English poets whose work shows the influence of Shelley (and whose does not?), and may be traced back to the great master himself. The lyric of Shelley, it must be remembered, is not, like the German, a development of the popular song, but is the poetical expression of the prolonged and passionate contemplation of a speculative idea. Besides Shelley, and perhaps Victor Hugo, it is scarcely fair to Swinburne to mention any modern poet as exercising great influence on his style. All his so-called models, Baudelaire, Walt Whitman, or Landor, breathe the same air, the air of the modern social revolution; and this 'elective affinity', of course, effects a certain likeness in their mode of expression: still here is no imitation of any of them. More discernible, as we think, is the influence of the masterpieces of Greek and Hebrew literature. If the pathetic strophes and antistrophes of the 'Ode on the Insurrection in Candia' remind us of the grandeur of Æschylus, the 'Eve of Revolution', with the 'trumpets of the four winds of the world', has quite as decidedly the weird, strange character of Ezekiel or the Apocalypse. Some of Swinburne's stanzas, in which he shows a greater variety and beauty than any other English poet, bear evidence of a thorough study of Dante. The sonnets, for instance, those on Barbès, the French republican, whose life was saved by Victor Hugo's lines, and the paraphrase of Michelangelo's celebrated inscription on the 'Night', in that entitled 'In San Lorenzo', are models of symmetry. The stanzas of the 'Eve of Revolution' might (except the two last verses) be divided exactly according to Dante's theory into '*pedes* and *versus*' (*De Vulg. Eloq.*)[1] and lastly, in the 'Christmas Antiphones', with their artificial middle rhyme, Italian influence seems undeniable.

To conclude; we regard Swinburne as of all English poets the most highly endowed with the purely poetic gift; and there is little doubt of his rank amid the poets of all time but for his fatal wantonness and exuberance of power, the restraint of which, as Goethe says, is the note of the true master:

> *So ist's mit aller Bildung auch beschaffen:*
> *Vergebens werden ungebund'ne Geister*
> *Nach der Vollendung reiner Höhe streben;*
> *Wer Grosses will, muss sich zusammenraffen,*
> *In der* Beschränkung *zeigt sich erst der* Meister,
> *Und das Gesetz nur kann uns Freiheit geben.*[2]

---

[1] See especially Dante's *De Vulgari Eloquentia*, Book ii, chapters x–xii. Though the Latin words signify 'feet' and 'verses', in discussing the *canzone* Dante does not use the words in their present meanings, referring instead to divisions of the musical setting into melodic sections.

[2] From a sonnet beginning '*Natur und Kunst sie scheinen sich zu fliehen*': 'So it is with all self-cultivation: in vain unfettered spirits strive to reach the heights; whoever wishes to be great must hold himself in check, first must through restraint show himself the master. Only through law can we achieve freedom.'

# 18. Swinburne on Robert Buchanan's self-revelations

## 1872

*Under the Microscope*, discussing topics several critics had raised —the merits of Byron, Tennyson, Walt Whitman particularly— answered some of Swinburne's critics—foremost among them an anonymous writer for the *Quarterly Review*, Alfred Austin (cf. No. 13), and, above all, Robert Buchanan, author of the article and book attacking D. G. Rossetti and the 'fleshly school' (for a fuller discussion see the Introduction, section IV). The following extract, part of the invective aimed at Buchanan, relies chiefly on the device of turning Buchanan's own words against him. The text, that of my critical edition in *Swinburne Replies*, is used by special permission of the Syracuse University Press, owner of the copyright.

A notable example of this latter sort was not long since (in his *Fors Clavigera*) selected and chastised by Mr. Ruskin himself with a few strokes of such a lash as might thenceforward, one would think, have secured silence at least, if neither penitence nor shame, on the part of the offender. This person, whose abuse of Mr. Carlyle he justly described as matchless 'in its platitudinous obliquity',[1] was cited by the name of one Buchanan—

> ὅστις ποτ' ἐστίν, εἰ τόδ' αὐ-
> τῷ φίλον κεκλημένῳ—[2]

but whether by his right name or another, who shall say? for the god of song himself had not more names or addresses. Now yachting among

---

[1] 'Notable example' refers to abuse of Carlyle. In reality Ruskin describes Buchanan's abuse as 'unmatchable . . . for obliquitous platitude in the mud-walks of literature' (*The Works of John Ruskin*, ed. Cook and Wedderburn, xxvii, 180).

[2] Æschylus, *Agamemnon*, ll. 160–1: 'Whosoever he be, if by this name it well pleaseth him to be invoked' (tr. Herbert Weir Smyth).

the Scottish (not English) Hebrides;[1] now wrestling with fleshly sin (like his countryman Holy Willie)[2] in 'a great city of civilization'; now absorbed in studious emulation of the *Persæ* of Æschylus or the 'enormously fine' work of 'the tremendous creature' Dante;[3] now descending from the familiar heights of men whose praise he knows so well how to sing, for the not less noble purpose of crushing a school of poetic sensualists whose works are 'wearing to the brain'; now 'walking down the streets' and watching 'harlots stare from the shop-windows', while 'in the broad day a dozen hands offer him indecent prints'; now 'beguiling many an hour, when snug at anchor in some lovely Highland loch, with the inimitable, yet questionable, pictures of Parisian life left by Paul de Kock'; landsman and seaman, Londoner and Scotchman, Delian and Patarene Buchanan.[4] How should one address him?

> *Matutine pater, seu Jane libentiùs audis?*[5]

As Janus rather, one would think, being so in all men's sight a natural son of the double-faced divinity. Yet it might be well for the son of Janus if he had read and remembered in time the inscription on the statue of another divine person, before taking his name in vain as a word wherewith to revile men born in the ordinary way of the flesh:—

> Youngsters! who write false names, and slink
> behind
> The honest garden-god to hide yourselves,
> Beware![6]

[1] In *The Fleshly School of Poetry, and Other Phenomena of the Day* Buchanan wrote: 'At the time of the publication ['The Fleshly School of Poetry' in the *Contemporary Review*] I myself was yachting among the Scottish Hebrides.'

[2] 'Holy Willie' is the hypocritical speaker in Burns's 'Holy Willie's Prayer'. Buchanan mentioned his desire to emulate Æschylus in *The Drama of Kings* (London, 1871), 452. For the comment on Dante and the three following quotations, see *The Fleshly School*, 11, 77, 82, 86.

[3] Lest it should seem impossible that these and the like could be the actual expressions of any articulate creature, I have invariably in such a context marked as quotations only the exact words of this unutterable author, either as I find them cited by others or as they fall under my own eye in glancing among his essays. More trouble than this I am not disposed to take with him. [Swinburne's note.]

[4] Cf. Horace, *Carm.*, III, iv, 64: '*Delius et Patareus Apollo*', associating Apollo with Delos, the island on which he was born, and Patara, the seat of his worship in Asia Minor.

[5] Horace, *Sermones*, II, vi, 20: 'O father of the morning, or Janus, if you would prefer to be so addressed' (tr. H. W. Wells).

[6] From W. S. Landor's 'Inscription on a Plinth in the Garden of Mnestheus at Lampsacus', except for 'Beware' replacing Landor's 'Take heed unto your ways!'

In vain would I try to play the part of a prologuizer before this latest rival of the Hellenic dramatists, who sings from the height of 'mystic realism', not with notes echoed from a Grecian strain, but as a Greek poet himself might have sung, in 'massive grandeur of style',[1] of a great contemporary event. He alone is fit, in Euripidean fashion, to prologuize for himself.

Πολὺς μὲν ἐν γραφαῖσι κοὐκ ἀνώνυμος
ψεύστης κέκλημαι Σκότιος,[2] ἄστεως τ᾽ ἔσω,
ὅσοι τε πόντου τερμόνων τ᾽ Ἀτλαντικῶν
ναίουσιν ἔξω σκάφεσι νησιωτικοῖς,
τοὺς μὲν τρέφοντας θώψ ἀπὸ γλώσσης σέβω,
ὅσοι δ᾽ ἀποπτύουσί μ᾽ ἐμπίπτω λαθών.[3,4]

He has often written, it seems, under false or assumed names; always doubtless 'with the best of all motives', that which induced his friends in his absence to alter an article abusive of his betters and suppress the name which would otherwise have signed it, that of saving the writer from persecution and letting his charges stand on their own merits; and this simple and very natural precaution has singularly enough exposed his fair fame to 'the inventions of cowards'[5]—a form of attack naturally intolerable though contemptible to this polyonymous moralist. He was not used to it; in the cradle where his genius had been hatched he could remember no taint of such nastiness. Other friends than such had fostered into maturity the genius that now lightens far and wide the fields of poetry and criticism. All things must have

[1] The quotations refer to Buchanan's claims for *The Drama of Kings* in a note at the end of that work, 'On Mystic Realism: A Note for the Adept'.

[2] For the occasions on which the word σκότιος is to be spelt with a capital Σ, the student should consult the last-century glossaries of Lauder and Macpherson. [Swinburne's note.]

[3] There are other readings of the two last lines:

τοὺς δεσπότας μὲν δουλιᾷ σαίνω φρενί,
ὅσοι δὲ μ᾽ἀγνοοῦσιν (Cod. Var. ὅσοισι δ᾽εἰμ᾽ ἄγνωτος) κ:τ:λ

[Swinburne's note.]

[4] Remembering the words of Aphrodite in the Prologue to *Hippolytus* by Euripides (ll. 3 ff.), Swinburne composes lines suitable to Buchanan: 'Great among written works and not nameless, I am called a shady liar within the city; and to those who dwell beyond the limits of the Atlantic Ocean in island ships and who nourish me I give lip service as a flatterer, but those who spurn me I attack covertly' (tr. L. R. Lind). The 'other readings' of the last two lines in Swinburne's note: 'The masters I fawn upon with slavish heart, but those who do not know me [variant MS reading,] to whom I am unknown, etc.' 'Lauder and Macpherson' and their 'last-century glossaries' (in note 2) are introduced for verisimilitude. Swinburne's 'capital' for the Greek word seems to imply a pun on 'Scot'.

[5] This and the preceding quoted phrase are from the preface to *The Fleshly School*.

their beginnings; and there were those who watched with prophetic hope the beginnings of Mr. Buchanan; who tended the rosy and lisping infancy of his genius with a care for its comfort and cleanliness not unworthy the nurse of Orestes; and took indeed much the same pains to keep it sweet and neat under the eye and nose of the public as those on which the good woman dwelt with such pathetic minuteness of recollection in after years. The babe may not always have been discreet;

νέα δὲ νηδὺς αὐτάρκης τέκνων·[1]

and there were others who found its swaddling clothes not invariably in such condition as to dispense with the services of the 'fuller';

γναφεὺς τροφεύς τε ταὐτὸν εἰχέτην τέλος.[2]

In effect there were those who found the woes and devotions of Doll Tearsheet or Nell Nameless[3] as set forth in the lyric verse of Mr. Buchanan calculated rather to turn the stomach than to melt the heart. But in spite of these exceptional tastes the nursing journals, it should seem, abated no jot of heart or hope for their nursling.

> Petit poisson deviendra grand
> Pourvu que Dieu lui prête vie.[4]

Petit bonhomme will not, it appears. The tadpole poet will never grow into anything bigger than a frog; not though in that stage of development he should puff and blow himself till he bursts with windy adulation at the heels of the laurelled ox.[5]

When some time since a passing notice was bestowed by writers of another sort on Mr. Buchanan's dramatic performance in the part of Thomas Maitland, it was observed with very just indignation by a literary ally that Mr. Rossetti was not ashamed to avow in the face of heaven and the press his utter ignorance of the writings of that poet— or perhaps we should say of those poets.[6] The loss was too certainly his

---

[1] Æschylus, *Choephoroi*, l. 757: 'Children's young inwards work their own relief' (tr. Smith).

[2] *Ibid.*, l. 760: 'Laundress [Swinburne's 'fuller'] and nurse had the same office.'

[3] Shakespeare's Doll Tearsheet and Buchanan's Nell follow the same calling.

[4] La Fontaine, *Fables*, V, iii: 'The little fish will get big provided God grants him life.'

[5] An allusion to the Aesopic fable in which a frog trying to blow himself up to ox-size bursts.

[6] 'The Fleshly School of Poetry', the article Buchanan had signed 'Thomas Maitland', charged that Rossetti's 'Jenny' had been suggested by Buchanan's poems. In 'The Stealthy School of Criticism' (*Athenaeum*, 16 December 1871, 792-4), Rossetti denied having any knowledge of those poems. Nevertheless Buchanan repeated the remark in his book.

own. It is no light thing for a man who has any interest in the poetic production of his time to be ignorant of works which have won from the critic who of all others must be most competent to speak on the subject with the authority of the most intimate acquaintance, such eloquence of praise as has deservedly been lavished on Mr. Buchanan. A living critic of no less note in the world of letters than himself has drawn public attention to the deep and delicate beauties of his work; to 'the intense loving tenderness of the coarse woman Nell towards her brutal paramour, the exquisite delicacy and fine spiritual vision of the old village schoolmaster',[1] &c. &c. This pathetic tribute to the poet Buchanan was paid by no less a person than Buchanan the critic. Its effect is heightened by comparison with the just but rigid severity of that writer's verdict on other men—on the 'gross' work of Shakespeare, the 'brutal' work of Carlyle, the 'sickening and peculiar' work of Thackeray, the 'wooden-headed', 'hectic', and 'hysterical' qualities which are severally notable and condemnable in the work of Landor, of Keats, and of Shelley. In like manner his condemnation of contemporary impurities is thrown into fuller relief by his tribute to the moral sincerity of Petronius and the 'singular purity' of Ben Jonson. For once I have the honour and pleasure to agree with him; I find the 'purity' of the author of *Bartholomew Fair* a very 'singular' sort of purity indeed. There is however another play of that great writer's, which, though it might be commended by his well-wishers to the special study of Mr. Buchanan, I can hardly suppose to be the favourite work which has raised the old poet so high in his esteem. In this play Jonson has traced with his bitterest fidelity the career of a 'gentleman parcel-poet',[2] one Laberius Crispinus, whose life is spent in the struggle to make his way among his betters by a happy alternation and admixture of calumny with servility; one who will fasten himself uninvited on the acquaintance of a superior with fulsome and obtrusive ostentation of good-will; inflict upon his passive and reluctant victim the recitation of his verses in a public place; offer him friendship and alliance against all other poets, so as 'to lift the best of them out of favour'; protest to him, 'Do but taste me once, if I do know myself and my own virtues truly, thou wilt not make that esteem of Varius, or Virgil, or

---

[1] From 'On My Own Tentatives' in Buchanan's *David Gray, and Other Essays*. Most of the comments that follow about authors ranging from Shakespeare to Shelley appear in the same book, and others appear in 'Tennyson's Charm', *Saint Pauls Magazine*, 1872, x, 282–303.

[2] This phrase and the next four quoted passages are from Ben Jonson's play *The Poetaster*.

Tibullus, or any of 'em indeed, as now in thy ignorance thou dost; which I am content to forgive; I would fain see which of these could pen more verses in a day or with more facility than I.' After this, it need hardly be added that the dog returns to his vomit, and has in the end to be restrained by authority from venting 'divers and sundry calumnies' against the victim aforesaid 'or any other eminent man transcending him in merit, whom his envy shall find cause to work upon, either for that, or for keeping himself in better acquaintance, or enjoying better friends'; and the play is aptly wound up by his public exposure and ignominious punishment. The title of this admirable comedy is *The Poetaster; or, His Arraignment*; and the prologue is spoken by Envy.

It is really to be regretted that the new fashion of self-criticism should never have been set till now. How much petty trouble, how many paltry wrangles and provocations, what endless warfare of the cranes and pigmies might have been prevented—and by how simple a remedy! How valuable would the applauding comments of other great poets on their own work have been to us for all time! All students of poetry must lament that it did not occur to Milton for example to express in public his admiration of *Paradise Lost*. It might have helped to support the reputation of that poem against the severe sentence passed by Mr. Buchanan on its frequently flat and prosaic quality. And, like all truly great discoveries, this one looks so easy now we have it before us, that we cannot but wonder it was reserved for Mr. Buchanan to make: we cannot but feel it singular that Mr. Tennyson should never have thought fit to call our attention in person to the beauties of *Maud*; that Mr. Browning should never have come forward, 'motley on back and pointing-pole in hand',[1] to bid us remark the value of *The Ring and the Book*; that Mr. Arnold should have left to others the task of praising his 'Thyrsis' and *Empedocles*. The last-named poet might otherwise have held his own even against the imputation of writing 'mere prose' which now he shares with Milton: so sharp is the critical judgment, so high the critical standard, of the author of *The Book of Orm*.

However, even in the face of the rebuke so deservedly incurred by the avowal of Mr. Rossetti's gross and deplorable ignorance of that and other great works from the same hand, I am bound in honesty to admit that my own studies in that line are hardly much less limited. I

[1] Browning's *Sordello*, l. 30.

cannot profess to have read any book of Mr. Buchanan's; for aught I know, they may deserve all his praises; it is neither my business nor my desire to decide. But sundry of his contributions in verse and prose to various magazines and newspapers I have looked through or glanced over—not, I trust, without profit; not, I know, without amusement. From these casual sources I have gathered—as he who runs may gather —not a little information on no unimportant matters of critical and autobiographical interest. With the kindliest forethought, the most judicious care to anticipate the anxious researches of a late posterity, Mr. Buchanan has once and again poured out his personal confidences into the sympathetic bosom of the nursing journals. He is resolved that his country shall not always have cause to complain how little she knows of her greatest sons. Time may have hidden from the eye of biography the facts of Shakespeare's life, as time has revealed to the eye of criticism the grossness of his works and the purity of his rival's; but none need fear that the next age will have to lament the absence of materials for a life of Buchanan. Not once or twice has he told in simple prose of his sorrows and aspirations, his struggles and his aims. He has told us what good man gave him in his need a cup of cold water, and what bad man accused him of sycophancy in the expression of his thanks. He has told us what advantage was taken of his tender age by heartless publishers, what construction was put upon his gushing gratitude by heartless reviewers. He has told us that he never can forget his first friends; he has shown us that he never can forget himself. He has told us that the versicles of one David Gray, a poor young poeticule of the same breed as his panegyrist (who however, it should in fairness be said, died without giving any sign of future distinction in the field of pseudonymous libel), will be read when the works of other contemporaries 'have gone to the limbo of affettuosos'. (May I suggest that the library edition of Mr. Buchanan's collected works should be furnished with a glossary for the use of students unskilled in the varieties of the Buchananese dialect?[1] Justly contemptuous as he has shown himself of all foreign affectations of speech or style in an English writer, such a remarkable word in its apparent defiance of analogy as the one last quoted is not a little perplexing to their ignorance. I hardly think it can be Scotch; at least to a southern eye it bears no recognizable affinity to the language of Burns.) In like manner, if we may trust the evidence of Byron, did Porson prophesy of Southey that his epics would be read

---

[1] In his remarks on 'the fleshly school', Buchanan severely criticized Rossetti's diction.

when Homer and Virgil were forgotten,[1] and in like manner may the humblest of his contemporaries prophesy that Mr. Buchanan's idyls will be read by generations which have forgotten the idyls of Theocritus and of Landor, of Tennyson and of Chénier.

In that singularly interesting essay on 'his own tentatives' from which we have already taken occasion to glean certain flowers of comparative criticism Mr. Buchanan remarks of this contemporary that he seems rather fond of throwing stones in his (Mr. Buchanan's) direction.[2] This contemporary, however, is not in the habit of throwing stones; it is a pastime which he leaves to the smaller fry of the literary gutter. These it is sometimes not unamusing to watch as they dodge and shirk round the street-corner after the discharge of their popgun pellet, with the ready plea on their lips that it was not this boy but that—not the good boy Robert, for instance, but the rude boy Thomas. But there is probably only one man living who could imagine it worth his contemporary's while to launch the smallest stone from his sling in such a direction as that—who could conceive the very idlest of marksmen to be capable of taking aim unprovoked at so pitiful a target. Mr. Buchanan and his nursing journals have informed us that to his other laurels he is entitled to add those of an accomplished sportsman. Surely he must know that there are animals which no one counts as game— which are classed under quite another head than that. Their proper designation it is needless here to repeat; it is one that suffices to exempt them from the honour and the danger common to creatures of a higher kind. Of their natural history I did not know enough till now to remark without surprise that specimens of the race may be found which are ambitious to be ranked among objects of sport. For my part, as long as I am not suspected of any inclination to join in the chase, such an one should be welcome to lay that flattering unction to his soul,[3] and believe himself in secret one of the nobler beasts of game: even though it were but a weasel that would fain pass muster as a hart of grice.[4] It

---

[1] According to Byron, the friendship of Landor and Southey 'will probably be as memorable as his own epics which (as I quoted to him ten or twelve years ago in "English Bards") Porson said could be remembered when Homer and Virgil are forgotten, and not till then' (quoted in a note to the Appendix of *The Two Foscari; Letters and Journals*, ed. R. E. Prothero, vi, 389).

[2] From *David Gray, and Other Essays*, 291: 'A gifted young contemporary, who seems fond of throwing stones in my direction, fiercely upbraids me for writing "Idylls of the gallows and the gutter", and singing songs of "costermongers and their trulls".'

[3] Cf. *Hamlet*, III, iv, 145.

[4] Swinburne's phrase for 'hart of grease' or 'fat hart'.

must no doubt be 'very soothing'[1] to Mr. Buchanan's modesty to imagine himself the object of such notice as he claims to have received; but we may observe from how small a seed so large a growth of self-esteem may shoot up:—

$$\sigma\mu\iota\kappa\rho o\hat{\upsilon}\ \gamma\acute{e}\nu o\iota\tau'\ \mathring{a}\nu\ \sigma\pi\acute{e}\rho\mu\alpha\tau o\varsigma\ \mu\acute{e}\gamma\alpha\varsigma\ \pi\acute{\upsilon}\theta\mu\eta\nu.[2]$$

From a slight passing mention of 'idyls of the gutter and the gibbet', in a passage referring to the idyllic schools of our day, Mr. Buchanan has built up this fabric of induction; he is led by even so much notice as this to infer that his work must be to the writer an object of especial attention, and even (God save the mark!) of especial attack. He is welcome to hug himself in that fond belief, and fool himself to the top of his bent;[3] but he will hardly persuade any one else that to find his 'neck-verse' merely repulsive[4]—to feel no responsive vibration to 'the intense loving tenderness' of his street-walker as she neighs and brays over her 'gallows-carrion'—is the same thing as to deny the infinite value, the incalculable significance, to a great poet, of such matters as this luckless poeticule has here taken into his 'hangman's hands'.[5] Neither the work nor the workman is to be judged by the casual preferences of social convention. It is not more praiseworthy or more pardonable to write bad verse about costermongers and gaol-birds than to write bad verse about kings and knights; nor (as would otherwise naturally be the case) is it to be expected that because some among the greatest of poets have been born among the poorest of men, therefore the literature of a nation is to suffer joyfully an inundation or eruption of rubbish from all threshers, cobblers, and milkwomen who now, as in the age of Pope, of Johnson, or of Byron, may be stung to madness by the gadfly of poetic ambition. As in one rank we find for a single Byron a score of Roscommons, Mulgraves, and Winchilseas, so in another rank we find for a single Burns a score of Ducks, Bloomfields, and Yearsleys.[6] And if it does not follow that a poet must be great if

---

[1] Swinburne was fond of this quoted phrase from Mr. Pecksniff's remarks in *Martin Chuzzlewit*, chapter 9.

[2] Æschylus' *Choephoroi*, l. 204: 'From a little seed may spring a mighty stock' (tr. Smyth).

[3] *Hamlet*, III, ii, 401.

[4] Usually 'neck-verse' refers to a verse from the Bible formerly used to test the literacy of those trying to save their necks by claiming benefit of clergy. Here Swinburne apparently uses the expression of Buchanan's poem about a character sentenced to be hanged.

[5] *Macbeth*, II, ii, 28.

[6] Swinburne considers these poets mediocre: Wentworth Dillon, fourth Earl of Roscommon (c. 1633–1685); John Sheffield, third Earl of Mulgrave (1648–1721); Anne

he be but of low birth, neither does it follow that a poem must be good if it be but written on a subject of low life. The sins and sorrows of all that suffer wrong, the oppressions that are done under the sun, the dark days and shining deeds of the poor whom society casts out and crushes down, are assuredly material for poetry of a most high order; for the heroic passion of Victor Hugo's, for the angelic passion of Mrs. Browning's. Let another such arise to do such work as 'Les Pauvres Gens' or the 'Cry of the Children', and there will be no lack of response to that singing. But they who can only 'grate on their scrannel-pipes of wretched straw'[1] some pitiful 'idyl' to milk the maudlin eyes of the nursing journals must be content with such applause as their own; for in higher latitudes they will find none.

Finch, Countess of Winchilsea (1661–1720); Stephen Duck (1705–1756); Robert Bloomfield (1766–1823), and Mrs. Anne Yearsley (1756–1806).

---

[1] *Lycidas*, l. 124.

# 19. A. C. Hilton: 'Octopus'

1872

Arthur Clement Hilton (1851–1877) wrote for the *Light Green*, a magazine of two issues (1872), which he established while at Cambridge University, the best of the parodies of Swinburne. The fact that 'Dolores' has been the most frequently parodied of Swinburne's poems casts light on an aspect of the poet's reputation.

## OCTOPUS[1]

### By ALGERNON CHARLES SIN-BURN

STRANGE beauty, eight-limbed and eight-handed,
  Whence camest to dazzle our eyes?
With thy bosom bespangled and banded
  With the hues of the seas and the skies;
Is thy home European or Asian,
  O mystical monster marine?
Part molluscous and partly crustacean,
  Betwixt and between.

Wast thou born to the sound of sea-trumpets?
  Hast thou eaten and drunk to excess
Of the sponges—thy muffins and crumpets,
  Of the seaweed—thy mustard and cress?
Wast thou nurtured in caverns of coral,
  Remote from reproof or restraint?
Art thou innocent, art thou immoral,
  Sinburnian or Saint?

Lithe limbs, curling free, as a creeper
  That creeps in a desolate place,
To enrol and envelop the sleeper
  In a silent and stealthy embrace,
Cruel beak craning forward to bite us,

[1] Written at the Crystal Palace Aquarium. [Author's note.]

Our juices to drain and to drink,
Or to whelm us in waves of Cocytus,
  Indelible ink!

O breast, that 'twere rapture to writhe on!
  O arms 'twere delicious to feel
Clinging close with the crush of the Python,
  When she maketh her murderous meal!
In thy eight-fold embraces enfolden,
  Let our empty existence escape;
Give us death that is glorious and golden,
  Crushed all out of shape!

Ah! thy red lips, lascivious and luscious,
  With death in their amorous kiss!
Cling round us, and clasp us, and crush us,
  With bitings of agonized bliss;
We are sick with the poison of pleasure,
  Dispense us the potion of pain;
Ope thy mouth to its uttermost measure
  And bite us again!

# 20. E. C. Stedman on Swinburne

## 1875

To Edmund Clarence Stedman, Wall Street broker, critic, and poet, Swinburne wrote some of his most important autobiographical letters, and Stedman became his most effective American champion. The following extracts include the first and last part of Stedman's essay.

From chapter xi, 'Latter-Day Singers: Algernon Charles Swinburne', in Edmund Clarence Stedman's *Victorian Poets* (sixth edition: Boston, 1882; first edition, 1875).

Ten years have passed since this poet took the critical outposts by storm, and with a single effort gained a laurel-crown, of which no public envy, nor any lesser action of his own, thenceforth could dispossess him. The time has been so crowded with his successive productions—his career, with all its strength and imprudence, has been so thoroughly that of a poet—as to heighten the interest which only a spirit of most unusual quality can excite and long maintain.

We have just observed the somewhat limited range of William Morris's vocabulary. It is composed mainly of plain Saxon words, chosen with great taste and musically put together. No barrenness, however, is perceptible, since to enrich that writer's language from learned or modern sources would disturb the tone of his pure English feeling. The nature of Swinburne's diction is precisely opposite. His faculty of expression is so brilliant as to obscure the other elements which are to be found in his verse, and constantly to lead him beyond the wisdom of art. Nevertheless, reflecting upon his genius and the chances of his future, it is difficult for any one to write with cold restraint who has an eye to see, an ear to hear, and the practice which forces an artist to wonder at the lustre, the melody, the unstinted fire and movement, of his imperious song.

## I.

I wish, then, to speak at some length upon the one faculty in which Swinburne excels any living English poet; in which I doubt if his equal has existed among recent poets of any tongue, unless Shelley be excepted, or, possibly, some lyrist of the modern French school. This is his miraculous gift of rhythm, his command over the unsuspected resources of a language. That Shelley had a like power is, I think, shown in passages like the choruses of *Prometheus Unbound*, but he flourished half a century ago, and did not have (as Swinburne has) Shelley for a predecessor! A new generation, refining upon the lessons given by himself and Keats, has carried the art of rhythm to extreme variety and finish. Were Shelley to have a second career, his work, if no finer in single passages, would have, all in all, a range of musical variations such as we discover in Swinburne's. So close is the resemblance in quality of these two voices, however great the difference in development, as almost to justify a belief in metempsychosis. A master is needed to awake the spirit slumbering in any musical instrument. Before the advent of Swinburne we did not realize the full scope of English verse. In his hands it is like the violin of Paganini. The range of his fantasias, roulades, arias, new effects of measure and sound, is incomparable with anything hitherto known. The first emotion of one who studies even his immature work is that of wonder at the freedom and richness of his diction, the susurrus of his rhythm, his unconscious alliterations, the endless change of his syllabic harmonies—resulting in the alternate softness and strength, height and fall, riotous or chastened music, of his affluent verse. How does he produce it? Who taught him all the hidden springs of melody? He was born a tamer of words: a subduer of this most stubborn, yet most copious of the literary tongues. In his poetry we discover qualities we did not know were in the language—a softness that seemed Italian, a rugged strength we thought was German, a blithe and debonair lightness we despaired of capturing from the French. He has added a score of new stops and pedals to the instrument. He has introduced, partly from other tongues, stanzaic forms, measures and effects untried before; and has brought out the swiftness and force of metres like the anapestic, carrying each to perfection at a single trial. Words in his hands are like the ivory balls of a juggler, and all words seem to be in his hands. His fellow-craftsmen, who alone can understand what has been done in their art, will not term this statement extravagance. Speaking only of his command over language and metre, I have a right to reaffirm, and to show by many illustrations, that he is the most sovereign of rhythmists. He compels the inflexible elements to his use. Chaucer is more limpid, Shakespeare more kingly, Milton loftier at times, Byron has an unaffected power— but neither Shelley nor the greatest of his predecessors is so dithyrambic, and no one has been in all moods so absolute an autocrat of verse. With equal gifts, I say, none *could* have been, for Swinburne comes after and profits by the art of all. Poets often win distinction by producing work that differs from what has gone before. It seems as if Swinburne, in this ripe period, resolved to excel others by a mastery of known melodies, adding a new magic to each, and going beyond the range of the farthest. His amazing tricks of rhythm are those of a gymnast out-leaping his fellows. We had Keats, Shelley, and Coleridge, after Collins and Gray, and Tennyson after Keats, but now Swinburne adds such elaboration, that an art which we thought perfected seems almost tame. In the first place, he was born a prodigy,—as much so as Morphy[1] in chess; added to this he is the product of these latter days, a phenomenon impossible before. It is safe to declare that at last a time has come when the force of expression can no further go.

I do not say that it has not gone too far. The fruit may be, and here is, too luscious; the flower is often of an odor too intoxicating to endure. Yet what execution! Poetry, the rarest poetic feeling, may be found in simpler verse. Yet again, what execution! The voice may not be equal to the grandest music, nor trained and restrained as it should be. But the voice is there, and its possessor has the finest natural organ to which this generation has listened.

Right here it is plain that Swinburne, especially in his early poems, has weakened his effects by cloying us with excessive richness of epithet and sound: in later works, by too elaborate expression and redundancy of treatment. Still, while Browning's amplification is wont to be harsh and obscure, Swinburne, even if obscure, or when the thought is one that he has repeated again and again, always gives us unapproachable melody and grace. It is true that his glories of speech often hang upon the slightest thread of purpose. He so constantly wants to stop and sing that he gets along slowly with a plot. As we listen to his fascinating music, the meaning, like the libretto of an opera, often passes out of mind. The melody is unbroken: in this, as in other matters, Swinburne's fault is that of excess. He does not frequently admit the sweet discords,

---

[1] Paul Charles Morphy (1837–1884), thought by some to have been the greatest chess player of all time.

of which he is a master, nor relieve his work by simple, contrasting interludes. Until recently his voice had a narrow range; its effect resulted from changes upon a few notes. The richness of these permutations was a marvel, yet a series of them blended into mannerism. Shelley could be academic at times, and even humorous; but Swinburne's monotone, original and varied within its bounds, was thought to be the expression of a limited range of feeling, and restricted his early efforts as a dramatic lyrist.

The question first asked, with regard to either a poet or singer, is, Has he voice? and then, Has he execution? We have lastly to measure the passion, imagination, invention, to which voice and method are but ministers. From the quality of the latter, the style being the man, we often may estimate the higher faculties that control them. The principle here involved runs through all the arts of beauty and use. A fine vocal gift is priceless, both for itself and for the spiritual force behind it. With this preliminary stress upon Swinburne's most conspicuous gift, let us briefly examine his record, bethinking ourselves how difficult it is to judge a poet who is obscured by his own excess of light, and whose earlier verses so cloyed the mind with richness as to deprive it of the judicial taste.

[Sections II, III and IV of the essay are omitted.]

## V.

Taine brings a great cloud of examples to show that each period shapes the work and fortunes of its authors, but it is equally true that men of genius create new modes, and often determine the nature of periods yet to come. Swinburne may live to see the time and himself in correspondence. To me he seems the foremost of the younger school of British poets. The fact that a man is not yet haloed with the light that comes only when, in death or in hoary age, he recalls to us the past, need not debar him from full recognition. A critic must be quick to estimate the present. For some years, as I have observed the successive efforts of this poet, a feeling of his genius has grown upon me, derived not only from his promise, but from what he actually has done. If he were to write no more, and his past works should be collected in a single volume,—although, as in the remains of Shelley, we might find little narrative-verse, what a world of melody, and what a wealth of imaginative song! It is true that his well-known manner would pervade the book; we should find no great variety of mood, few studies of visible objects, a meagre reflection of English life as it exists today. Yet a subtle observer would perceive how truly he represents his own time, and to a poet this compendium would become a lyrical handbook, a treasured exposition of creative and beautiful design.

Acknowledging the presence of true genius, minor objections are of small account. A poet may hold himself apart, or from caprice may do things unworthy of his noblest self, but we think of him always as at his best. The gift is not so common; let us value it while it is here. Let us also do justice to the world—to the world that, remembering its past errors, no longer demands of great wits that they should wholly forego madness. Fifty years ago, and Swinburne, for his eccentricities and disdain, might have been an exile like Byron and Shelley, or, for his republicanism, imprisoned like Leigh Hunt. We have learned that poets gather from strange experiences what they teach in song. If rank unwholesome flowers spring from too rich a soil, in the end a single fruitful blossoming will compensate us for the sterile *fleurs du mal* of youth. Lastly, Swinburne has been said to lack application, but ten years of profuse and consecutive labors refute the charge. Works like his are not produced without energy and long industrious hours. If done at a heat, the slow hidden fire has never ceased its burning. Who shall dictate to a poet his modes and tenses, or his choice of work? But all this matters nothing; the entire host of traditional follies need not abash us if, with their coming, we have a revival of the olden passion and the olden power.

# *ERECHTHEUS*

## 1876

---

## 21. John Addington Symonds, review, *Academy*

8 January 1876, ix, 23–4

*Erechtheus* was the first and indeed the only book by Swinburne that was almost unanimously praised. The review by John Addington Symonds is more knowledgeable than others, the work of a poet and man of letters who had been a special student of Greek literature, though he is now remembered chiefly for his studies in the Renaissance.

---

Lycurgus the orator gives the following argument of the lost tragedy of *Erechtheus* by Euripides:—

They say that Eumolpus, the son of Poseidon and Chione, came with the Thracians to conquer Attica; and that at that time Erechtheus, who had for wife Praxithea, the daughter of Cephisus, reigned in Athens. When, therefore, a great army was about to assault the land, the king sent to Delphi, and enquired how he might obtain a victory over his enemies. The god answered that he would win, if he slew his daughter before such time as the forces engaged in battle. This, in obedience to the oracle, he did, and drove the foemen forth from Attica.

From other sources we learn that the name of the daughter, thus sacrificed for the welfare of Athens, was Chthonia, and that two of her sisters having vowed not to survive her, slew themselves. It also appears that in the decisive battle Erechtheus killed Eumolpus with his own hand, and was himself destroyed by a thunderbolt from Zeus. Erechtheus was reputed to have been autochthonous, or sprung from the

Attic soil in marriage with Hephaestus. He and Praxithea were the parents of Oreithyia, whom the north wind whirled away to Thrace, and of Procris the unhappy bride of Cephalus. How Euripides handled the whole of this mythological material in his lost drama is uncertain; but it is clear from a long speech of fifty-five lines preserved by Lycurgus, that in the person of Praxithea he nobly illustrated his favourite female virtue of εὐψυχία—the firm and lofty spirit in a woman, which subordinated all personal affections and domestic charities to public heroism, and to the duty demanded from her by the State. Had the tragedy been preserved entire, we cannot doubt that both mother and daughter, Praxithea and Chthonia, would have taken rank beside Makaria and Iphigeneia.[1]

Mr. Swinburne in the play before us has selected the same leading motive of Chthonia's sacrifice, and has interwoven with it all the fabulous material which gives variety and colour to the legend of Erechtheus. The skill with which he has disengaged the splendid human heroism of Praxithea and Chthonia from this background of intricate and sombre mythology, and has concentrated all the interest of his drama on their two personalities, reserving the other elements of the fable for lyrical treatment in the choruses, for descriptions which produce a sense of relief, and for allusions which deepen the tragic pathos, proves the most consummate mastery of dramatic art. His *Erechtheus* is not a bare imitation of a lost tragedy by Euripides. It *is* a Greek play written in the English tongue, in the creation of which the poet has not merely adopted the forms of the Attic drama, but has thought and felt, selected his chief subject and distributed his subordinate incidents, precisely as a Greek playwright would have done. The harmony of all the parts is perfect. The tone is maintained with unerring tact. Not one word is spoken, not one note is struck, and not one sentiment is suggested which could jar upon the sympathies or tax the intelligence of an ancient Greek. And yet our *Erechtheus* is as living to us now as it would have been to an Athenian. The humanity of the two heroines, in their self-sacrifice and piety and measureless love, is so perfect that no archaisms of scholarship, mythology, and alien superstition can divide them from our affection.

[1] Makaria, a daughter of Heracles and Deianira, volunteered to die in fulfilment of an oracle in order that the children of Heracles and the Athenians might win a victory over the forces of Eurystheus. Euripides' *The Children of Heracles* introduces her in this role. Iphigenia, the daughter of Agamemnon, after her father had killed a sacred stag, was to be sacrificed in order to appease the goddess Artemis and thus enable the Greek fleet to sail—a situation portrayed by Euripides in *Iphigenia at Aulis*.

It is worth while pausing for a moment to consider the point on which the action turns. Athens, though as yet but a young city, the child of rocky Attica, and the nursling of Pallas, has a sense of her high destinies. For her sake gods have been in combat. Pallas and Poseidon stood against each other, and Pallas conquered. Now, the wrath of Poseidon assails the virgin city, and the armies of his son Eumolpus threaten like a wave to overwhelm her. By the mysterious will of heaven it is decreed that only Chthonia's death can secure life for the State. This sacrifice is demanded of Praxithea, the mother, who has already seen one daughter ravished from her side by Boreas. It is demanded of the child herself, who has nothing but her young life to yield. Both mother and daughter obey without a murmur, conscious, indeed, of the dreadful price they have to pay, but confirmed in their constancy by faith in heaven, and by the certainty they feel that such a city as Athens will one day be, is worth the loss of all particular lives. Such patriotism is always noble; it never fails to supply a theme for impassioned poetry. But if we remember what Athens has been in the history of the freedom and of the glory of the human spirit, then the self-devotion of Chthonia and the self-forgetfulness of Praxithea touch us not merely with admiration but also with a deep sense of personal gratitude. This is the powerful motive which the poet holds at his disposal; and it may be easily imagined that both lustre and dignity are added to it by the praises with which the experience of the past has enabled him to exalt the worth of the land for whom her daughter dies. It is a passion before which the ordinary motives of romantic poetry—love, jealousy, ambition—hang their diminished heads. Perhaps the greatest evidence of Mr. Swinburne's genius in this drama is this, that having chosen an essentially classic subject, and having treated it in a rigorously classic style, he has at the same time vitalised it with emotion which, though more antique than modern, still compels our own particular sympathy. In hearing the speech of Athena at the termination of the action, even the modern audience will feel that consolation of the noblest and most spiritual kind is offered, not only to the citizens of Erechtheus and the widowed queen, but also to themselves, because the poet has convinced them that the drama of Athens was the drama of liberty, and that on the fate of Athens hung the fate of civilized humanity. It is for the spiritual citadel of all mankind, the city glorious of thought and freedom, that Chthonia dies; and the promise of Athena is for us the voice of history anticipated. Such is the high and noble theme of Mr. Swinburne's youngest poem. To such altitudes, rarely scaled by the feet of poets in the modern age, has he ascended.

It is conceivable that some other poet might have seen the grandeur of the subject of *Erechtheus*, and, in attempting it, might have failed fully to enlist our human sympathies. In the heroines of Euripidean tragedy, for example, there is an element of frigid stoicism which repels our love as much as their self-sacrifice attracts it. This peril Mr. Swinburne, by his vivid realisation of the maternal and filial relations between Praxithea and Chthonia, has not so much avoided as annihilated. The sublimity of self-devotion to the public good can never be called cold or stern, when the patients of this exalted enthusiasm love each other as these do. To quote passages in support of this remark would be impossible in a notice of the kind which I have undertaken. The whole of the two scenes which are devoted to Praxithea and her daughter (lines 361–554 and lines 863–1134) would have to be transcribed.

At this point, it may be said in passing that the character-interest of the play is concentrated upon the two women, and that the greatest amount of artistic pains has been bestowed upon Praxithea. Her $\mathring{\eta}\theta os$, as a god-fearing, reverent, law-loving, intensely affectionate, yet nobly disinterested woman—a woman for whom the sanctities and charms of domestic life, dear as they are, exist only as a part of a wider spiritual sphere from which they draw their vitality—is presented to us with the utmost consistency, traced with delicacy, and firmly sustained. Praxithea is as real and full in personality as the Antigone of Sophocles. Erechtheus occupies the second place in the composition. To have brought him into equal prominence with Praxithea and Chthonia would have been to confuse the drama with divided interests. For the rest, the heralds and messengers stand of course upon a third plane; while Athena, like a being of another world, speaks once and speaks authoritatively with the clear voice of a goddess and the tenderness of a protective saint.

One of the difficulties of the subject has been hinted in the previous paragraph. Chthonia saves Athens; that is the central point of the play; at the same time Erechtheus is slain in battle, and two of Chthonia's sisters kill themselves. It is impossible to combine these subsidiary incidents into more than a formal harmony with the main motive. Yet even here Mr. Swinburne has contrived a dramatic success, by rendering them the means of bringing Athena upon the stage and placing in her lips the prophecy of Athenian greatness. It was necessary that blow on blow should crush the patient faith-abiding hearth of Praxithea, and that the city in the hour of its salvation should be reduced to mourning, in order that the appearance of the *deus ex machina* should be justified. In this way only could the perfection of Praxithea's character, as beautiful in chastened joy as in courageous sorrow, be exhibited, and the play conclude on such a note as this last speech of hers:—

> O queen Athena, from a heart made whole
> Take as thou givest us blessing; never tear
> Shall stain for shame nor groan untune the song,
> That as a bird shall spread and fold its wings
> Here in thy praise for ever, and fulfil
> The whole world's crowning city crowned with thee
> As the sun's eye fulfils and crowns with sight
> The circling crown of heaven. There is no grief
> Great as the joy to be made one in will
> With him that is the heart and rule of life
> And thee, God born of God; thy name is ours,
> And thy large grace more great than our desire.

In respect to form, the *Erechtheus* is constructed upon pure classic principles, and will bear the most minute scrutiny that the scholar can give. If it be fashioned upon the style of any one of the three Attic tragedians, it is probably to Aeschylus that we should look for Mr. Swinburne's model. The first and the seventh Choruses (see lines 95–238, and lines 1283–1447) recall similar lyric movements in the *Supplices* and the *Septem Contra Thebas*; while the presence of only two actors on the stage at the same time is Aeschylean. Very true, again, to the spirit of Aeschylean art is the whole mythology of the powers of sea and earth in conflict. As personality is given to the winds and the waves, so language and imagery are created for them by the poet. It would be a mistake, however, to regard *Erechtheus* as a study after Aeschylus. The knowledge of Greek dramatic art which it displays, is comprehensive and complete; and it is clear that Mr. Swinburne has freely availed himself of all resources of the genuine Attic stage which suited his purpose. In this play, as before in *Atalanta*, he is particularly successful in his use of stichomuthia, or dialogue conducted by the interchange of single lines. According to Greek usage, he employs this form of conversation for the conveyance of covert speech and *double entendre* (see pp. 15, 23, 88), and also for defiant bandying of words between antagonistic personages (see p. 38). Instances of both Iambic and Trochaic stichomuthia occur in places where a more sedate and a more animated utterance are severally required. The part of the

Messenger, again, is used with fine effect. The speech which describes the death of Chthonia (lines 1191–1340) has all the beauty of similar descriptions in Euripides; while the Athenian Herald's narrative of the decisive battle (1487–1584) is marked by Aeschylean pomp of diction. It is probable, however, that the student of classic literature will derive most pleasure from the kommos, or lyrical dialogue sustained between Chthonia and the Chorus just before her death (lines 1087–1134). It begins, after the appearance of Chthonia upon the stage, with a kind of antiphonal litany, the girl chaunting one long grave line of prayer and farewell, the Chorus returning answer with a shorter line of consolatory response; and it concludes with a monody sung by Chthonia. In the whole of this passage the Greek outline is traced with a pure and simple precision beyond praise.

It remains still to speak of the Chorus, of which Mr. Swinburne has made liberal use. Counting long and short together, there are no fewer than nine choric movements in the play. The first, which is eddying, clamorous, Aeschylean, sets forth the old strife of Poseidon and Athena, invokes the protection of heaven in the dire calamity of Athens, and adverts to the tales of Oreithyia and Procris. The second expresses the sense of mysterious awe inspired by the oracle communicated to Erechtheus. The third, which is a real triumph of lyrical genius, describes the rape of Oreithyia by the stormful north wind. In the fourth, the coming sacrifice of Chthonia is foreseen, and the pathos of it is enhanced by reflections upon death and life. The fifth dwells upon that love of loves, which is stronger than all love, the mysterious affection of earth's children for the earth, and the yearning toward one another of earth and fire in the love embraces that begat a brood autochthonous for Attica. This chorus is important for the main motive of the tragedy, as a lyrical expression of the enthusiasm which supports Praxithea and Chthonia. The sixth very briefly contrasts Niobe with Praxithea. The seventh describes war and the terror of battle, the darkness which shrouded the sun's light while the armies were engaging, and the clinging in their sore need of Athena's citizens to the hope of help from Phoebus. The eighth, which is short, but very true to Greek feeling, expresses the joy felt for the deliverance of the city, mingled with a dread lest some mysterious curse should cling about it for the outpoured maiden's blood. This prepares the audience for the appearance of Athena, who alone can reassure her citizens and give the certainty of plenitude of peace and growing fame for ever. The ninth and last lyrical utterance of the Chorus is the ten concluding lines of the tragedy. Whether general readers will find as much in the lyrical passages of *Erechtheus* to admire, separated from the drama, as they found in *Atalanta*, may perhaps be questioned. The scholar, on the contrary, will recognise in them a still greater fidelity to Greek thought and feeling, a more intimate and organic connexion between their themes and the motives of the drama. There is no competent reader who, after sufficient study of the play, will not agree with us in recognising the sublime beauty of the subject, the faith and purity and reverence which mark its large and deep humanity, and the exquisiteness of its artistic workmanship. *Erechtheus* is, in truth, a masterpiece, considered not merely as a reproduction of classical art, but also as a poem which appeals to men of all nations and of all times.

# 22. W. K. Clifford on *Songs before Sunrise*

## 1877

W. K. Clifford (1845–1879), an exceptionally able mathematician who taught at University College, London, and a thinker of rare promise, was a pioneer in the appreciation of an aspect of *Songs before Sunrise*. Like Swinburne, he admired Mazzini. In his lecture 'Cosmic Emotion' (*Nineteenth Century*, October 1877, ii, 411–29; reprinted in *Lectures and Essays*, ed. Leslie Stephen and Frederick Pollock, London, 1879)—'an emotion which is felt in regard to the universe or sum of things viewed as a cosmos or order'—the young idealist illustrated his views from *Songs before Sunrise*. In the following extract notes giving Clifford's references to volumes of poetry have been renumbered, and citation of particular poems has been added.

We arrive thus at a common principle, which at once distinguishes good actions from bad in the internal world, and which has created the external world, so far as it is living. This principle is, then, a fit object for cosmic emotion if we can only get rid of the vagueness of its definition. And it has this great advantage, that it does not need to be personified for poetical purposes. For we may regard the result of this mode of action, extended over a great length of time, as in some way an embodiment of the action itself. In this way the human race embodies in itself all the ages of organic action that have gone to its evolution. The nature of organic action, then, is to personify itself, and it has personified itself most in the human race.

But before we go further two things must be remarked. First, the very great influence of life in modifying the surface of the earth, so great as in many cases to be comparable to the effects of far ruder changes. Thus we have rocks composed entirely of organic remains, and climate changed by the presence or absence of forests. Secondly, although we have restricted our cosmos to the earth in space, and to the history of life upon it in time, there is no necessity to maintain the restriction. For we must suppose that organic action will always take place when the elements which are capable of it are present under the requisite physical conditions of temperature, light, and environment. It is therefore in the last degree improbable that it is confined to our own planet.

In this principle, therefore, we must recognise the mother of life, and especially of human life; powerful enough to subdue the elements and yet always working gently against them; biding her time in the whole expanse of heaven, to make the highest cosmos out of inorganic chaos; the actor, not of all the actions of living things, but only of the good actions; for a bad action is one by which the organism tends to become less organic, and acts for the time as if inorganic.

To this mother of life, personifying herself in the good works of humanity, it seems to me that we may fitly address a splendid hymn of Mr. Swinburne's, whose meaning if I mar or mistake by such application, let the innocency of my intent plead for pardon with one into whose work it is impossible to read more or more fruitful meaning than he meant in the writing of it:—

> Mother of man's time-travelling generations,
>   Breath of his nostrils, heart-blood of his heart,
> God above all Gods worshipped of all nations,
>   Light above light, law beyond law, thou art.
>
> Thy face is as a sword smiting in sunder
>   Shadows and chains and dreams and iron things;
> The sea is dumb before thy face, the thunder
>   Silent, the skies are narrower than thy wings.
>
>         .     .     .     .     .     .
>
> All old grey histories hiding thy clear features,
>   O secret spirit and sovereign, all men's tales,
> Creeds woven of men thy children and thy creatures,
>   They have woven for vestures of thee and for veils.
>
> Thine hands, without election or exemption,
>   Feed all men fainting from false peace or strife,
> O thou, the resurrection and redemption,
>   The godhead and the manhood and the life.[1]

Still our conception is very vague. We have only said '*good action* has created the life of the world, and in so doing has personified itself in

[1] 'Mater Triumphalis', *Songs Before Sunrise*.

humanity; so we call it the mother of life and of man'. And we have defined good action to be that which makes an organism more organic. We want, therefore, to know something more definite about the kind of action which makes an organism more organic.

This we can find, and of a nature suitable for cosmic emotion, by paying attention to the difference between molar and molecular movement. We know that the particles even of bodies which appear to be at rest are really in a state of very rapid agitation, called molecular motion, and that heat and nerve-discharge are cases of such motion. But molar motion is the movement in one piece of masses large enough to be seen.

Now the peculiarity of living matter is that it is capable of combining together molecular motions, which are invisible, into molar motions, which can be seen. It therefore appears to have the property of moving spontaneously, without help from anything else. So it can for a little while; but it is then obliged to take molecular motion from the surrounding things if it is to go on moving. So that there is no real spontaneity in the case. But still its changes of shape, due to aggregation of molecular motion, may fairly be called *action from within*, because the energy of the motion is supplied by the substance itself, and not by any external thing. If we suppose the same thing to be true for a complex organism that is true for a small speck of living matter—that those changes in it which are directly initiated by the living part of the organism are the ones which distinguish it from inorganic things, and tend to make it more organic—then we shall have here the nearer definition of organic action. It is probable that the definition as I have stated it is rather *too* precise—that the nature of the action, in fact, varies with circumstances in the complex organism, but is always nearly as stated.

Let us consider what this means from the internal point of view. When I act from within, or in an organic manner, what seems to me to happen? I must appear to be perfectly free, for, if I did not, I must be made to act by something outside of me. 'We think ourselves free,' says Spinoza, 'being conscious of our actions, and not of the causes which determine them.' But we have seen reason to believe that although there is no physical spontaneity, yet the energy for such an action is taken out of myself—*i.e.* out of the living matter in my body. As, therefore, the immediate origin of my action is in myself, I really am free in the only useful sense of the word. 'Freedom is such a property of the will,' says Kant, 'as enables living agents to originate events independently of foreign determining causes.'

The character of an organic action, then, is freedom—that is to say, *action from within*. The action which has its immediate antecedents within the organism has a tendency, in so far as it alters the organism, to make it more organic, or to raise it in the scale. The action which is determined by foreign causes is one in regard to which the organism acts as if inorganic, and in so far as the action tends to alter it, it tends also to lower it in the scale.

It is important to remember that only a part of the body of a complex organism is actually living matter. This living matter carries about a quantity of formed or dead stuff; as Epictetus says, ψυχάριον εἶ βάσταζον νεκρόν—'a little soul for a little bears up this corpse which is man'.[1] Only actions originating in the living part of the organism are to be regarded as actions from within; the dead part is for our purposes a portion of the external world. And so, from the internal point of view, there are rudiments and survivals in the mind which are to be excluded from that *me*, whose free action tends to progress; that *baneful strife which lurketh inborn in us* is the foe of freedom—*this let not a man stir up, but avoid and flee.*

The way in which freedom, or action from within, has effected the evolution of organisms, is clearly brought out by the theory of Natural Selection. For the improvement of a breed depends upon the selection of *sports*—that is to say, of modifications due to the overflowing energy of the organism, which happen to be useful to it in its special circumstances. Modifications may take place by direct pressure of external circumstances; the whole organism or any organ may lose in size and strength from failure of the proper food, but such modifications are in the downward, not in the upward, direction. *Indirectly* external circumstances may of course produce upward changes; thus the drying up of axolotl ponds caused the survival of individuals which had 'sported' in the direction of lungs. But the *immediate* cause of change in the direction of higher organization is always the internal and quasi-spontaneous action of the organism.

> Freedom we call it, for holier
> Name of the soul's there is none;
> Surelier it labours, if slowlier,
> Than the metres of star or of sun;

[1] The Greek is quoted in a footnote to the 'Hymn to Proserpine', *Poems and Ballads*. 'I am aware of the difficulties which beset Dr. Beale's theory of germinal matter, as they are stated by Mr. G. H. Lewes; but however hard it may be to decide what *is* living matter, and what is formed stuff, the distinction appears to me to be a real one, to the extent, at least, of the use here made of it' (Clifford's note).

Slowlier than life into breath,
Surelier than time into death,
It moves till its labour be done.[1]

The highest of organisms is the social organism. To Mr. Herbert Spencer, who has done so much for the whole doctrine of evolution and for all that is connected with it, we owe the first clear and rational statement of the analogy between the individual and the social organism, which, indeed, is more than an analogy, being in many respects a true identity of process, and structure, and function. Our main business is with one property which the social organism has in common with the individual—namely, this, that it aggregates molecular motions into molar ones. The molecules of a social organism are the individual men, women, and children of which it is composed. By means of it, actions which, as individual, are insignificant, are massed together into the important movements of a society. Co-operation, or *band-work*, is the life of it. Thus it is able to 'originate events independently of foreign determining causes', or to act with freedom.

Freedom in a society, then, is a very different thing from anarchy. It is the organic action of the society as such; the union of its elements in a common work. As Mr. Spencer points out, society does not resemble those organisms which are so highly centralized that the unity of the whole is the important thing, and every part must die if separated from the rest, but rather those which will bear separation and reunion, because, although there is a certain union and organization of the parts in regard to one another, yet the far more important fact is the life of the parts separately. The true health of society depends upon the communes, the villages and townships, infinitely more than on the form and pageantry of an imperial government. If in them there is band-work, union for a common effort, converse in the working out of a common thought, then the Republic *is*, and needs not to be made with hands, though Caesar have his guns in every citadel. None the less it will be part of the business of the Republic, as she grows in strength, to remove him. So long as two or three are gathered together, freedom is there in the midst of them, and it is not until society is utterly divided into its elements that she departs:—

Courage yet! my brother or my sister!
Keep on! Liberty is to be subserv'd, whatever occurs;
That is nothing, that is quell'd by one or two failures, or any number of failures,
Or by the indifference or ingratitude of the people, or by any unfaithfulness,

[1] 'To Walt Whitman in America', *Songs before Sunrise*.

174

Or the show of the tushes of power, soldiers, cannon, penal statutes.
Revolt! and still revolt! revolt!
What we believe in waits latent forever through all the continents, and all the
    islands and archipelagos of the sea;
What we believe in invites no one, promises nothing, sits in calmness and light,
    is positive and composed, knows no discouragement,
Waiting patiently, waiting its time.

.   .   .   .   .   .   .   .   .   .

When liberty goes out of a place, it is not the first to go, nor the second or third
    to go,
It waits for all the rest to go—it is the last.
When there are no more memories of heroes and martyrs,
And when all life, and all the souls of men and women are discharged from any
    part of the earth,
Then only shall liberty, or the idea of liberty, be discharged from that part of
    the earth,
And the infidel come into full possession.[1]

So far our cosmic conception is external. Starting with organic action,
as that which has effected the evolution of life and all the works of life,
we have found it to have the character of freedom, or action from
within, and in the case of the social organism we have seen that freedom
is the organic action of society as such, which is what we call the
Republic. The Republic is the visible embodiment and personification
of freedom in its highest external type.

But the Republic is itself still further personified, in a way that leads
us back with new light to the conception of the internal cosmos. The
practice of band-work, or comradeship, the organic action of society,
has so moulded the nature of man as to create in it two specially human
faculties—the conscience and the intellect. Conscience is an instinctive
desire for those things which conduce to the welfare of society; intellect
is an apparatus for connecting sensation and action, by means of a
symbolic representation of the external world, framed in common and
for common purposes by the social intercourse of men. Conscience and
reason form an inner core in the human mind, having an origin and a
nature distinct from the merely animal passions and perceptions; they
constitute the soul or spirit of man, the universal part in every one of us.
In these are bound up, embalmed and embodied, all the struggles and
searchings of spirit of the countless generations which have made us
what we are. Action which arises out of that inner core, which is

---

[1] 'To a Foil'd European Revolutionaire', *Leaves of Grass*, Whitman.

prompted by conscience and guided by reason, is *free* in the highest sense of all; this at last is *good* in the ethical sense. And yet, when we act with this most perfect freedom, it may be said that it is not we that act, but Man that worketh in us. He whose life is habitually governed by reason and conscience is the free and wise man of the philosophers of all ages. The highest freedom, then, is identical with the Spirit of Man—

> The earth-god Freedom, the lonely
>    Face lightening, the footprint unshod,
> Not as one man crucified only
>    Nor scourged with but one life's rod;
> The soul that is substance of nations,
> Reincarnate with fresh generations;
>    The great god Man, which is God.[1]

The social organism itself is but a part of the universal cosmos, and like all else is subject to the uniformity of nature. The production and distribution of wealth, the growth and effect of administrative machinery, the education of the race, these are cases of general laws which constitute the science of sociology. The discovery of exact laws has only one purpose—the guidance of conduct by means of them. The laws of political economy are as rigid as those of gravitation; wealth distributes itself as surely as water finds its level. But the use we have to make of the laws of gravitation is not to sit down and cry 'Kismet!' to the flowing stream, but to construct irrigation works. And the use which the Republic must make of the laws of sociology is to rationally organise society for the training of the best citizens. Much patient practice of comradeship is necessary before society will be qualified to organise itself in accordance with reason. But those who can read the signs of the times read in them that the kingdom of Man is at hand.

[1] 'To Walt Whitman in America', *Songs before Sunrise*.

# POEMS AND BALLADS:
# SECOND SERIES

## 1878

## 23. Theodore Watts, *Athenaeum*

### 6 July 1878, 7–9

According to his biographers, Theodore Watts (later Watts-Dunton), wrote the unsigned reviews of Swinburne's books in the *Athenaeum* from 1877 to 1899. In what he says of the poet's use of alliteration and his 'intellectual strength' the reviewer is aiming at current critical prepossessions.

This long expected volume will not disappoint the admirers of Mr. Swinburne's poetry. At least, it will not disappoint those who had the insight to perceive what a vast advance upon *Poems and Ballads* was the *Songs before Sunrise*. In this volume, as in that, there is the same passion for anapaestic and dactyllic rhythms, and the same mastery over them; there is the same lofty aspiration and belief in the high destiny of man, and there is the same equal balance of those forces which we call 'intellectual' against those forces which we ascribe to genius. For, never was there a greater mistake than the common one of supposing that, because Mr. Swinburne is not a concise writer, therefore his intellect lags behind his genius. 'Hertha', the 'Hymn of Man', and the more daring portions of *Atalanta* showed, to any truly critical mind, that intellectually Mr. Swinburne is second to almost none of his contemporaries.

It seems necessary, however, to digress a little in order to explain clearly what we mean; for the subject has hitherto been left untouched by the critics, though of some importance in poetic criticism.

It is obvious that English anapaestic and dactyllic verse must be diffuse, or it will become doggrel. The moment the poet tries to 'pack' his anapaestic or dactyllic line as he can pack his iambic line, his versification becomes rugged, harsh, pebbly; becomes so of necessity. Nor is this all: anapaestic and dactyllic verse must in English be alliterative, or the same pebbly effect begins to be felt. The anapaestic line is so full of syllables that, in a language where the consonants dominate the vowels (as they do in English), these syllables grate against each other, unless their corners are artfully bevelled by one of the only two smoothing effects at the command of the English versifier—alliteration or an obtrusive use of liquids. For instance, in an iambic line, such a free use of both these effects, liquefication and alliteration, as occurs in Mr. Swinburne's 'Lisp of leaves and ripple of rain' would be intolerable; yet, as an anapaestic line, it is one of the finest in the language.

This makes Mr. Swinburne's poetry appear diffuse; and working so much in anapaestic and dactyllic movements as he does, it explains, though it does not altogether justify, his undoubtedly excessive use of alliteration in iambic or trochaic movements, where this bevelling is not so indispensable. When the 'divine guide' has really strongly seized a lyrist he must—it might almost be said—write in anapaests or dactyls. And, as a lyrist, he must be musical—whatever he sacrifices for that end. Now, with the exception of Shelley (for Coleridge's fervour is all imaginative—never personal), Mr. Swinburne is the first purely lyrical genius—judging from his work—in the English language. We say, 'judging from his work'; for, what Collins would have been had he succeeded Shelley it would be as presumptuous to say as it would be presumptuous to say what Marlowe would have been in an age not devoted to drama, and what Crashaw would have been in an age not corrupted by euphuism.

So dominant with Mr. Swinburne is the delight of lyrical movement, that even in iambics the anapaestic dance *will* come up, as we see in such lines as this, in 'In the Bay',—

> For surely, brother and master and lord and king,—

(where, note in passing, that, at once, he passes into the anapaestic liquefication), and, as is still more obvious in the prologue to 'Tristram and Iseult' (published in an annual called *Pleasure*), and in the 'Sailing of the Swallow' (published in the *Gentleman's Magazine*), where the anapaestic undulations impart a billowy movement to the lines, which sometimes suggests Homeric hexameters, and sometimes suggests the leap of M. Hugo's verse in the second series of *La Légende des Siècles*.

And, again, the blank verse of *Bothwell* is far more lyrical than Flet-cher's own.

In testing the amount of intellectual vigour behind the work of any artist, the first thing to ask is, What are the conditions under which an artist works? Having done this in regard to Mr. Swinburne's verse, we, for our part, have come to a conclusion which no amount of popular criticism would drive us from—that, in intellectual agility, and even in intellectual strength, Mr. Swinburne has, among contemporary English poets, no superior, unless it be Mr. Browning.

What we have said upon the relation between the 'dancing move-ments' and diffuseness is illustrated very forcibly by the opening poem of this volume, 'The Last Oracle', where the poet's intellectual strength —while wasting, so to speak, in its struggle with form, as Laocoön's strength wasted in his struggle with the serpent—is as unmistakably apparent as though it were not being wasted at all; perhaps more so.

In iambic movement the finest poem in the volume is the one on Marlowe, called 'In the Bay', and here there is, as was to be expected, much more 'packing'. This is sure to be more admired than 'The Last Oracle', but it is not so rare and noticeable a work. The conclusion is especially fine:—

[quotes the last three stanzas of 'In the Bay']

That Mr. Swinburne could, before he surrendered himself entirely up to the witchery of anapaests, be concise enough, is rendered apparent by his earliest iambic writing, and especially by the early translations of Villon, which form an interesting feature of this volume. Mr. Swin-burne has given us but very little translation; and, unless we had seen these renderings of Villon, we should have said that his muse was not well adapted to translation; and especially it might have been supposed that it was but ill-adapted to rendering Villon—the most concise of all French poets, and whose temperament was the very opposite of Mr. Swinburne's. For, widely different as are Horace, Dante, Villon, and Burns, these four must always in true criticism be classed together and by themselves in regard to their instinctive method of using language as an artistic medium. More than any others, they realized in poetry the power of verbal parsimony, and to this they made everything yield. As an ounce of duck-shot is to a quarter of an ounce bullet, so is a line by any one of these to any other poet's line in its power of 'striking home'.

These translations, however, are marvellous, both for vitality and for closeness. 'The Complaint of the Fair Armouress' is, in our judgment, quite as notable a triumph of translation as Mr. D. G. Rossetti's 'Ballad of Dead Ladies'. It happens, however, that those lines in the translation, which more than all others showed the perfection of the translator's work, he has—in his determination not to mar the beauty of the poem by reproducing the mediaeval coarseness of the original—omitted; replacing them by asterisks.

There is also a translation of one of Victor Hugo's beautiful poems upon children. To translate anything of Victor Hugo's must be a labour of love with Mr. Swinburne, but to render a poem upon children must be a specially grateful task. If a critic should wish to say the gracious thing to Mr. Swinburne, it would be to compare him to Victor Hugo. Such splendid praise has never, perhaps, been lavished by one living poet upon another as the fiery English lyrist has lavished upon the great Frenchman, who is at once fiery lyrist, fiery dramatist, and fiery novelist. 'My master', 'the greatest living poet',—such are the phrases Mr. Swinburne always adopts when speaking of Victor Hugo, —to whom *Bothwell* was dedicated,—to whom we may expect to find some allusion on almost every page of his brilliant and too rapturous prose.

No wonder, then, if, in the volume before us, besides this translation, we come upon three poems addressed to M. Hugo. And it may be said that Mr. Swinburne's language,—which, since the chastening labour that produced *Bothwell* is, though undoubtedly needing compression, nearer, at its best, to the great style than any other contemporary Englishman's—is never so lofty and never so Titanic as when he is addressing the Gallic Titan. Readers of the *Athenaeum* are familiar with the sonnet beginning:—

> He had no children, who for love of men,
>   Being God, endured of Gods such things as thou,
> Father; nor on his thunder-beaten brow
> Fell such a woe as bows thine head again.

Another sonnet will be new to them:—

[quotes 'Victor Hugo in 1877']

And here, again, we come upon a subject so tempting and so suggestive that it is impossible to pass it by. Indeed, in discussing it we do not digress; but, on the contrary, probe to the very heart's core of Hugo's poetic work as well as of Mr. Swinburne's. Victor Hugo, if more reticent in lavishing praise upon the young bard, is certainly in no way chary in expressing his admiration of him. He speaks of him as 'the great English poet'; and, at the Voltaire gathering the other day, he sent an invitation to him to come and sit by his side. Yet, surely, to a superficial inquiry, nothing can be more paradoxical and anomalous than such a duo of 'mutual admiration' between men, one of whom is the English exponent of the doctrine of *l'art pour l'art*, the other the most notable example of rebellion against that doctrine—the most notable instance of a first-class imagination wing-clipped and strangled by ethics and teleology that European literature has shown since Spenser.

Yet, the moment the inquiry is pursued beyond the surface the anomaly vanishes. It is perceived that the kinship between these two lies much deeper than those superficial similarities, which are obvious to all. It is perceived that, over and above such familiar and obvious points of similarity between them as power of the 'long stroke'—an artless belief in the simplest and most familiar rhythmical effects quite inconceivable in men with such a mastery over those highest effects which, being above 'self-conscious' art, can only come to the inspired singer—such again as a lawless, reckless 'unpacking of the heart', which is mostly poetry, but sometimes rhetoric—it is perceived that, besides these and many other points of superficial similarity, there is this, that the apostle of the doctrine of *l'art pour l'art* is no true apostle at all, but is just as ethical and just as teleological as M. Hugo himself. They are both 'God-intoxicated men' as much as ever Spinoza was.

That this should not have been seen on the publication of the first series of *Poems and Ballads* is another proof of the condition into which English criticism has sunk—another evidence of that separation between philosophy and *belles lettres* which, since the dominance of the Baconian experimental philosophy in this country, has been widening every year.

This is the truth then; as inevitably as the needle sets to the pole so do all Mr. Swinburne's imaginings and cogitations set towards teleology and the 'painful riddle of the earth'.[1] It obtrudes itself everywhere. Even Sappho, in the very height of her unholy passion, forgets, in Mr. Swinburne's hands, all about Anactoria, and begins to challenge the inscrutable ways of God. In the 'Sailing of the Swallow' Tristram stops in his love-passages to discourse of pantheism and evolution. And 'Dolores'—what is that but a wail from the bed of vice?—a Jeremiad on the misery of pleasure? In Mr. Swinburne's poetry teleology and ethical

---

[1] Cf. Tennyson's 'Palace of Art', l. 213: 'the riddle of the painful earth'.

preaching are positively in the way. They are almost more in the way than in M. Hugo's. The latter does grant his readers some respite. Mr. Swinburne, like Shelley, grants almost none. From the perpetual ethics of his poetry we turn for relief to the 'sweet paganism' of Keats, of Mr. Tennyson, and the author of the *Epic of Hades*.[1]

What, then, is the difference between these two—between M. Hugo and Mr. Swinburne? Simply this, that—while both are in revolt against 'the things that be'—M. Hugo's revolt is against society—against the conventions of man; whereas Mr. Swinburne's revolt—springing as it does from a more subtle, though perhaps less brilliant, intelligence—is against God as a concept of man's. M. Hugo, agonized at the spectacle of *Les Misérables*, arraigns society, saying—'All this misery has come because you, Society, have departed from the laws of a benevolent God.' Mr. Swinburne—passing by society as being unworthy of castigation,—says, 'All this misery comes from God, inasmuch as He permits it; for if He is omniscient and omnipotent—as a God must be to deserve that name,—His foreseeing is foredooming.' M. Hugo's sophism lies in ignoring the fact that society is a shadow—is simply a convenient *word*,—used to express an aggregate of individuals struggling from primitive darkness towards the light. Mr. Swinburne's sophism lies in not sufficiently realizing the fact that what he abuses as 'God' is not God at all, but a certain little pulsation of a certain little mass of 'animal pap'—a man's brain. In both cases, the abuse, it may be said, does no great harm; still, as it results in a waste of force in the abuser, it is, perhaps, hardly worth while to indulge in it. Such points of similarity as these between Victor Hugo and Mr. Swinburne are fundamental; points which place them quite outside the domain of pure art, which knows nothing of society and nothing of God.

Yet there is this great difference, that, whereas the passage of a decade over Mr. Swinburne's head is attended with the usual results of such a passage over the heads of all poets and all men—the passage of five decades over M. Victor Hugo's head has worked no effect whatsoever upon him. In this, the French poet stands absolutely alone, not only in French literature, but perhaps in all literature. With other men the law of growth is seen working as inevitably as, in the physical world, it works in the animal and vegetable organism. Not that time itself is a factor, or anything more than a mere condition for factors to work in; but over the head of whatsoever organism time may pass—be it poet or be it potato—there is that within it which grows: in the one

[1] A poem (1876–77) by Lewis Morris.

case, it advances with a certain march from sprout to leaf, from leaf right on to seed; in the other it advances from blind and lawless power—perhaps from blind and lawless rebellion—to that lawfulness and self-governance—that 'philosophic mind' which, as Wordsworth tells us, 'the years' should bring.

In the physical world there is no exception to this rule; in the mental world there is none save in one case—that of Victor Hugo. If he was barbaric when, years ago, he threw himself into the Romantic movement, how much more barbaric is he now! If he was as empty of wisdom, as devoid of the 'sweet amber light of philosophy' as Pierre Vidal, then *Le Pape*, and his speech about Voltaire have just shown us that he is at this moment more empty of wisdom than ever—safer than ever from that demon of 'philosophy' which Keats tells us would 'clip an angel's wing'. The rebel against society is a brilliant boy of eighty years; let us see what has become of the rebel against 'God'.

In every powerful mind there must be more or less of the Titanic temper. Plunged, it knows not whence nor why, in the midst of this long πόλεμος πατὴρ πάντων[1]—confronted as it is with the enormities of Nature's apparent 'cruelty',—deafened as it is by the 'sobs and cries of suffering man'—beaten pitilessly back, with bruised and bleeding wings, whenever it tries to pass the bars—every great and vigorous young soul must raise the standard of revolt against that *Something* that might have given us a Cosmos and gives us apparently a chaos. But as time goes on the poet's vision grows wider; he begins to see that, even if Nature is indeed as wicked as she seems to him, our only defence against that wickedness is to band together against the common enemy, and that, in order to band together, we must be good.

Having arrived at this,—that, notwithstanding all superficial contradictions, the universe, without a preponderance of good over evil, could not work at all; that in the deepest sense, goodness and absolute life are indeed synonymous terms; and that if this is not fully shown here, it is because it must be fully shown elsewhere;—that not to come to this conclusion is to prove oneself a shallow thinker—a bad logician, —having arrived at this—as a first-rate intelligence always must—the young poet begins to see that if blasphemy is not quite so wicked as he had hoped, it is more foolish and meaningless than he now likes to remember. He begins to see that, although the real God, 'of whose im-

---

[1] 'Strife the father of all.' Apparently adapted from Heraclitus' Fragment 53, where war is described as father and king of all, a god who is 'both creator and created' (see G. S. Kirk, *Heraclitus: The Cosmic Fragments* [1954], 245 ff.).

mensity the universe is but the superficial film', cannot be offended in this way, any more than the man who, with a blade of grass, lifts an ant from destruction, can be offended by the raising of angry antennae on the part of the little creature to whom the blade seems a warlike spear, —yet blasphemy is an offence against man. He learns, moreover, that, though our passions are part of us, they must be dominated by 'the lordship of the soul', or they will certainly tear us to death; and that to fire these passions unduly is again to wrong man. He learns, in short, that though the earth is not heaven, it is nevertheless crusted with gems or stones according to the eyes that see and the feet that walk, and that there is something, at least, that will really stand the *cui bono* test—the affections.

M. Hugo always felt this; and morally there was no need of growth, whatever need there was of philosophical expansion. Mr. Swinburne, with much finer philosophical acuteness than M. Hugo, did need it, and such a growth is so apparent in him that we consider the second series of *Poems and Ballads* the most striking book—apart from its pricelessness as a body of poetry—that has appeared in England for some years. It is full of such tender writing as this upon the death of Barry Cornwall:—

[quotes 'In Memory of Barry Cornwall']

*Erechtheus* lifted him from the rank of fine poets to the rank of great poets. And, notwithstanding the violence of some of the political sonnets, this volume is in no way unworthy of the position he has taken. Moreover, it displays a love of nature such as was not seen in his previous books.

# 24. Maupassant on Swinburne

## 1891

Maupassant happened to be near at hand in October 1868 when Swinburne narrowly escaped drowning, being swept out to sea by 'treacherous undercurrents' while swimming at Étretat, on the Norman coast. The incident led to Maupassant's becoming acquainted with the English poet. His personal impressions, possibly somewhat coloured after a considerable lapse of time, helped to shape and to reflect the image of Swinburne in France (see Introduction, the last part of section III). The following extract includes everything of special interest, the part omitted being an insignificant factual statement. The translation was made especially for this book by Violette Lang (Mrs. Cecil Y. Lang).

Guy de Maupassant's 'Notes on Algernon Charles Swinburne' introducing Gabriel Mourey's translation of *Poems and Ballads* into French prose (Paris, 1891), v–x.

It is very difficult to speak to the French public about an English poet like Mr. Swinburne, when, as in my case, one does not know his language. I once met this poet, whose strange countenance is most interesting, extremely disturbing even, for he made on me the impression of a kind of Edgar Allan Poe, idealized and sensualized, of a writer with a soul more exalted, more depraved, more in love with what is strange and monstrous, more curious—groping after and suggesting subtle, unnatural refinements of life and thought—than the soul of the American poet, itself suggestive merely of phantoms and terrors. The impression I have retained from my several meetings with him is perhaps of the most extravagantly artistic person alive in the world today.

He is at once an artist in the ancient mode and in the modern. A poet adept in lyric and epic, in love with rhythm, poet of the *epos*,[1]

[1] Since Maupassant uses both '*épique*' and '*épopée*', in the latter instance he may well have had in mind the kind of material of which epics are made. In English *epic* and *epopee*

filled with the spirit of Greece, he is also one of the most refined and subtle of those explorers of nuance and sensation who constitute the new schools of poetry.

This is how I met him: I was very young, spending the summer on the beach at Étretat. One morning about ten o'clock some sailors came up screaming that a swimmer was drowning under the Porte d'Amont. They got a boat, and I accompanied them. The swimmer, unaware of the terrible tidal current of this archway, had been swept away, and then had been rescued by a fishing boat behind this Porte, usually called the Petite Porte.

I learned in the evening of the same day that the reckless bather was an English poet, Mr. Algernon Charles Swinburne, who was staying for some days with another Englishman with whom I had sometimes chatted on the pebbly beach, Mr. Powell, the owner of a small cottage that he had christened Chaumière Dolmancé.

This Mr. Powell astonished the countryside by an extremely solitary life that seemed bizarre to bourgeois eyes and to sailors little accustomed to English fantasies and eccentricities. Hearing that I had tried, too late, to bring aid to his friend, he sent me an invitation to lunch for the following day. The two men were waiting for me in a pretty garden, shady and cool, at the back of a low Norman house, built of stone and roofed with thatch. They were both short of stature, Mr. Powell fat, Mr. Swinburne thin—thin and startling at first glance—a sort of fantastic apparition. It was then that, seeing him for the first time, I thought of Edgar Poe. His forehead was very high under his long hair, and his face became gradually narrower towards a slight chin shadowed with a meagre tuft of beard. A very light moustache hovered over remarkably thin, tight lips, and his neck, which seemed to have no end, joined that head—alive with clear, fixed, penetrating eyes—to a torso without shoulders, the top of his chest seeming hardly wider than his forehead. This virtually supernatural character was shaken all over by nervous spasms. He was very cordial and very hospitable; and the extraordinary charm of his intelligence captivated me at once.

During the whole of lunch we talked about art, literature, humanity, and the opinions of those two friends cast over everything a kind of disturbing, macabre light, for they had a way of seeing and understanding that made them seem like diseased visionaries, drunken with a poetry magical and perverse.

---

are synonymous, whereas *epos* can mean 'a series of events of special dignity or magnitude'. (Strictly speaking, of course, Swinburne did not write an epic.)

Some bones were lying around on the tables, among them a flayed hand—that of a parricide, it seems—whose dried-up blood and muscles still clung to the white bones. They showed me fantastic sketches and photographs, a whole store of incredible bibelots. A pet monkey was sneaking about, grimacing and inconceivably droll, full of tricks and pranks, not just a monkey but a mute friend of his masters, the treacherous enemy of newcomers.

As I was told later, the monkey was hanged by one of the Englishmen's young servants (he resented the animal). The dead monkey was buried in the middle of the lawn, in front of the door of the cottage. To mark his grave they ordered an enormous block of granite, engraved simply with the name 'Nip', on top of which, as in oriental cemeteries, was placed a birdbath.

Several days later I was again invited by these eccentric Englishmen to lunch on spitted monkey, specially ordered at Le Havre from a dealer in exotic animals. The very odour of this roast, when I entered the house, made me apprehensive, and the horrible taste of the animal rid me, once and for all, of any desire to try such a dish again.

But Messrs. Powell and Swinburne were delightful in their fantasy and lyricism. They recounted Icelandic legends, translated by Mr. Powell, of a gripping and terrible novelty. Swinburne spoke of Victor Hugo with boundless enthusiasm.

I never saw him again. Another foreign writer, a very great one, the most intellectual man I have ever met—by which I mean gifted with the most clear-sighted intuitions about humanity, the most comprehensive philosophy, the most independent opinions on every subject —the Russian novelist, Ivan Turgenev, often translated Swinburne's poems for me, with keen admiration. He criticized them also. But every artist has his faults. It is enough to be an artist. . . .

# 25. F. W. H. Myers on Swinburne's *Weltanschauung*

## 1893

Myers (1843-1901), poet, essayist, and special student of psychic phenomena, shared with Swinburne classical attainments and especially an enthusiasm for Sappho. His essay on the modern poets was notable (in its time) for being a serious estimate of Swinburne's thought.

From 'Modern Poets and the Meaning of Life', *Nineteenth Century*, January 1893, xxxiii, 93-111 (93-100, for the part dealing with Swinburne); reprinted in *Science and a Future Life with Other Essays* (1893).

> But earth's dark forehead flings athwart the heavens
> Her shadow crown'd with stars—and yonder—out
> To northward—some that never set, but pass
> From sight and night to lose themselves in day.
> I hate the black negation of the bier,
> And wish the dead, as happier than ourselves
> And higher, having climb'd one step beyond
> Our village miseries, might be borne in white
> To burial or to burning, hymn'd from hence
> With songs in praise of death, and crown'd with flowers!
>
> TENNYSON.

Wordsworth, Darwin, Tennyson—the three greatest Englishmen of our century—all now have passed away. *Greatest* I call them, not for personal faculties alone, which are hard to compare as between the many men of genius whom our age has produced, but because it seems to me that these men's faculties have achieved most in the most important directions, in the intuition, discovery, promulgation of fundamental cosmic law. And by cosmic law I here mean, not such rules merely as may hold good universally for matter, or motion, or abstract quantities, but principles which, even if as yet but dimly and narrowly understood, may conceivably be valid for the whole universe, on all possible planes of being. Of such principles, we have as yet but three— Uniformity, Conservation, Evolution. We believe that all operations in the universe obey unchanging law. We believe that all matter and all energy known to us are indestructible. And we believe that all physical and vital operation in the universe is at present following certain obscurely discernible streams of tendency, whose source and goal are alike unknown. The first of these laws lies at the root of all Science; the second at the root of Physics; the third at the root of Biology.

It is not, of course, with any one of these three laws that the work of Wordsworth or of Tennyson is connected. Of a *fourth* cosmic principle, to which, as I hold, they have helped to introduce mankind, there will be mention later on. Meantime my purpose is briefly to review the work of Tennyson and of our two great poets who survive—Browning I must omit for want of space—in reference to its most serious or philosophical import.[1] And such criticism, if it is to have any real value, must needs start thus *ab ovo*,[2] and must take account of the speculative or ethical standpoint from which each poet writes. Nor can such standpoint be any longer indicated by words which merely express inclusion or non-inclusion among the adherents of any definite form of faith.

For the change which is coming over our questionings of the universe affects the poet not less intimately, if less directly, than it affects the *savant* or the philosopher. The conceptions which he breathes in from the intellectual atmosphere are no longer traditional, but scientific; no longer catastrophic, but evolutionary; no longer planetary, but cosmical. He may still feel that certain facts in human history have had a unique importance for man. But he must recognise that in order to understand those very facts we must endeavour to understand the universe around us. That universe cannot have changed appreciably in two thousand years. Taking it as a whole, what was going on then must be going on now.

Yet if the poet endeavours to nourish himself on cosmical laws, he soon finds how ill-suited they are for the sustenance of the human heart. They are the offspring, not of philosophical musing or generous emotion, but of observations, experiments, computations, conducted

---

[1] I may perhaps refer the reader to a paper on 'Tennyson as Prophet' in this Review for March 1889. I have reason to believe that the line there taken, based in part upon his own conversation, was not unacceptable to Lord Tennyson. [Myers's note.]

[2] 'From the egg' (or beginning).

with an entire absence of ethical preoccupation. Imperfectly understood in themselves, they are yet more difficult to translate into formulae which will answer the questions that we most wish to ask. Does the law of the uniformity of Nature cancel all that has been held as miracle or revelation, or may so-called miracle and revelation themselves form a stable element in the succession of cause and effect? Does the law of the conservation of energy condemn man's consciousness to extinction when the measurable energies which build up his chemical texture pass back into the inorganic world, or may his conscious life be a form of activity which, just because it is not included in our cycle of mutually transformable energies, is itself in its own proper form as imperishable as they? What does evolution mean, when we get below the obviously superficial terms in which we now describe it as progressing from the simple to the complex, from the homogeneous to the heterogeneous, and the like? Does it apply to the moral, or only to the material world? In its application to the material world, is it in any sense continuous and eternal, or is it always temporary and truncated, as must needs be the case with our planetary and solar evolution, and may conceivably be the case with all the stellar evolution which we perceive or infer? And if it applies to the moral future of mankind, is it truncated there also, as must be the case if man exists only while he can inhabit the surface of a planet which, at the best, is only warranted habitable for a few million years, or has it the continuity and eternity for which man's personal immortality alone would offer scope?

And, broadly, if the alien and impersonal character of all these laws convinces us that the universe is in no way constructed to meet the moral needs of man, can we then discern its purport?—is any effort possible to us, or must we drift helplessly with the cosmic stream?

It so happens that the respective attitudes of Mr. Swinburne and Mr. William Morris towards these fundamental problems are specially interesting in two opposite ways—with Mr. Swinburne, from his extraordinary intellectual detachment from the ordinary emotions of humanity; with Mr. Morris, from the intensity with which he personally shares those emotions.

Mr. Swinburne's case is a very unusual one. His temperament, it need hardly be said, is one of exceptional keenness and fervour; but he has himself explained that this fervour is elicited mainly by poetry and by the aspects of Nature. The name which the poet assumes in his principal autobiographical poem, 'Thalassius', or Child of the Sea—like the symbolical parentage of the Sun-God which he assigns to

himself—is significant of a nature for which these elemental relationships rank as primary passions, and which finds its intensest stimulus
in flooding light and stormy ocean. Not, of course, that a temperament
so vivid has wholly escaped strong personal feeling. Thalassius describes
both a sad experience of love, and also a period of reckless wandering,
'by many a vine-leafed, many a rose-hung road'. But from this wandering he feels, in his allegory, the Sea, his mother, recall him,

> And charm him from his own soul's separate sense
> With infinite and invasive influence,
> That made strength sweet in him and sweetness strong,
> Being now no more a singer, but a song.

To no poet, perhaps, was this last line ever more justly applicable. The
idea is further developed in a passage from 'On the Cliffs', where the
poet addresses the nightingale—in whom also the intensity and volume
of song seem to transcend the actual personal emotion:—

> We were not marked for sorrow, thou and I,
> For joy nor sorrow, sister, were we made,
> To take delight and grief to live or die,
> Assuaged by pleasures and by pains affrayed,
> That melt men's hearts or alter; we retain
> A memory mastering pleasure and all pain,
> A spirit within the sense of ear and eye,
> A soul behind the soul, that seeks and sings,
> And makes our life move only with its wings.

The essential isolation—the view of life as from without—which
follows on this character, is described in 'Thalassius':—[1]

> From no loved lips and on no loving breast
> Have I sought ever for such gifts as bring
> Comfort, to stay the secret soul to sleep,
> The joys, the loves, the labours, whence men reap
> Rathe fruit of hopes and fears,
> I have made not mine; the best of all my days
> Have been as those fair fruitless summer strays,—
> Those waterwaifs which but the sea-wind steers,—
> Glad flakes of foam and flowers on footless ways
> Which take the wind in season and the sun,
> And when the wind wills is their season done.

One marked element of the poet's youthful training has not yet

[1] An oversight for 'On the Cliffs'.

been mentioned. This was the influence of Walter Savage Landor—an influence pointing mainly towards the worship of Liberty. And it is well for the world that this early bias was implanted, and that in after years the last of 'the world's saviours'—the representative, for poetry even more than for history, of the last great struggle where all chivalrous sympathies could range themselves undoubtingly on one side—should have received a crown of song such as had scarcely before been laid at the feet of any living hero. But since Mazzini's work was done, there has been no struggle which has called forth the poet's sympathy with equal clearness. 'Republic' was a word with which he was wont to conjure; but we have just seen one of the three largest empires of the world turned into a republic without producing a stanza from Mr. Swinburne, or indeed any appreciable result except a fall in stocks.

The fact is that, fortunately for mankind, Liberty is becoming a matter for the statesman to define rather than for the poet to invoke; and that the denunciation of tyranny is falling into the same obsolescence which has already overtaken the glorification of personal prowess as a theme of song. The youths who bore their swords in myrtles are almost as remote from us now as the youth who dragged his enemy round the walls of Troy. We thrill to the old music; but that *motif* can be worked afresh no more. Liberty represents the next stage of progress after Peace and Plenty; when men, having attained by forceful government to security of property, are inevitably urged by the mere weight of multitude to arrange their laws in such fashion as the greatest number suppose to make for their greatest happiness. This may be done with tardy clumsiness, or with that hastier clumsiness which we term Revolution. But the obstacles to this process in civilised countries are no longer picturesque; and the poet, though not yet the statesman, has already to face that difficulty which John Stuart Mill felt in the background. When we have rectified all the anomalies which the Radical Reformer—not yet the Socialist—can discover, what are we to turn to next? For that perplexity, as he has told us, Mill found a solution which met the needs of his individual soul. It lay in the study of the poems of Wordsworth. But although this was in fact (as I shall later try to show) the best line of thought open to that philosopher, there is here no hint of fresh general occupation for the human race as a whole. Rather it suggests to us, what the subsequent history of thought has confirmed, that we are now thrown back upon fundamental problems; that before the race can make out for itself a new practical ideal—such as Plenty and Liberty were once to the many, and such as

Science is now to the few—we must somehow achieve a profound re-adjustment of our general views of the meaning of life and of the structure of the universe.

And, in fact, with this great upheaval of thought Mr. Swinburne, by the mere force of circumstances, finds himself largely concerned. It is not that his main interest is in philosophical speculation; his main interest is in literature and poetry. But he has the intelligence to catch, the voice to utter, whatever speculation is in the air around him; and assuredly some of the utterances to which his receptive but, so to say, detached and disinterested genius prompts him, surpass Lucretius himself in the singularity of their divergence from the traditional stream of human thought and song.

We are bound to face the possibility that the human race came into existence from the operation of purely physical causes, and that there may therefore be in all the universe no beings higher than ourselves; not even the remote and indifferent gods of the Lucretian heaven. By many modern minds, in whom the sense of pity for unmerited suffering and the desire for ideal justice have become passionately strong, this conception, which absolutely negatives the possibility of any pity or justice more efficacious than our own, is felt as an abiding nightmare, which seems from time to time to deepen into a terrible reality. This is the mood of mind illustrated in its extreme form in Tennyson's 'Despair'. Yet this very hypothesis has inspired one of Mr. Swinburne's most exultant poems, the magnificent 'Hymn of Man', too well known to need more than a few lines of quotation:—

In the grey beginning of years, in the twilight of things that began,
The word of the earth in the ears of the world, was it God? was it man? . . .
When her eyes new-born of the night saw yet no star out of reach;
When her maiden mouth was alight with the flame of musical speech;
When her virgin feet were set on the terrible heavenly way,
And her virginal lids were wet with the dew of the birth of the day; . . .
Did her heart rejoice, and the might of her spirit exult in her then,
Child, yet no child of the night, and motherless mother of men?

*Æneadum genetrix*,[1] so sang Lucretius in the same tone long ago, personifying, with a half-ironical enthusiasm, the blind Power which ruled his world; which had no care for human virtue or human pain:—

*Nec bene promeritis capitur, nec tangitur ira.*[2]

[1] Lucretius, *De Rerum Natura*, l. 1: 'mother of Aeneas and his descendants'.
[2] *Ibid.*, ii, 651: [The nature of divinity] 'is neither propitiated with services nor touched by wrath' (tr. W. H. D. Rouse).

Still more striking is the long passage in which Tristram of Lyonesse proudly avows, before the great spectacle of the universe, the inevitable nothingness of man.

> Ay, what of these? but, O strong sun! O sea!
> I bid not you, divine things! comfort me,
> I stand not up to match you in your sight;
> Who hath said ye have mercy toward us, ye who have might? . . .
> For if in life or death be aught of trust,
> And if some unseen just God or unjust
> Put soul into the body of natural things,
> And in Time's pauseless feet and world-wide wings,
> Some spirit of impulse and some sense of will,
> That steers them thro' the seas of good and ill,
> To some incognisable and actual end,
> Be it just or unjust, foe to man or friend,
> How should we make the stable spirit to swerve,
> How teach the strong soul of the world to serve, . . .
> The streams flow back toward whence the springs began,
> That less of thirst might sear the lips of man?

Mr. Swinburne, of course, knows as well as anybody what answer man, in all his insignificance, makes to such appeals as these. When Tristram asks:—

> Hath he such eyes as, when the shadows flee,
> The sun looks out with to salute the sea?

we answer: Nay, but he has eyes that can weep: and therefore in a moral universe no 'great blazing lump', be it sun or Sirius, could be of so much account as he.

But in these poems at any rate we have the most striking extant record of an important phase of thought. We have the strict materialistic synthesis clad in its most splendid colouring, and its most inexorable scorn of men.

Growing out of this there is another phase of thought which also Mr. Swinburne has presented with singular fire. That is the resolve that even if there be no moral purpose already in the world, man shall put it there; that even if all evolution be necessarily truncated, yet moral evolution, so long as our race lasts, there shall be; that even if man's virtue be momentary, he shall act as though it were an eternal gain. This noble theme inspires the verses called 'The Pilgrims', too familiar for long quotation here:—

—Is this so sweet that one were fain to follow?
Is this so sure where all men's hopes are hollow,
 Even this your dream, that by much tribulation
 Ye shall make whole flawed hearts and bowed necks straight?
—Nay, though our life were blind, our death were fruitless,
Not therefore were the whole world's high hopes rootless;
 But man to man, nation would turn to nation,
 And the old life live, and the old great word be great.

Fine as this is, there is a vagueness about the offered promise which leaves the wisdom of the Pilgrims' self-sacrifice open to more than one criticism. For, on the one hand, Science looks coldly on the notion of interfering with our present well-being for the advantage of distant generations—preferring to remind us that we know so little of the conditions of life even a hundred years hence that, with the best intentions, it would be no easy matter to benefit anyone more remote than our grandchildren; and, on the other hand, the gentle cynical philosophy which spoke through the mouth of M. Renan bids us note that, inasmuch as man's whole existence may very possibly be the *mauvaise plaisanterie*[1] of some irresponsible Power, it will be judicious so to act as to be able at the worst to assure ourselves that we have never been completely taken in.

Whatever, indeed, of wisdom rather than of cynicism this advice contains has been exemplified by Mr. Swinburne's career; for he has given himself whole-heartedly to an object which is neither selfish nor unworthy, and yet which is in some sense independent of what the universe may be or do. I need not say that I mean the Art of Poetry; which for himself forms an adequate issue from these deeper perplexities, although it is ill-adapted for mankind at large, since it absolutely requires the possession of genius. A world of amateur art is not in itself an ideal.

Poetic imagination leads Mr. Swinburne, as is natural, to the expression of various other moods of mind, not necessarily consistent with the mood of 'The Pilgrims'. Thus the Lucretian satisfaction at liberation from the terrors of religion forms the theme of a beautiful roundel:—

We have drunken of Lethe at last, we have eaten of lotus;
 What hurts it us here that sorrows are born and die?
We have said to the dream that caressed and the dread that smote us,
  Good-night and good-bye.

[1] 'Mischievous pleasantry.'

Or sometimes he dwells simply upon the fact that we die, and that our loves perish with us; but dwells on it somehow as with an intelligence interested in noting that fact, rather than with a heart that feels it as inmost pain.

> Or they loved their life through, and then went whither?
> And were one to the end—but what end who knows?
> Love deep as the sea as a rose must wither,
> As the rose-red seaweed that mocks the rose.
> Shall the dead take thought for the dead to love them?
> What love was ever as deep as a grave?
> They are loveless now as the grass above them,
> Or the wave.

I know not what in the easy brilliancy of these lines gives the impression that they are an imaginative description of the inhabitants of some other planet, or at least that Thalassius is as much concerned for his seaweed as for anything else. And of all Swinburne's poems, perhaps the most wonderful, with melody farthest beyond the reach of any other still living man, is that 'Garden of Proserpine', whose close represents in well-known words the deep life-weariness of men who have had enough of love. There is here far more than the Lucretian satisfaction in the thought that we shall sleep tranquilly through the hazardous future as we slept tranquilly through the raging past— *ad confligendum venientibus undique Poenis*[1]—when all the perils which menaced Rome were as nothing to us yet unborn. No, there is here a profounder renouncement of life; there is the grim suspicion which has stolen into many a heart, that we do in truth feel within us, as years go by, a mortality of spirit as well as flesh; that the 'bower of unimagined flower and tree' withers inevitably into a frozen barrenness from which no new life can spring:—

> And love, grown faint and fretful,
> With lips but half regretful
> Sighs, and with eyes forgetful
> Weeps that no loves endure.

When we turn from Swinburne to William Morris we pass into a very different emotional clime. Similar as the two poets are in thoroughness of artistic culture and in width of learning, the personal temperaments which their poems reveal are in some sense comple-

---

[1] *De Rerum Natura*, iii, 833: 'While from all quarters the Carthaginians were coming to the conflict' (tr. Rouse).

mentary. In Swinburne we have seen the vivid but detached intelligence rendering in turn with equal eloquence, and apparently with equal satisfaction, every attitude of mind which the known cosmic laws, construed strictly as against man's hopes, can be shown to justify. . . .

# 26. George Saintsbury: 'Mr. Swinburne'

## 1895

George Saintsbury (1845–1933), prolific literary critic and historian, was a journalist and editor before his appointment to the chair of English at Edinburgh University in 1895, the year in which he published *Corrected Impressions: Essays on Victorian Writers*, from which this essay comes. 'Mr. Swinburne' is used by permission of the publisher, William Heinemann.

I do not suppose that anybody now alive (I speak of lovers of poetry) who was not alive in 1832 and old enough then to enjoy the first perfect work of Tennyson, has had such a sensation as that which was experienced in the autumn of 1866 by readers of Mr. Swinburne's *Poems and Ballads*. And I am sure that no one in England has had any such sensation since. The later revelation had indeed been preceded by more signs and tokens than the earlier. Tennyson's first work had passed unknown or had been laughed at; at least two remarkable volumes (not to mention *The Queen Mother and Rosamond*) had already revealed to fit readers what there was in Mr. Swinburne. The chorus in *Atalanta*, 'Before the beginning of years', had attracted the highest admiration from impartial and unenthusiastic judges, while it had simply swept younger admirers off their legs with rapture; and the lyrics of *Chastelard* had completed the effect in the way of exciting, if not of satisfying, expectation.

Now we were told, first, that a volume of extraordinarily original verse was coming out; now, that it was so shocking that its publisher repented its appearance; now, that it had been reissued, and was coming out after all. The autumn must have been advanced before it did come out, for I remember that I could not obtain a copy before I went up to Oxford in October, and had to avail myself of an expedition to town to 'eat dinners' in order to get one. Three copies of the precious volume, with 'Moxon' on cover and 'John Camden Hotten' on title page, accompanied me back that night, together with divers maroons for the purpose of enlivening matters on the ensuing Fifth of November. The book was something of a maroon in itself as regards the fashion in which it startled people; and perhaps with youthful readers the hubbub did it no harm. We sat next afternoon, I remember, from luncheon time till the chapel bell rang, reading aloud by turns in a select company 'Dolores' and 'The Triumph of Time', 'Laus Veneris' and 'Faustine', and all the other wonders of the volume. There are some who say that after such a beginning critical appreciation is impossible—the roses bloom too aggressively by the not at all calm Bendemeer[1] when it is read again, and the pathetic and egotistic fallacies hide the truth from sight. If it were so, it were little use attempting to 'correct impressions' in this or any similar matter. But I do not think so meanly of the human intellect. There is practically nothing for which it is impossible to 'allow', nothing which may not be 'ruled out'. And though I feel that the maroons and the memories would make me a shamefully biased judge of Mr. Swinburne personally, that I should if I were on a jury let him off on any accusation, and if I were a judge give him the smallest possible sentence the law allowed, a critical opinion of his works is a different matter. Everybody must keep a conscience and mind it somewhere; and, for my part, I pride myself on keeping and minding it here.

Yet I have no hesitation in saying that after these years I find myself disposed to alter very little of the estimate which I made of the *Poems and Ballads* as we read them 'midst triptychs and Madonnas', as another poet sings, on that November Sunday. Mr. Swinburne has done a very great deal of work since, and I suppose not his wildest admirer would maintain that it has all or most of it been at the level of the best parts of the *Poems and Ballads*. There are even, I believe, as there usually are, archaics in Swinburnianism who hold that it has never been really merry since *Atalanta* itself; and, on the other hand, there are more sober Swinburnians who perhaps question whether the poet's very best has been seen except at intervals and in somewhat small proportion since the second *Poems and Ballads* of 1878. Nor is it necessary to spend much time in displaying the faults of this most captivating of the poets of the second half of the nineteenth century in England. The danger of them, and to some extent the damage of them, was seen in his very earliest work. The astonishing fertility of his command of language and of metre, the vast volume and variety of his verbal music, were

[1] A river in Thomas Moore's *Lalla Rookh*, associated with a memory of childhood, a nightingale's song, and roses.

almost perilously near to 'carrying him away' then, and no doubt have more and more actually done so. I do not think that Mr. Swinburne has ever written a single piece of verse that can be called bad, or that does not possess qualities of poetry which before his day would have sufficed to give any man high poetical rank. But he has always wanted discipline who never wanted music or eloquence; and the complaint that his readers sometimes find themselves floating on and almost struggling with a cataract of mere musical and verbal foam-water is not without foundation. Of late years, too, his extraordinary command of metre has led him to make new and ever new experiments in it which have been too often mere *tours de force*, to plan sea-serpents in verse in order to show how easily and gracefully he can make them coil and uncoil their enormous length, to build mastodons of metre that we may admire the proportion and articulation of their mighty limbs. In other words, he has sometimes, nay, too often, forgotten the end while exulting in his command of the means.

And yet, if we take the very latest of his works, how vast an addition to the possibilities of poetical delight do we see in it when compared with what English readers already had forty years ago, or even thirty! Although Mr. Swinburne's indebtedness to the late Laureate is of course immense, as must have been that of any man born when he was born, it happened most fortunately that his natural genius inclined him to the mode exactly opposite to Tennyson's. I have already endeavoured to show in these papers that, though that great poet could sing in divers tones, he always most inclined, and was most happily inspired when he did incline, to the mode of slow and languid singing. Mr. Swinburne's most natural gift is exactly the other way. His muse can 'toll slowly' when she chooses; but she has always an impulse to quicken, and is almost always happiest in quick time. Take, for instance, that famous poem already referred to, the great *Atalanta* chorus. It is stately enough, and certainly not very frolic in tone. But what a race and rush there is about it! What a thunder and charge of verse! It is almost impossible even to read it slowly. Take again the not less exquisite song in *Chastelard*, 'Between the sundown and the sea'. Here there is an appearance of languor; there are no trisyllabic feet, none of the extraneous aids to, or signs of, rhythmical speed. And yet the measure hurries rather than lags, the rhymes seem to invite each other to respond and speed the response, the beginnings of the lines catch up and send on the ends, the ends generate fresh beginnings almost before they have ceased. So in the two magnificent pieces that come almost on the threshold of the *Poems and Ballads* the same irrepressible impulse may be observed. The quatrain in which 'Laus Veneris' is written is one of the least lightly moving in appearance of all English measures, and yet it too grows tumultuous; while the intricate and massive stanza of 'The Triumph of Time' swells and swings like a wave.

In these cases the poet's idiosyncrasy is to some extent working against and subduing forms which do not lend themselves readily to it. But where the forms are congenial, the effect is too remarkable to have escaped even the most careless remark: and these pieces have in consequence supplied the most popular if not the most characteristic of Mr. Swinburne's poems. In that wonderful metre of 'Dolores' and the Epilogue to the first *Poems and Ballads* which Mr. Swinburne adapted from Praed by shortening the last line,[1] 'the sound of loud water' and 'the flight of the fires' both embody themselves in words. The mighty rush of the 'Hymn to Proserpine', the galloping charge of the 'Song in Time of Revolution', the dancing measures of 'Rococo', and many others, attain what, speaking in jargon, one might call the maximum velocity of any British poet. It is sometimes, as, for instance, in 'A Song in Time of Revolution', very nearly impossible to make speech accompany the words at the rate which seems as if it were required. You gabble and stumble in trying to keep up with the poet's speed. And by degrees Mr. Swinburne developed and perfected that faculty of his which has been already noticed—the faculty of arranging his measures in a sort of antiphony, where, as in very quick chanting, the alternate lines seem to catch up their forerunners almost before these have finished.

The two best examples of this curious gift known to me, and two of the very best things he has ever done, are the poems in the second volume of *Poems and Ballads*, entitled 'At a Month's End' and the 'Dedication to Captain Richard Burton'. I have sometimes had a fancy that I should like to hear

> The night last night was strange and shaken:
> More strange the change of you and me.
> Once more for the old love's love forsaken,
> We went down once more towards the sea,

with these unmatched passages which follow the lines,

> As a star sees the sun and falters,
> Touched to death by diviner eyes,

[1] Swinburne may have owed more to Thomas Holley Chivers (1809–1858) than to Praed. See, for instance, Swinburne's letter of May 18, 1886 (Lang, v, 143–4), quoting some of Chivers's lines.

As on the old gods' untended altars
The old fire of withered worship dies,

sung by alternate semi-choruses, the second tripping up the first a little.
Nor is such a motion as this,

Nine years have risen and eight years set
Since there by the well-spring our hands on it met,

to be found anywhere in English poetry earlier. The verse does not
merely run, it *spins*, gyrating and revolving in itself as well as proceeding on its orbit: the wave as it rushes on has eddies and backwaters
of live interior movement. All the metaphors and similes of water,
light, wind, fire, all the modes of motion, inspire and animate this
astonishing poetry.

Now if there is any truth in the view which was given in the last paper
of Mr. Swinburne's poetical virtue, it will be seen at once that there is
a special danger of uncritical admiration of him. The charm of the
latest—let us hope not the last—of the Laureates is not an impetuous
charm: it does not take you by a *coup de main*;[1] but it never lets you go
when it has once taken you. Has this other kind of poetical assault, this
*ivresse*[2] *de M. Swinburne* (to borrow the phrase *ivresse de Victor Hugo*
which was long ago used of the great French poet who was the God
of Mr. Swinburne's idolatry), the opposite defect of its opposite quality?
Does it hold you with a grasp as insecure as the first onset of it is
tempestuous? Is Mr. Swinburne a poetical Prince Rupert?[3] There are
some who say so. I seem to remember words of a very distinguished
person, my own contemporary, about a man's 'forgetting the *Poems
and Ballads* he used to spout'. All I can say is that I myself do not do
anything of the kind. There are, as I take it, three kinds of literary lovers,
as perhaps of other. There are those who only love one or a very few
things and cleave to it or them. Perhaps this is the most excellent way,
though I own I do not think so. There are the inconstants who love
and who ride away. And there are those who are polygamous but

---

[1] 'Surprise' or 'unexpected stroke'.

[2] 'Rapture', 'intoxication'.

[3] As commander of a corps of cavalry in the Civil War, Prince Rupert of Bavaria
(1619–1682) distinguished himself, particularly in initial onslaughts, but some ultimate
defeats have been attributed to his rashness.

faithful; that is to say, who constantly add to their loves, but never drop, forget, or slight the old. I boast myself to be of the last. In fact, why should a rational lover of poetry ever tire of Mr. Swinburne? That poet may have done things not wholly worthy of him, but no one is obliged to read them. He may have, even in his best things, been sometimes led astray by want of judgment in politics or religion or philosophy, by undue flux of language or of verse. But these things can be ignored or skipped. The virtue of the virtuous part remains; and I dare swear that it will be found at the second reading and the tenth and the hundredth as distinct as at the first by those who can get beyond and above mere novelty.

It is, if not the most philosophical, one of the most effectual of tests to consider a very strong literary mannerism or manner in its imitations. Mr. Swinburne, Heaven knows, has been imitated enough. Kingsley says somewhere that Amyas Leigh's companions proved the presence of mosquitoes on the Magdalena 'as well as wretched men could'. Reviewers did the same with the influence of Mr. Swinburne. For years his metres, his phrasing, his alliteration, his repetition of words, were the very *cophinus* and *foenum* of the poetaster,[1] the sole equipment and furniture with which he started his dreadful trade. And did one poetaster or poet during all these years achieve anything with them that was not either designed or unconscious parody and that was worth anything? Not one stanza, not one line. Some of the designed parodies were very funny; some of the undesigned ones funnier still. But that is a proof of excellence, not of inferiority. It is when a thing is imitable, not when it is parodiable, that it stands confessed as second-rate. And Mr. Swinburne, like other poets on the right side of the line, is not imitable—at any rate, he has not been imitated. They have gotten his fiddle but not his rosin: they can pile on alliteration, and be biblical in phrase, and trench on things forbidden in subject, and make a remarkably dull Italian into a god, and a great but not rationally great Frenchman into a compound of Shakespeare and Plato.[2] They can write lines in twenty-seven syllables or thereabouts if necessary; but they can't write poetry. Mr. Swinburne can and does.

There are, no doubt, several differences between poetical and other intoxication, but perhaps the chief difference is this. You can test the

---

[1] 'Basket' and 'hay'. Saintsbury probably had in mind the use of the two words in Juvenal's Satire iii, 13-15: ' . . . but now the holy fount and grove and shrine are let out to Jews, who possess a basket and a truss of hay for all their furnishings.'

[2] Saintsbury of course thinks of Mazzini and Hugo.

strength of the liquids odious to Sir Wilfrid Lawson[1] in two ways—by dipping a Sykes's hydrometer in them, or by actually imbibing and waiting to see whether they 'get you forrarder'.[2] In the case of poetry, only the latter test is available: you are yourself the hydrometer. Consequently it is exceedingly difficult to refer matters to any common standard. 'This is this to me and that to thee.' And it is nowhere so difficult as in the case of a poet like Mr. Swinburne, whose poetical appeal consists wholly or mainly in this quality of impassioning and exhilarating. He does not tell a story very well; his strictly dramatic faculty is not, I think, put by better judges of drama than I am very high. He is not a poetical schoolman and a poetical satirist like Dryden, nor a poetical epigrammatist and conversationalist like Pope. What is more remarkable considering his century, he is not by any means consummate or even eminent as a painter in words. His sea-pieces put aside, it may be said of his descriptions that, beautiful as they are, they are rather decorative or conventional than strictly pictorial, they do not bring the actual sights before the eyes with the simple force of Tennyson, or with the elaborate and complex force of Rossetti and Mr. Morris. What he is first of all is an absolutely consummate artist in word-music of the current and tempestuous kind, and an unfailing player on those moods of passion or of thought which are akin to his own. And if he fails in either of these two branches of his appeal, I should say that it must be not so much his fault as that of his audience. Music requires an ear to hear as well as a voice to sing it; and when Mr. Guppy remarked that 'there are chords in the human breast',[3] his aposiopesis might have been filled as well as in any other way by the words 'which, if their quality be not of the right kind, will fail to respond to the very deftest player'. It may possibly be a fault of Mr. Swinburne's that he lends himself rather ill to mere dispassionate admiration. I doubt myself whether any poet of a very high class can be dispassionately appreciated: but certainly he cannot. You must, to quote one of his own finest passages, be somewhat in the mood to

> Hear through star-proof trees
> The tempest of the Thyiades,[4]

---

[1] An advocate of temperance (1829-1906).

[2] A colloquial expression for 'enable you to make headway'.

[3] In chapter 20 of Dickens' *Bleak House*. Mr. Guppy observes that 'there are chords in the human mind — —'

[4] Cf. 'Prelude' to *Songs before Sunrise*:

> We too have tracked by star-proof trees
> The tempest of the Thyiades. . . .

or you must be in the mood of reaction after such a hearing, in order to enjoy him fully. 'And what for no?' There is no *senatus consultum de Bacchanalibus*[1] as far as books are concerned; and I confess a certain contempt for any one who cannot get excited over print and paper.

And after all there is a vast residuum when this merely personal excitement (which from my own experience I should say is quite as likely to be felt a little before fifty as a little after twenty) has subsided. There is the astonishing revelation of the metrical powers of English: for, though we knew them to be infinite before, this of itself does not take the very least thing off from the blush of each fresh instalment of the infinite surprises. There is the endless amusement of analysing the means (as to a certain limited effect is possible) by which these musical and emotional effects are produced. There is the pleasure of tracing what is, in so literary and scholarly a poet as Mr. Swinburne, the great and complicated indebtedness to the masters of Greece and of Rome, of Italy and of France, but most of all to those of England. And there is what is most delightful of all to the true lover of poetry and literature, the delight of finding out how much it is impossible to account for.

For to this we always come, and in this I believe consists the greatest and most lasting enjoyment of every kind of beauty. If you ever could find out exactly why it is beautiful, the thing would become scientific and cease to be interesting. But you cannot, and so there is at once the joy of possession and the ardour of the unattained. You read for the first, the twentieth, or the hundredth time 'The Garden of Proserpine', or 'Ilicet', or 'A Wasted Vigil'. There is the first stage of pleasure, a purely uncritical enjoyment. Then there is the second stage, in which you sit down and take your critical paper and pencil, and put down: metre so much; alliteration so much; ingenious disposition of vowel sounds so much; criticism of life so much; pathetic fancy so much; to having read it when SHE was present, or absent, or cross, or kind, or something, so much; literary reminiscence so much. And then there is the third, when you have totted these items up and found that they do not come to anything like the real total, that there is an infinite balance of attraction and satisfaction which you cannot explain, which is fact, but an unsolved, unanalysed, ultimate fact. The poetry which has come to mean this to a lover of poetry never gets stale, never loses charm, never seems the same, or rather, always being the same in one way, is always fresh in another.

[1] The decree of the Roman Senate that abolished celebration of Bacchanalian Mysteries (186 B.C.).

Among such poetry I, for my part, rank a very large proportion of Mr. Swinburne's earlier work, and not a very little of his later. If it were ever going to pall on me, I think it pretty certainly must have palled by this time. And what is more, there is the comforting reflection that anything in which one has taken delight so long is secure from palling by the very fact. The accumulation of delighted remembrance is a delight in itself: what has been has been, and therefore must ever continue to be. The constantly repeated thought and sensation has become an entity, a thing in itself, a possession for ever, by the very dint of having been so long and so often possessed.

# 27. William Morton Payne: 'Algernon Charles Swinburne'

## 1897

William Morton Payne (1858–1919) became associate editor of the Chicago *Dial*, a periodical to which he contributed some reviews of Swinburne's books. In 1905 he published *Selected Poems of Swinburne* and in 1907 *The Greater English Poets of the Nineteenth Century*, in which the last chapter is devoted to the poet, and which once more emphasized the value of Swinburne's later work.

*Library of the World's Best Literature*, ed. Charles Dudley Warner.

---

Early in the eighties, there were living in England six great poets, whose work had given to the later Victorian era of English song a splendour almost comparable to that of the Elizabethan and later Georgian periods. All of these poets but one have now passed away (Rossetti in 1882, Arnold in 1888, Browning in 1889, Tennyson in 1892, and Morris in 1896), leaving Mr. Swinburne in solitary preeminence. In this year of the Queen's Jubilee he is left with no possible rival among the living; and stands as the Victorian poet *par excellence* in a peculiarly literal sense, for he was born in the year of her Majesty's accession to the throne, which makes his sixty years conterminous with the sixty years of her reign. So little has been made public concerning that life, that his personality has remained even more closely veiled than was that of Tennyson; and the facts at the command of the biographer are of the most meagre description. He was the son of a distinguished officer of the Royal Navy; and on his mother's side, descended from the third Earl of Ashburnham. He was educated at Balliol College, Oxford, but left in 1860 without taking a degree. A journey to Italy followed; made chiefly for the purpose of paying a tribute of affectionate admiration to the old poet Landor, then nearing the close of his days in Florence. The greater part of Mr. Swinburne's life has been spent in England: for a time he lived in London with the Rossetti brothers and Mr. George Meredith; but for many years past his home has been at Wimbledon, where he has kept house with Mr. Theodore Watts-Dunton, the distinguished critic and the closest of his friends.

Mr. Swinburne made his first appearance in literature as a dramatic poet; and published in rapid succession the four dramas—*Rosamond*[1] (1860), *The Queen Mother* (1860), *Atalanta in Calydon* (1865), and *Chastelard* (1865). The first of these works has for its subject the idyl and tragedy of Henry II at Woodstock, the second the massacre of St. Bartholomew, and the last an episode in the early life of Mary Stuart at the French court.[2] *Atalanta in Calydon* is a noble tragedy upon a Greek theme, and written in as close a reproduction of the Greek manner as it is likely to be given to any modern poet to achieve. These four works gained for their author a considerable reputation with cultivated readers, yet made no direct appeal to the wider public. But the situation became changed in the year that followed the appearance of *Chastelard*—the year of the famous *Poems and Ballads* (1866). It is hardly an exaggeration to say that no other volume of English poetry published before or since, ever created so great a sensation as this. If Byron awoke to find himself famous the day after the first cantos of *Childe Harold* made their appearance, Mr. Swinburne awoke to find himself both famous and notorious. For the *Poems and Ballads* not only showed that a new poet had arisen with a voice of his own, and possessed of an absolutely unexampled command of the resources of English rhythm, but they also showed that the author deemed fit for poetical treatment certain passional aspects of human life concerning which the best English tradition had hitherto been one of reticence. The unerring instinct of sensational journalism at once sought out for discussion these poems (perhaps a dozen in number) of questionable propriety; and before the year was over, the volume had become the subject of a discussion so ample and so heated that a parallel is hardly to be found in the history of English literature.

This discussion has proved peculiarly unfortunate for the poet's fame; since there has grown out of it a legend which still persists in the popular consciousness, and which embodies a view of the poet so distorted and so grotesquely untrue, that those who are acquainted with his work as a whole can only smile helplessly and wait for time to set matters right. The facts of the matter are simply these: The *Poems and*

---

[1] *The Queen-Mother and Rosamond* was a volume containing two plays.
[2] The scene is really Edinburgh.

*Ballads* was essentially a first book. Its contents had been written for the most part by a mere boy, long before their collection into a volume; and bear about the same relation to his mature work as is borne by the vapourings of Shelley's *Queen Mab* to *Prometheus Unbound* and 'Epipsychidion'. The objectionable pieces are few in number, and probably no one regrets more than the author himself the defective taste which permitted them to be preserved. 'They are obviously,' to quote from a recent critic, 'the hasty and violent defiance hurled in the face of British Philistinism by a youthful writer, who, in addition to the exuberance of his scorn of conventions, was also, it is plain, influenced by a very boyish desire to shock the dull respectabilities of the average Philistine.' But the unfair critical onslaught upon these poems (utterly ignoring the many pure and elevated numbers found in the same volume) was so noisy that its echo has been prolonged; and the opinion still obtains in many quarters that sensuality is the chief attribute of a poet who in reality might be charged with the fault of excessive spirituality, so far above earth and so tenuous is the atmosphere in which he has his intellectual being. If we accept Milton's dictum that poetry should be simple, sensuous, and passionate, it may be admitted that Mr. Swinburne has passion (although mainly of the intellectual sort), but he is rarely simple; while in sensuous charm he is distinctly inferior to more than one of his contemporaries.

The even-minded critic of Mr. Swinburne's poetry thirty years ago (and there were such, notable among them being Richard Grant White and Mr. Stedman) might discern from an examination of the five works already mentioned, the leading traits that so many other volumes were to develop. There were already then evident the astonishing virtuosity in the use of English metres; the linguistic faculty, by virtue of which the poet composed Greek, Latin, and French verses with as much apparent readiness as English; the imitative power which made it possible for him to write like Chaucer, or the poets of the old ballad and the miracle play; the spiritual insight which made *Atalanta* so much more than a mere imitation of Greek tragedy; the hero-worship which is so generous a trait of his character; the defence of religion against theology and priestcraft; and the intense love of liberty that breathes through all his work.

Since the year which made Mr. Swinburne's name familiar to all lovers of English poetry, his activity has been unceasing. Productions in prose and verse have flowed from his pen at the rate of about a volume annually; the complete list of his works embracing upwards of thirty volumes, about one-third of which are studies in literary criticism. Although these latter volumes form an important section of his writings, they must be dismissed with a few words. There are three collections of miscellaneous critical essays; separate monographs of considerable bulk upon Shakespeare, Ben Jonson, Victor Hugo, and William Blake, briefer monographs upon George Chapman and Charlotte Brontë; a highly controversial examination of certain literary reputations, *Under the Microscope*; and several pamphlets more or less polemical in character. *A Year's Letters*, which is a sort of prose novelette, was written for periodical publication under the pseudonym 'Mrs. Horace Manners'; but has never been reprinted. There are also many critical studies to be found in the pages of the English monthly reviews; notable among them being a nearly complete series of papers which examine in close detail the work of the Elizabethan dramatists, and constitute, together with the published volumes on Shakespeare, Jonson, and Chapman, the most exhaustive and scholarly commentary that has yet been produced upon that important body of English poetry. The style of these prose writings is *sui generis*, and as astonishing in its way as that of Carlyle. It defies imitation; which is probably fortunate, since it is not an altogether admirable style. But with all its vehemence, its verbosity, and its recondite allusiveness, it has somehow the power to carry the reader with it; sweeping away his critical sense for the time being, and compelling him to share in both the occasional prejudices and the frequent enthusiasms of the writer. And after due allowance has been made for the temperamental qualities of Mr. Swinburne, and for the extravagances of his diction, there will be found to remain a residuum of the highest critical value; so that it may fairly be said that he has illuminated every subject that he has chosen to discuss.

In dealing with the volumes of poetry—about a score in number—of which nothing has yet been said, we are confronted with an *embarras de richesses*. Chronologically, the earliest of them is the *Songs before Sunrise* (1871), and the latest *The Tale of Balen* (1896). Perhaps the first thing that should be said about them, in view of still current misconceptions, is that whatever taint of sensuality clung to the productions of the poet's youth, the work of his manhood is singularly free from any offense of this sort. In its dramatic portions, it handles the noblest of themes with superb creative power, and deals with them in grave harmonious measures; in its lyrical portions, it clothes an almost austere ideal of conduct in melodies whose beauty is everlasting. The dramatic poems include *Erechtheus*, a Greek tragedy fully as fine as *Atalanta*, and exhibiting more of artistic restraint; the two works *Bothwell* and *Mary Stuart*, which complete the magnificent trilogy begun by *Chastelard*; *Marino Faliero*, a Venetian subject treated with splendid effect; *Locrine*, a tragedy suggested by Milton's *Comus*, and upon a theme dealt with by an unknown Elizabethan dramatist; and *The Sisters*, a comparatively unimportant domestic tragedy. Strongly dramatic in spirit, although in form a narrative in rhymed couplets, the tale of *Tristram of Lyonesse* completes the list of Mr. Swinburne's longer poetical works down to *The Tale of Balen*, which is essentially a verse paraphrase of a section of the *Morte d'Arthur* of Malory. The lyrical division of Mr. Swinburne's work includes two additional series of *Poems and Ballads*; the impassioned volume of *Songs before Sunrise*, inspired by the Italian revolutionary movement, and dedicated to Mazzini—a work which is probably the highest and most sustained expression of the poet's lyrical powers; the *Songs of Two Nations*, which includes the great 'Song of Italy', the superb 'Ode on the Proclamation of the French Republic', and the fierce sonnets called 'Dirae'; the *Songs of the Springtides*, whereof 'Thalassius'—a sort of spiritual autobiography, in which the poet pays the noblest of his many tributes to the memory of Landor —is the first and the greatest; the *Studies in Song*, which includes the wonderful lyrical group inspired 'By the North Sea'; the *Tristram* volume, which contains, besides the titular poem, many other pieces —among them 'A Dark Month', the group of songs which has made their author the supreme English poet of childhood; *A Century of Roundels*; *A Midsummer Holiday*; and *Astrophel*. Mention should also be made, as illustrating the lighter aspect of Mr. Swinburne's genius, of the anonymously published *Heptalogia; or The Seven against Sense*, a collection of the cleverest parodies ever written, in which the poet travesties his own style with no less glee than the style of half a dozen of his contemporaries. If one would seek for further indications of his sense of humour, they may be found in the poem 'Disgust', which parodies Tennyson's 'Despair', and in the 'Report of the Proceedings on the First Anniversary Session of the Newest Shakespeare Society'.

The mere enumeration of Mr. Swinburne's works requires so much space that little remains for any general comment upon them. It should be said that he early outgrew the doctrine of 'art for art's sake', and has made his verse more and more the ally of great and worthy causes. Such ardent and whole-souled admiration of man for man as finds expression in his many poems to Landor, Hugo, and Mazzini, to say nothing of his many tributes to lesser men, is hardly paralleled in literature. And the sweep of his lyre becomes even more impressive when its strings are plucked in behalf of France crushed beneath the heel of the usurper; of Italy struggling to be free. The fierce indignation with which he inveighs against all the social, political, and religious forces that array themselves against the freedom of the body and soul of man, the glowing patriotism which fires his song when its theme is the proud heritage of achievement to which every Englishman is born, and the prophetic inspiration which imparts to him the vision of a regenerated humanity, and all the wonder that shall be when 'the world's great age begins anew' and 'the golden years return'[1]—these are indeed subjects for the noblest sort of poetical expression; and they are the very warp and woof of the many-coloured verbal fabric that has come from Mr. Swinburne's loom. And with these great words spoken for mankind in the abstract there comes also a personal message, exalting the virtues of heroism, and sacrifice of self, and steadfast devotion to high impersonal ends—a message that finds its highest embodiment is such poems as 'Super Flumina Babylonis', and 'The Pilgrims', and 'Thalassius'; a message that enforces as fine an ethical ideal of individual conduct as may be found anywhere in English literature.

[1] From Shelley's *Hellas*, the first two lines of the final chorus, 1060-1.

# 28. 'An Imaginary Correspondence'

*Punch*, 30 July 1902, cxxiii, 60

---

'An Imaginary Correspondence' (quoted by special permission of *Punch*, owner of the copyright) satirized Swinburne's preference for outspoken language as illustrated by his essay on Dickens. Here, as in 'The Appreciations of Algernon' in its following issue, *Punch* exaggerated obvious tricks of style.

---

### AN IMAGINARY CORRESPONDENCE

(*Which may be supposed to have passed between the Editor of the* Quarterly Review *and Mr. A. C. Swinburne when the proofs of the latter's signed article on Charles Dickens were being revised for the press.*)

DEAR SIR,—In going through the proofs of your valuable article on DICKENS I came across the expression 'Blatant Booby'. As the application of this description to persons from whom one may differ in opinion is somewhat unusual in modern literary controversy, perhaps you might like to modify it?

Yours faithfully,
THE EDITOR.

DEAR SIR,—I utterly and entirely refuse and decline to make or accept any change or alteration whatsoever in the expression you mention. When I think a man a 'booby' I call him a 'booby'.

Yours faithfully,
A. C. SWINBURNE.

DEAR SIR,—In writing of Mr. ANDREW LANG's prefaces to DICKENS I see you say, 'The offence becomes an outrage, the impertinence becomes impudence, when such rubbish is shot down before the door-step of CHARLES DICKENS.' Is not this rather too strong a description?

Yours faithfully,
THE EDITOR.

DEAR SIR,—Certainly not! In this epicene age, when the cautious criticaster bedecks and beslavers the words and works of every imbecile impostor, it is utterly right and entirely necessary that such expressions should be used. A short shift and a lang drop for such fellows!

Yours ferociously,

A. C. SWINBURNE.

DEAR SIR,—In your 'DICKENS' article I see you speak of 'the chattering duncery and the impudent malignity of so consummate and pseudo-sophical a quack as GEORGE HENRY LEWES'. You also write of the same gentleman's 'insolent and idiotic impeachments'. Could you see your way to toning down these expressions, as they are calculated to give pain to many?

Yours faithfully,

THE EDITOR.

SIR!—The suggestion that I should mar or modify the nervous intensity and virile vigour of my incomparable style to placate the prejudices or soothe the susceptibilities of a plethoric public is incompetent and idiotic. Nor would the public thank me for complying with that inane suggestion. To whittle away and water down my virulent vituperation and vehement invective would deprive my article of the peculiar flavour which differentiates it from the critical utterances of the groundlings. There is really nothing to say about CHARLES DICKENS that has not been said fifty times over already. All that can be done is to say it in a thoroughly trenchant manner. This I have set myself to do. And the fellow who says I have not done it is a blatant booby, an arrant ass, a preposterous pedant, and an incomparable imbecile.

Yours in a towering passion,

A. C. SWINBURNE.

# 29. Swinburne: a backward glance

1904

Swinburne's *Dedicatory Epistle* introducing his *Collected Poems* of 1904, addressed to Theodore Watts-Dunton, contains his most extended discussion of his own work. The extracts that follow will indicate that he did not forget his critics: the first recalls the reception of *Poems and Ballads*, and the second is his response to a recurring complaint of bookishness (see the last part of section VI of the Introduction).

To my best and dearest friend I dedicate the first collected edition of my poems, and to him I address what I have to say on the occasion.

You will agree with me that it is impossible for any man to undertake the task of commentary, however brief and succinct, on anything he has done or tried to do, without incurring the charge of egoism. But there are two kinds of egoism, the furtive and the frank: and the outspoken and open-hearted candour of Milton and Wordsworth, Corneille and Hugo, is not the least or the lightest of their claims to the regard as well as the respect or the reverence of their readers. Even if I were worthy to claim kinship with the lowest or with the highest of these deathless names, I would not seek to shelter myself under the shadow of its authority. The question would still remain open on all sides. Whether it is worth while for any man to offer any remarks or for any other man to read his remarks on his own work, his own ambition, or his own attempts, he cannot of course determine. If there are great examples of abstinence from such a doubtful enterprise, there are likewise great examples to the contrary. As long as the writer can succeed in evading the kindred charges and the cognate risks of vanity and humility, there can be no reason why he should not undertake it. And when he has nothing to regret and nothing to recant, when he finds nothing that he could wish to cancel, to alter, or to unsay, in any page he has ever laid before his reader, he need not be seriously troubled by the inevitable consciousness that the work of his early youth is not and cannot be unnaturally unlike the work of a very young man. This would be no excuse for it, if it were in any sense bad work: if it be so, no apology would avail; and I certainly have none to offer.

It is now thirty-six years[1] since my first volume of miscellaneous verse, lyrical and dramatic and elegiac and generally heterogeneous, had as quaint a reception and as singular a fortune as I have ever heard or read of. I do not think you will differ from my opinion that what is best in it cannot be divided from what is not so good by any other line of division than that which marks off mature from immature execution—in other words, complete from incomplete conception. For its author the most amusing and satisfying result of the clatter aroused by it was the deep diversion of collating and comparing the variously inaccurate verdicts of the scornful or mournful censors who insisted on regarding all the studies of passion or sensation attempted or achieved in it as either confessions of positive fact or excursions of absolute fancy. There are photographs from life in the book; and there are sketches from imagination. Some which keen-sighted criticism has dismissed with a smile as ideal or imaginary were as real and actual as they well could be: others which have been taken for obvious transcripts from memory were utterly fantastic or dramatic. If the two kinds cannot be distinguished, it is surely rather a credit than a discredit to an artist whose medium or material has more in common with a musician's than with a sculptor's. Friendly and kindly critics, English and foreign, have detected ignorance of the subject in poems taken straight from the life, and have protested that they could not believe me were I to swear that poems entirely or mainly fanciful were not faithful expressions or transcriptions of the writer's actual experience and personal emotion. But I need not remind you that all I have to say about this book was said once for all in the year of its publication: I have nothing to add to my notes then taken,[2] and I have nothing to retract from them. To parade or to disclaim experience of passion or of sorrow, of pleasure or of pain, is the habit and the sign of a school which has never found a disciple among the better sort of English poets, and which I know to be no less pitifully contemptible in your opinion than in mine. . . .

Not to you or any other poet, nor indeed to the very humblest and

[1] The American edition (1905) reads 'thirty-eight years'. See Introduction, xlii, for a discussion of the date of the *Dedicatory Epistle*.

[2] *Notes on Poems and Reviews*.

simplest lover of poetry, will it seem incongruous or strange, suggestive of imperfect sympathy with life or deficient inspiration from nature, that the very words of Sappho should be heard and recognised in the notes of the nightingales,[1] the glory of the presence of dead poets[2] imagined in the presence of the glory of the sky, the lustre of their advent and their passage felt visible as in vision on the live and limpid floorwork of the cloudless and sunset-coloured sea. The half-brained creature to whom books are other than living things may see with the eyes of a bat and draw with the fingers of a mole his dullard's distinction between books and life: those who live the fuller life of a higher animal than he know that books are to poets as much part of that life as pictures are to painters or as music is to musicians, dead matter though they may be to the spiritually still-born children of dirt and dullness who find it possible and natural to live while dead in heart and brain. Marlowe and Shakespeare, Æschylus and Sappho, do not for us live only on the dusty shelves of libraries.

[1] In 'On the Cliffs'.
[2] In 'In the Bay'.

# 30. Oliver Elton: 'Mr. Swinburne's Poems'

## 1907

Oliver Elton (1861–1945) had engaged in private tutoring and reviewing and had lectured on English literature in Owens College, Manchester, before his appointment in 1901 as King Alfred Professor of English Literature at the institution which soon became the University of Liverpool. His chapter on Swinburne in *Modern Studies* (used by permission of Edward Arnold [publishers], owner of the copyright) was preceded by reviews in the *Speaker* during 1904 and 1905, and his more mature and rounded estimate of the poet appeared in his *Survey of English Literature 1780–1880* (1920), iv, 55–84.

*Modern Studies* (1907), 208–27.

I. Preface to the Collected Edition: The Ode. II. Conception of Beauty found in Rossetti, Morris, Burne-Jones, and in Mr. Swinburne. III. First Series of 'Poems and Ballads': The Youthful Love of Death. IV. Transition to 'Songs Before Sunrise': Inspiration from Italy and Mazzini. V. Second Series of 'Poems and Ballads': Greek Plays. VI. 'Tristram of Lyonesse.' VII. 'The Tale of Balen.'

### I.

After a generation, Mr. Swinburne's verse comes out in a collected form, happily under the author's care, and without alteration of the text. There is 'nothing that he could wish to cancel, or to alter, or to unsay, in any pages he has ever laid before his reader'. This is very well, for his earlier writings, at any rate, are now historic, and any change, even for the better, would change their nature. His preface on his own poetry is a happy example of his critical prose. It is untouched by the flagrant volubility of enormous panegyric or superlative damnation which often covers up the clearness and gravity of Mr. Swinburne's judgments on literature. Well we know that style, where the shot is so weighty and well aimed, but is discharged with a furious waste of powder, and even at times with an inconvenient recoil. But in this preface, with its proud and unfailing dignity of retrospect, one of the greatest critics amongst English poets judges himself and makes awards, as few English poets have done, between his own works. We need not expect that his choice should be ours. Such pieces as 'In the Bay' and 'On the Cliffs', which he singles out from amongst those 'inspired by the influence of places' as of deeper appeal to himself, may perhaps belong, in point of performance, to the large class of his lyrics that can be termed self-echoes—beautiful enough, but with a beauty that the author has himself already excelled in its own kind, and therefore not so much alive in our memory as their predecessors in our love. But 'A Forsaken Garden', which he ranks as to its associations with those others, had a new freshness of landscape and a new intensity of rhythm, which brings it into a different class of lovely things. The poet's re-reading of these pieces has begotten a passage of lyrical prose that stands with 'A Forsaken Garden' itself:—

Not to you or any other poet, or indeed to the very humblest and simplest lover of poetry, will it seem incongruous or strange, suggestive of imperfect sympathy with life or deficient inspiration from nature, that the very words of Sappho should be heard and recognized in the notes of the nightingales, the glory of the presence of dead poets imagined in the presence of the glory of the sky, the lustre of their advent and their passage felt visible as in vision on the live and limpid floorwork of the cloudless and sunset-coloured sea.

Some words from the same preface touch on the species and aspirations of the ode, 'considered as something above all less pure and absolute song by the very law of its being', and defined, if not rigidly by the correspondent forms of strophe that are based on Pindar's, still so as to exclude the sham Pindaric and such 'lawless lyrics of irregular and uneven build as Coleridge' used. They throw light on Mr. Swinburne's conception of his own highest task as a poet as well as on his fundamentally Hellenic sympathies as a lyrist. Whether, in the nature of things, one kind is inherently greater or more central than another kind of lyrical perfection, his own briefer songs, 'Love laid his sleepless head' and 'A Match', even when confronted with the 'Ode to Victor Hugo' and the choruses in 'Atalanta', may leave us questioning. Any primacy that the ode may possess, it possibly gains, not only from the larger sweep and more elaborate resonance of its form, but from the suggestion, whether overt or underlying, of some great and public emotion uttered by a throng of performers to a larger throng of responsive hearers, and celebrated in triumphal or burial procession. From this point of view, which seems to imply some actual event or the memory of one, in order to awaken sufficient resonance in the heart, those odes, where, as in Wordsworth's on the 'Intimations of Immortality', the poet is his own audience and the subject is a pure idea, however legitimate and splendid they be, would fall furthest from the original and fullest conception of the species; not because of their irregular measures, but by the restriction of their imagined audience, to one person, who is the poet himself, and by the failure of the mind's eye to furnish any scene or visible centre for their emotion. By Mr. Swinburne no such experiment is ever risked; for the choruses in his Greek plays, and his 'Hymn of Man', and his 'Ode to Victor Hugo', one and all presuppose, if not always an actual occurrence, still some unison of many spirits in a common admiration or passion, which is of the essence of the ode; and in these pieces, whether they be more or less perfect than the little lyrics and elegies, we should be dull to ignore a special pride of rhythm and ambition of wing, that answer faithfully enough to the poet's now expressed promotion of the ode above all other forms of song.

## II.

Mr. Swinburne began his poetic life as a member of a school; and by a school of artists more is meant than when we speak of a school of herrings, darting and gleaming about in one place indistinguishably. It is a band of men, working so as to stamp their separate souls, be it through forms or colours or melodies (which may themselves often enough betray an inner likeness), upon moods or ideas that animate them all: so that their work as a whole may without absurdity be regarded as a single poem, or work of art, conceived in honour of a single series of ideas. The stronger each member of the band, the firmer his hold, though the greater his individual expression, of those ruling ideas. So it was with William Morris, Rossetti, Burne-Jones, and so with the youngest-born and youngest-natured of them all, who is still with us and at work. The more they diverged, the plainer was their engrossment with pure beauty, with visible beauty, and especially with the beauty of the feminine form, which came to be looked on, even by the halest of the four, as a typical vesture or symbol of Beauty herself, and perhaps also as the 'sovran shrine'[1] of Melancholy. Common to them all, therefore, was the mystical will to go behind Beauty and have its meaning; and here they parted company and each of them spoke for himself. Rossetti saw the spiritual call in face and form, and desired the spirit through his desire of the body, and at last did not know the one desire from the other, and pressed on, true mystic as he was, in ever-narrowing circles, to some third thing that seemed to lie behind both desires. Some such impulse, as we have said, was not absent in Morris, though it hardly went further than the delicious complaint and unrest of the *Earthly Paradise*; but after a time, in his prose romances, he came to find little more in beauty than the object of natural human longing, and the shrine, not of Melancholy, but of affections and tender graces. The frank desire that is told of in these stories is that of the young man for young-eyed beauty. A third of the group, the painter, feeling that 'soul is form, and doth the body make',[2] embodied abstract emotions or dreams, after Spenser's way, but embodied them in figures of his own dream-life, figures in which the two sexes are not always markedly contrasted; and he exhibited different phases of Love—Love weary, or Love cruel, or Love incurably remote; or, more often, Love at pause and transparent and void of quality, like a clean empty cup of crystal. Akin to this, but less seated in the dream-world and more stinging in expression, was the conception of beauty that inspired the first series of *Poems and Ballads*. Thus in the work of the four artists there is enough unity to earn them the title of a historic school, whose flowering-time was from about 1855 to about 1880. No other school has since arisen in Britain, except that slighter but authentic one of the young Irish writers, whose vision of beauty, and the manner of whose mystical utterance, is very different. The prologue and the epilogue to Mr. Swinburne's lyrical writings show the endurance of his affection for the two friends, to whom he pays noble tribute in lines that fly lightly like birds from crest to crest of the breaking wave. Written in the same measure, both are offered to Burne-Jones, with whom, in the new dedication, is joined the name of William Morris. The purged ethereal pathos of this utterance is more than a renewal of the writer's poetical youth.

> No sweeter, no kindlier, no fairer,
> No lovelier a soul from its birth

---

[1] Keats's 'Ode on Melancholy', l. 26.
[2] Spenser's 'Hymne in Honour of Beautie', l. 132.

Wore ever a brighter and rarer
  Life's raiment for life upon earth
Than his who enkindled and cherished
  Art's vestal and luminous flame
That dies not when kingdoms have perished
  In storm or in shame.

No braver, no trustier, no purer,
  No stronger and clearer a soul
Bore witness more splendid and surer
  For manhood found perfect and whole
Since man was a warrior and dreamer
  Than his who in hatred of wrong
Would fain have arisen a redeemer
  By sword or by song.

## III.

In his preface Mr. Swinburne recalls his past amusement over those critics of the first *Poems and Ballads* who 'insisted on regarding all the studies of passion and sensation attempted and achieved in it as either confessions of positive fact or excursions of absolute fancy'. This is a remark that might warn some of the critics of Shakespeare's *Sonnets*, who either sneer at them as a literary exercise or paw over them as Pepys-like confessions. To treat a poet as a diarist, or again to imagine him building his creations out of no experience, is to be blind to the first conditions of artistic handicraft. The critic has to do, not with the actual experience of the poet, but with the experience that the poet presents to him, blended as it is of memory and dreams and invention inscrutably. We had better not pry into that chemistry. Even if we were the Recording Angel, or God's spies, and knew the evidence, it would not help us to detect the creative process. Goethe, it has often been observed, left volumes of self-portrayal, and we are no nearer the secret of his work. The conception, in its greater or less nobility and clearness, and the execution, in its greater or less unity and rightness, are all that concern us in presence of a piece of art. From this, the only point of view, it may be fairly said that many of Mr. Swinburne's earlier pieces remain, to adapt a phrase of Poe's, not only poems of obscure emotion, but obscure poems of emotion, and the *Note* upon 'Dolores', 'Hesperia', and the rest, ought all the more to be now republished, if only as a prose poem in its own right. The pressmen of that earlier time, red with muddled and excited protest, often treated

Swinburne as one of the writers called by Baudelaire 'brutaux et pure-
ment épidermiques'.[1] But he was, in fact, a poet of the emotions, and
not merely or mainly of the sensations. Look at D'Annunzio's 'Il Peccato
di Maggio', where the sentimental hardness of the Latin, the solemn
inventory of the woman's body, the callow particularity, only suggest
the first amour of a collegian; and then turn to 'An Interlude', with its
light step and backward wistful look. One is a poem of sensation, the
other a poem of emotion—of emotion that comes short of anything
highly spiritual, but of emotion still:—

> I remember the way we parted,
>   The day and the way we met,
> You hoped we were both broken-hearted,
>   And knew we should both forget.

Even in the poems that are a pure record of delirium mingled with the
foretaste of heavy regret for its transiency, like 'In the Orchard', the
advantage remains with the English poet, for the taste of expected loss
is as strong upon his lips as the taste of present pleasure. And the harsher
and stranger among those *Poems and Ballads* were studies of idea as well
as of emotion and sensation. They are the first verses in England since
those of Donne to utter faithfully certain youthful moods of sick
revulsion, or of acrid satiety, or of hope idly recurrent, or of passion on
the ebb and self-regretting. They chronicle the invasion of hatred amid
the triumph of pleasure, and the stranding of light love on its own
shallow rocks; the balance of the soul in apathy, like the slow fluctua-
tion of a weed in the stream languid after the tidal wave; the cold-
handed visit of Retrospect, and the revulsion to the dreamy peace of the
Garden of Proserpine. These things are part of our youth, and it was
Swinburne who gave them words. They are far behind, and yet they
come back again in his art. It is an error to treat these poems as literary
followings of Baudelaire and Gautier, in whom some of their moods
and themes may doubtless be paralleled. The feeling, that recurs oftenest
and seems to govern all the rest, is easily definable and perfectly real,
and is most fully set forth in 'Ilicet'. It is that love of death which is felt
in youth or adolescence. It is a feeling much derided, and wholly
unaffected. Age looks on the end as an intruder, or as a timely gift of
nature, or as a natural process, or it does not think at all of the end,
which comes on before it is realized. But to youth in its dark hour the

---

[1] 'Brutal and purely epidermal.'

end is a treasure lusted for, it is the desire of no consciousness, it is the release from irritation, it is the crown of the garland of sleep. This is the burden of 'Ilicet' and of 'Félise':—

> No memory more of love or hate,
> No trouble, nothing that aspires,
> No sleepless labour thwarting fate,
> And thwarted; where no travail tires,
> Where no faith fires.

And again—

> Not for their love shall Fate retire,
> Nor they relent for our desire,
> Nor the graves open for their call.
> The end is more than joy and anguish,
> That lives that laugh and lives that languish,
> The poppied sleep, the end of all.

As old in poetry as Catullus, this permanent or recurring cry of mankind is repeated in *Poems and Ballads* with unwearied energy. The slightest curb on the feeling would spoil everything. There is no curb except on the expression, and this is why the verses live; for the controlled expression of uncontrolled feeling is essential to high lyric. No doubt there is a loftier weariness. Shakespeare was tired, not merely of the mirage of desire, but of that bitterness of mature experience, which in these young poems is wholly absent. Yet not for that is the right of the hastier and less-tired soul diminished to sing of its lightlier-earned fatigue, or to set into rhyme the strange measures of joy and grief that it has trodden.

## IV.

The repetitions in the first series of *Poems and Ballads* show that the poet was dissatisfied with his subjects, and was moving forward to larger ones. He ceased to find true matter for his imagination in the pathological idyll, or in the theme *Amor Mortis conturbat me*;[1] for the frame of mind that inspires such themes cannot, in its nature, last long, although it had called out his portentous creative power as a metrist, and had uttered itself in caressing triple rhymes, or undulant long stanzas unknown before. Some pieces in the same book announce the heroic age of Mr. Swinburne's poetry, which ran its course (if we

[1] Cf. Dunbar's refrain in 'Lament for the Makers': 'The fear of death ["*Timor mortis*" instead of "the desire for death", "*Amor mortis*"] disturbs me.'

exclude his dramas on English subjects) between the *Song of Italy* in 1867 and the *Erechtheus* of 1876. The lines 'To Victor Hugo' wind a clear horn of onset amid the amorous Asiatic timbrels of 1866; and the honours paid to Landor, the 'oldest singer that England bore', show the temper that was to animate, and perhaps to release, the genius of the youngest. The delicately pure and more than Sicilian grace of Landor's own elegy and idyll, and also his passion for the noble antique, sank into his scholar. The earliest creed of Mr. Swinburne may perhaps be read in the Greek memorial lines preceding *Atalanta* and addressed to Landor. The praise of the old man's potent passion for liberty, and of his stately talent for poetical sculpture, suddenly closes upon the note of 'Ilicet'. The enthusiasm of the born Hellenist mingles with the spirit of the Preacher[1]—who surely, contrary to common opinion, must have been a young man—as in some sad refrain of Theognis. But the English piece, already mentioned, written in Landor's honour, has something of Landor's own strictness in outline and high-bred beauty of phrase; and these were salutary stars for the poet of 'The Triumph of Time', with its beautiful profusion and verbal ebullience, to steer by. A clear political strain already exalts the verse of the younger republican aristocrat, and it is also heard, with less restraint, in the 'Song in Time of Revolution'. Mr. Swinburne's style at this time was greater and stronger than anything he had found to say. The result was that it often wreaked itself upon the air.

The full inspiration came from Italy, and the compelling voice was the voice of Mazzini, to whom the *Songs before Sunrise* and *A Song of Italy* are dedicated. Mr. Swinburne never offered any mere echo of Mazzini's doctrine.

I never pretended to see eye to eye with my illustrious friends and masters, Victor Hugo and Giuseppe Mazzini, in regard to the positive and passionate confidence of their sublime and purified theology.

Nor did he ever try to set forth in verse the whole of Mazzini's social and political religion. In this abstinence he was true to his lyrical and odic gift. A ruminative poet like Wordsworth—if ever Wordsworth could have risen to appreciate Mazzini's creed—would have covered a high tableland of leisurely blank verse with the abstract exposition of it. But in song and ode only a certain measure of such thinking can dissolve: if more is attempted, the result is a dreadful and dulling sediment of doctrine. The large emotions of fraternity and self-sacrifice

[1] See Eccl. i: i.

and ultimate hope are the lyric poet's true material, apart from all programmes and tactics. Also, Mr. Swinburne gave more expression to the revolutionary cry than his master. To Mazzini the overthrow of the existing order and the clamour for freedom, for freedom undefined, were a mere preface to the real work in hand.

We invoke (he says) a social world, a vast harmonious organization of the forces existing in undirected activity in that vast laboratory, the earth; and, in order to call this new world into being, and to lay the foundation of a pacific organization, we have recourse to those old habits of rebellion which consume our forces within the circle of individualism.

Not all of this idea is absorbed by the English poet; but some of it flowers in 'The Pilgrims' and in the 'Prelude' to the *Songs before Sunrise*. The 'Prelude' tells of the poet's escape from the exotic or orgiastic dreams of his younger fancy; but with the lure of the names— *Thyiades, Cotytto, Bassarid*—a gust of the old airs blows across the scene; and then, at the end, he turns again to the future and utters the public impulse of a whole era with a buoyant lyric passion that makes its own tune and flows without waste or riot and breaks into a beauty like that of the morning. The same is true of the 'Eve of Revolution', a poem of transcendent hope and insuperable will. Mazzini's vision is that of a perfected and pacified society; but his scholar rather dreams of such a vigilant heroic thinker as Mazzini himself, who risks his life but keeps his spirit free of fear and doubt during the unresting labours of his mortal lease.

These poems are surrounded by many more, which keep pace with the stages in the battle for Italian unity, or serve as inspiriting marches of comradeship in the pauses of the weightier music. 'Dirae', a sonnet-series that followed, is a frantic imprecation on the successive anniversaries of Garibaldi's check at Mentana, and is marred by Hugoesque virulence. The two worst influences on Mr. Swinburne's art have been Victor Hugo and the Authorized Version of the Bible. If only he had chosen Alfred de Vigny for his worship, what lapses and effusion had been spared! And almost every transference of scriptural style, by way of parody or irony, to erotic or anti-clerical rhetoric, has been a failure. There is no good reason why the noble manner of our old translators of Hebrew poetry should be thus misused. There is no cruder weapon for the expression of invective. One exception may be found in the poem called 'Before a Crucifix', where the rhetoric, if it does not quite find entrance, calls and clangs at the gate of the heart owing to the splendour of the rhythm. But among these odes and poems of liberation are found the highest and finest of Swinburne's lyrical writings. They are an eager, young-hearted accompaniment to the public events of the years 1866 to 1870. If at times they run to formless overflow, they are pure in phrasing and infallible in cadence. Of this poet it may too often be felt that his 'strength's abundance weakens his own heart'. The stream is so high in flood, that the banks are lost and the boundaries blurred, though the course is true and the higher landmarks visible. The series may be said to close with the 'Ode on the Proclamation of the French Republic'. Unity in Italy was won, but without the republic dreamed of by Mazzini; and Mr. Swinburne, who may not have felt drawn to celebrate what seemed a triumph marred, kept his paean for the France of 1871. In his later volumes there are many political verses, but not so many as might have been hoped that are fresh, adequate, and beautiful. Some, like those on Nelson, speak to all. The comminations on Gladstone and the Boers are not likely to please even fanatics. But the hopes declared in the *Songs before Sunrise*, if at some seasons they have faded out of sight, are in their nature lasting, like that high expression of them to which Mr. Swinburne rose in his fortunate hour.

## V.

The abstract and moral passion for mankind does not always wear long in an Englishman. Mr. Swinburne gave it voice in 1870; even in 1875, in the *Songs of Two Nations*, it is heard. It has not come to him from Comte with his quaint hierarchies, so dangerous if they were not mere nightmares, but from those Republican ardours of Mazzini, from the emancipation of Italy and France. Then Mr. Swinburne came back to themes which seem to have lain deeper in his blood; to Mary of Scotland, to our Renaissance drama, to Britain and her present hopes. But meanwhile he took leave of those free artists of France with whom his own affinity was strong. Rossetti had translated from Villon with even a more intimate sense of words than the younger poet, but his pent and searching spirit must have cared far less for that bright and blackguardly ballad-maker. Mr. Swinburne's 'Ballade' on Villon might have been made on a friend or companion who died yesterday:—

> Poor splendid wings so frayed and soiled and torn!
> Poor kind wild eyes so dashed with light quick tears!
> Poor perfect voice, most blithe when most forlorn.

It does not appear whether personal acquaintance inspired the laments on Gautier and Baudelaire; we hardly trace it in the faint and acrid immortelles that are laid upon their tombs in the Second Series of *Poems and Ballads*. There Mr. Swinburne is back once more in the land of inquisitive passion, of absorption in form, on the further side of good and evil. His public and political enthusiasm is in arrest. Few men cared so sublimely little for the general fates of the world as the authors of *Les Fleurs du Mal* and *Le Roi Candaule*; and rightly, for the world was not their business. It takes a Frenchman to be thorough, whether in his devotion or in his apathy to the hopes of man. There had been signs in 'Félise' of the study of Baudelaire; and Gautier's best-known and strangest, though not his greatest, piece of decoration, 'the golden book of spirit and sense',[1] had received a sonnet from his English brother; but the elegies of Mr. Swinburne on both poets ring deeper than those tributes, and rarely has a foreign writer earned a more glorious valediction from an English mourner than Baudelaire in 'Ave atque Vale':—

> For thee, O now a silent soul, my brother,
> Take at my hands this garland, and farewell.
> Thin is the leaf, and chill the wintry smell,
> And chill the solemn earth, a fatal mother,
> With sadder than the Niobean womb,
> And in the hollow of her breasts a tomb.

This part of the Second Series of *Poems and Ballads* is an elegy of the poet on himself, a farewell to his youth and its early masters, a pagan wayside ritual, an *ex voto* before he travels on, restless-hearted, with a scornful look askance at the peace of the Christian graveyards.

The Second Series appeared in 1878; and meanwhile more had been done. The two Hellenics, *Atalanta* and *Erechtheus*, belonging to the golden youth of the poet, are significantly reprinted, not amongst his plays, but amongst his lyrics and narratives. Their interest is far more than purely musical; but no poems leave a surer conviction that the untouched musical resources of the language are infinite; that no measure is so old as to be dead, and that when the right player comes the long burden of the metrical past is as nothing. And most of their glory lies in the rhymed measures of the choruses, which attain a longer sweep of line and a fuller rush of movement than all but the best of the *Poems and Ballads*. In his new preface Mr. Swinburne records his own preference to *Erechtheus* on the score of 'the whole being greater than

---

[1] From Swinburne's 'Sonnet (with a copy of *Mademoiselle de Maupin*)'.

the parts', while of the constructive power in *Atalanta* he can hardly say so much.

The two best things in these two Greek plays, the antiphonal lamentation for the dying Meleager and the choral presentation of stormy battle between the forces of land and sea, lose less by such division from the main body of the poem than would those scenes in *Bothwell* which deal with the turning-point in the life of Mary Stuart on the central and conclusive day of Carberry Hill.

Charged as these poems are with reminiscences of Greek tragedy, and carefully as they are laid out on the Greek convention, their predominantly lyric tone, overflowing even into dialogue and mono-logue, keeps them from being Greek in essence, and leaves them only the more original. They are, in soul and spirit, not so near even to the more decorative kind of ancient drama as *Samson Agonistes* is to the plays of Sophocles. It is less the thought than the sure mastery of swift-footed and magnificent cadence that remains upon the memory—a cadence new and young that has not yet spent itself in myriad self-echoes.

## VI.

Four years after the second *Poems and Ballads*, in 1882, came the romance *Tristram of Lyonesse*. The lyrical poet is trying, in a narrative metre, to sing and tell a story at the same time. The verse goes apace, but the manner is so expansive and diffusive that the tale goes slowly. The same tale can be stripped and presented in a short ballad, the leisurely psychology disappearing, and giving us instead the quick strokes of vital passion. There is an old Icelandic ballad on Tristram, where the refrain of seven words gives the heart of the story: *their doom was nought, save to part*; and this method is one for a concentrated, economical artist. But the old regular way, the spacious, tardy, and not less beautiful way of romancing, as it is seen in Chaucer's *Troilus and Creseide*, or in Morris's 'Story of Rhodope', is used in *Tristram of Lyonesse*: but here the movement is vehement and quick, there it is gentle and leisurely. The surging rollers of its rhyme advance rapidly and break loudly, but the shore is sometimes invisible, and the faces of the personages, the situation at a given moment, are obscured in the rumour and the spray. Our old heroic couplet has never been so hastened by the devices of overflowing line and trisyllabic bar and by the lightening of accent. Yet all such comparisons, which try to convey the impression of rapid *tempo*, are really out of place. For *Tristram* is a true romance, where the conception of time is abolished altogether. This is the distinguishing mark of a story where the real persons are only two or three, and the active world is a far-off murmur, not suffered to intrude otherwise. For time can only be measured in such a story by the interruptions of the world, and these are never suffered to happen. At the crises, no time passes; but the rapid absorbed life of a few instants in the heart of Iseult or Cressida belies all measurement by beats of the clock. Nor are the characters distinctly shown; for the subject of *Tristram* is not so much the long-canonized lovers as Love itself, and the epilogue on 'the light and sound and darkness of the sea' is in accord with their fates.

## VII.

The *Tale of Balen*, printed fifteen years later, is a greater poem and better done than *Tristram*, though its theme is not so great. It reaches the heart, through the ear, more surely, and the versification has a clearer beauty. It is another story of guilt, though fate is the guilty party and punishes the good and noble as if the guilt were theirs. The story is one of the large heroic episodes—the predestined, innocent, and mutual death of brother at the hand of brother, beguiled and environed by treacherous black magic. Tennyson tells the story too; but it is less suited than some other chapters of Malory to his far-sought felicity of decoration and his various but slowly-wheeling blank verse. Mr. Swinburne rides, as he tells us,

> Reining my rhymes into buoyant order
> Through honeyed leagues of the northland border;

and the gusty airs and thrilling scents of his own countryside pass into the aspiring fourfold rimes and pathetic refluent close of each stanza. The old harmony by contrast which pervaded *Poems and Ballads*, of the sense of joy with the countervailing sense of doom, is here with a difference: for it goes to a proud and manly march. Balen, *fey*, but jaunting with a high heart through omens and the invisible smiting foes that leave their prey in his path and vanish, and ever nearing the fratricidal field by the accursed castle, is he not the latest and perhaps the last creation of those romancers of a renewed Middle Age who first spoke in the 'Defence of Guenevere', now close on half a century ago? Yet, from the severe and rigid concentration of the youthful Morris, to the copious ease and generous magnificence of his friend, the step in workmanship is far. *Balen* shows that vigour of the Northern blood, wild-hearted and strong-headed, which befits a teller of tales in rhyme. The exotic and plaintive moods of the *Poems and Ballads* are still present, and intervene in undertone, and save the story from being no more than a capital Walter Scott ballad of killing and foray and perfunctory romance.

So long, so voluble, an interval after *Tristram*, and then, in *Balen*, a sudden resurrection of lyric power! The *Roundels*, with their odd, often ineffectual refrains, like childish gestures; the Third Series of *Poems and Ballads*, and *Astrophel*, and its companions, hard to remember; *A Midsummer Holiday*; all again and again stirring dimly the old fascination; many of these are the work of a wonderful improviser, so sure of doing his feat that he cannot fail if he tries, and his skill becomes involuntary and monotonous; he is heard at last with more surprise than pleasure. The composition is empty, the executant infallible; as if he had wagered how well he could do—nothing. The exertion of great skill *in vacuo* always becomes at last supremely painful. We blame ourselves for wearying of that with which no fault can be found, except that it is faultlessly null. Much of Mr. Swinburne's song and lyric for twenty years has been performance rather than creation. No one else could write it; it is sincere; but it perishes like the scud or the cloud-wreath, in the act of formation. His true power during that long interval lies in prose and drama. The present edition does not give the critical papers; the English dramas are contained in a separate one. Both justify a reissue more loudly than much that is here reprinted. The noble early commentary on Blake, now republished, is written with the sanity of a true poet; and the articles on the playwrights from Chapman to Heywood, produced mostly in the 'eighties, are even better as criticisms than the companion sonnets, superb in harmony and strenuous in effort but not always fortunate as poems. The reader of the prose and verse eulogies on Hugo sickens at the calls on his admiration; but *A Note on Charlotte Brontë* and others of the English studies abide, in their essential justice, their splendid praise, and their poetic insight. The evolution of Mr. Swinburne's dramatic style can be traced from the lyrism of *Chastelard*, through the epical tragedy of *Bothwell*, to the curt strength of *The Sisters*—where the phrasing is only just within the liberties of verse—and of *Rosamund, Queen of the Lombards*. This change has meant a sterner hold on character and historical truth, and an increase in pure brainwork. But his plays, like his prose writings, are very nearly a life-work in themselves, and would call for a respectful and a separate notice. Nor is the time yet ready for the final anthology which will be made by Time from the six volumes before us, with their rich variety, here so scantily chronicled, of landscape, and sea-piece, and ballad, and memorial ode. The fame of a profuse and unequal and unresting writer has of necessity to wait longer than that of one who, like Dante Gabriel Rossetti, winnows his work and saves only that which possesses the utmost intensity and perfection, and who is thus his own anthologist. Yet the ultimate garland of the more spendthrift singer may prove to be not less in quantity, as it will certainly not rank lower in beauty of its own noble order.

# 31. Max Beerbohm: 'No. 2 The Pines'

## 1920

Beerbohm's essay, readable and wisely sympathetic as it is, contains a touch of the kind of caricature found in the drawings of his *Pre-Raphaelite Circle*, as well as a bias traceable in part to opinion fostered by Gosse. It is nevertheless an engaging picture of Swinburne and of Watts-Dunton in their later years (see Introduction, section VI).

From *And Even Now* (1920) by special permission of William Heinemann and E. P. Dutton, owners of the copyright.

[*Early in the year* 1914 *Mr. Edmund Gosse told me he was asking certain of his friends to write for him a few words apiece in description of Swinburne as they had known or seen him at one time or another; and he was so good as to wish to include in this gathering a few words by myself. I found it hard to be brief without seeming irreverent. I failed in the attempt to make of my subject a snapshot that was not a grotesque. So I took refuge in an ampler scope. I wrote a reminiscential essay. From that essay I made an extract, which I gave to Mr. Gosse. From that extract he made a quotation in his enchanting biography. The words quoted by him reappear here in the midst of the whole essay as I wrote it. I dare not hope they are unashamed of their humble surroundings.—M. B.*]

In my youth the suburbs were rather looked down on—I never quite knew why. It was held anomalous, and a matter for merriment, that Swinburne lived in one of them. For my part, had I known as a fact that Catullus was still alive, I should have been as ready to imagine him living in Putney as elsewhere. The marvel would have been merely that he lived. And Swinburne's survival struck as surely as could his have struck in me the chord of wonder.

Not, of course, that he had achieved a feat of longevity. He was far from the Psalmist's limit. Nor was he one of those men whom one associates with the era in which they happened to be young. Indeed, if

233

there was one man belonging less than any other to Mid-Victorian days, Swinburne was that man. But by the calendar it was in those days that he had blazed—blazed forth with so unexampled a suddenness of splendour; and in the light of that conflagration all that he had since done, much and magnificent though this was, paled. The essential Swinburne was still the earliest. He was and would always be the flammiferous boy of the dim past—a legendary creature, sole kin to the phoenix. It had been impossible that he should ever surpass himself in the artistry that was from the outset his; impossible that he should bring forth rhythms lovelier and greater than those early rhythms, or exercise over them a mastery more than—absolute. Also, it had been impossible that the first wild ardour of spirit should abide unsinkingly in him. Youth goes. And there was not in Swinburne that basis on which a man may in his maturity so build as to make good, in some degree, the loss of what is gone. He was not a thinker: his mind rose ever away from reason to rhapsody; neither was he human. He was a king crowned but not throned. He was a singing bird that could build no nest. He was a youth who could not afford to age. Had he died young, literature would have lost many glories; but none so great as the glories he had already given, nor any such as we should fondly imagine ourselves bereft of by his early death. A great part of Keats' fame rests on our assumption of what he *would* have done. But—even granting that Keats may have had in him more than had Swinburne of stuff for development—I believe that had he lived on we should think of him as author of the poems that in fact we know. Not philosophy, after all, not humanity, just sheer joyous power of song, is the primal thing in poetry. Ideas, and flesh and blood, are but reserves to be brought up when the poet's youth is going. When the bird can no longer sing in flight, let the nest be ready. After the king has dazzled us with his crown, let him have something to sit down on. But the session on throne or in nest is not the divine period. Had Swinburne's genius been of the kind that solidifies, he would yet at the close of the nine-teenth century have been for us young men virtually—though not so definitely as in fact he was—the writer of *Atalanta in Calydon* and of *Poems and Ballads*.

Tennyson's death in '92 had not taken us at all by surprise. We had been fully aware that he was alive. He had always been careful to keep himself abreast of the times. Anything that came along—the Nebular Hypothesis at one moment, the Imperial Institute at another—won mention from his Muse. He had husbanded for his old age that which he had long ago inherited: middle age. If in our mourning for him there really was any tincture of surprise, this was due to merely the vague sense that he had in the fullness of time died rather prematurely: his middle-age might have been expected to go on flourishing for ever. But assuredly Tennyson dead laid no such strain on our fancy as Swinburne living.

It is true that Swinburne did, from time to time, take public notice of current affairs; but what notice he took did but seem to mark his remoteness from them, from us. The Boers, I remember, were the theme of a sonnet which embarrassed even their angriest enemies in our midst. He likened them, if I remember rightly, to 'hell-hounds foaming at the jaws'.[1] This was by some people taken as a sign that he had fallen away from that high generosity of spirit which had once been his. To me it meant merely that he thought of poor little England writhing under the heel of an alien despotism, just as, in the days when he really was interested in such matters, poor little Italy had writhen. I suspect, too, that the first impulse to write about the Boers came not from the Muse within, but from Theodore Watts-Dunton without. . . . 'Now, Algernon, we're at war, you know—at war with the Boers. I don't want to bother you at all, but I do think, my dear old friend, you oughtn't to let slip this opportunity of,' etc., etc.

Some such hortation is easily imaginable by any one who saw the two old friends together. The first time I had this honour, this sight for lasting and affectionate memory, must have been in the Spring of '99. In those days Theodore Watts (he had but recently taken on the -Dunton) was still something of a gadabout. I had met him here and there, he had said in his stentorian tones pleasant things to me about my writing, I sent him a new little book of mine, and in acknowledging this he asked me to come down to Putney and 'have luncheon and meet Swinburne'. Meet Catullus!

On the day appointed 'I came as one whose feet half linger.'[2] It is but a few steps from the railway-station in Putney High Street to No. 2. The Pines. I had expected a greater distance to the sanctuary— a walk in which to compose my mind and prepare myself for initiation. I laid my hand irresolutely against the gate of the bleak trim front-garden. I withdrew my hand, I went away. Out here were all the aspects of common modern life. In there was Swinburne. A butcher-

[1] Cf. 'The Transvaal', l. 13: 'To scourge these dogs, agape with jaws afoam'.
[2] An adaptation of 'In Memory of Walter Savage Landor', l. 21: 'I came as one whose thoughts half linger'.

boy went by, whistling. He was not going to see Swinburne. He could afford to whistle. I pursued my dilatory course up the slope of Putney, but at length it occurred to me that unpunctuality would after all be an imperfect expression of reverence, and I retraced my footsteps.

No. 2—prosaic inscription! But as that front-door closed behind me I had the instant sense of having slipped away from the harsh light of the ordinary and contemporary into the dimness of an odd, august past. Here, in this dark hall, the past was the present. Here loomed vivid and vital on the walls those women of Rossetti whom I had known but as shades. Familiar to me in small reproductions by photogravure, here they *themselves* were, life-sized, 'with curled-up lips and amorous hair'[1] done in the original warm crayon, all of them intently looking down on me while I took off my overcoat—all wondering who was this intruder from posterity. That they hung in the hall, evidently no more than an overflow, was an earnest of packed plenitude within. The room I was ushered into was a back-room, a dining-room, looking on to a good garden. It was, in form and 'fixtures', an in-alienably Mid-Victorian room, and held its stolid own in the riot of Rossettis. Its proportions, its window-sash bisecting the view of garden, its folding-doors (through which I heard the voice of Watts-Dunton booming mysteriously in the front room), its mantel-piece, its gas-brackets, all proclaimed that nothing ever would seduce them from their allegiance to Martin Tupper.[2] 'Nor me from mine', said the sturdy cruet-stand on the long expanse of table-cloth. The voice of Watts-Dunton ceased suddenly, and a few moments later its owner appeared. He had been dictating, he explained. 'A great deal of work on hand just now—a great deal of work.' . . . I remember that on my subsequent visits he was always, at the moment of my arrival, dicta-ting, and always greeted me with that phrase, 'A great deal of work on hand just now.' I used to wonder what work it was, for he pub-lished little enough. But I never ventured to inquire, and indeed rather cherished the mystery: it was a part of the dear little old man; it went with the something gnome-like about his swarthiness and chubbiness—went with the shaggy hair that fell over the collar of his eternally

---

[1] From 'The Leper', l. 12.

[2] Martin Tupper (1810-1889) was the author of a mediocre work in verse, *Proverbial Philosophy*, that enjoyed a tremendous vogue both in England and America, though derided by its more discerning readers. Partly because the name carries overtones of prosiness, Beerbohm uses 'Tupper' to recall an era. Note the later 'Tupperesque' and 'Tupperossettine', the latter combining the name with 'Rossetti'.

crumpled frock-coat, the shaggy eyebrows that overhung his bright little brown eyes, the shaggy moustache that hid his small round chin. It was a mystery inherent in the richly-laden atmosphere of The Pines. . . .

While I stood talking to Watts-Dunton—talking as loudly as he, for he was very deaf—I enjoyed the thrill of suspense in watching the door through which would appear—Swinburne. I asked after Mr. Swinburne's health. Watts-Dunton said it was very good: 'He always goes out for his long walk in the morning—wonderfully active. Active in mind, too. But I'm afraid you won't be able to get into touch with him. He's almost stone-deaf, poor fellow—almost stone-deaf now.' He changed the subject, and I felt I must be careful not to seem interested in Swinburne exclusively. I spoke of *Aylwin*. The parlourmaid brought in the hot dishes. The great moment was at hand.

Nor was I disappointed. Swinburne's entry was for me a great moment. Here, suddenly visible in the flesh, was the legendary being and divine singer. Here he was, shutting the door behind him as might anybody else, and advancing—a strange small figure in grey, having an air at once noble and roguish, proud and skittish. My name was roared to him. In shaking his hand, I bowed low, of course—a bow *de coeur*; and he, in the old aristocratic manner, bowed equally low, but with such swiftness that we narrowly escaped concussion. You do not usually associate a man of genius, when you see one, with any social class; and, Swinburne being of an aspect so unrelated as it was to any species of human kind, I wondered the more that almost the first impression he made on me, or would make on any one, was that of a very great gentleman indeed. Not of an *old* gentleman, either. Sparse and straggling though the grey hair was that fringed the immense pale dome of his head, and venerably haloed though he was for me by his greatness, there was yet about him something—boyish? girlish? childish, rather; something of a beautifully well-bred child. But he had the eyes of a god, and the smile of an elf. In figure, at first glance, he seemed almost fat; but this was merely because of the way he carried himself, with his long neck strained so tightly back that he all receded from the waist upwards. I noticed afterwards that this deportment made the back of his jacket hang quite far away from his legs; and so small and sloping were his shoulders that the jacket seemed ever so likely to slip right off. I became aware, too, that when he bowed he did not unbend his back, but only his neck—the length of the neck accounting for the depth of the bow. His hands were tiny,

even for his size, and they fluttered helplessly, touchingly, unceasingly.
Directly after my introduction, we sat down to the meal. Of course
I had never hoped to 'get into touch with him' reciprocally. Quite
apart from his deafness, I was too modest to suppose he could be
interested in anything I might say. But—for I knew he had once been
as high and copious a singer in talk as in verse—I had hoped to hear
utterances from him. And it did not seem that my hope was to be
fulfilled. Watts-Dunton sat at the head of the table, with a huge and
very Tupperesque joint of roast mutton in front of him, Swinburne
and myself close up to him on either side. He talked only to me. This
was the more tantalizing because Swinburne seemed as though he were
bubbling over with all sorts of notions. Not that he looked at either
of us. He smiled only to himself, and to his plateful of meat, and to the
small bottle of Bass's pale ale that stood before him—ultimate allowance of one who had erst clashed cymbals in Naxos. This small bottle
he eyed often and with enthusiasm, seeming to waver between the
rapture of broaching it now and the grandeur of having it to look
forward to. It made me unhappy to see what trouble he had in managing
his knife and fork. Watts-Dunton told me on another occasion that
this infirmity of the hands had been lifelong—had begun before Eton
days. The Swinburne family had been alarmed by it and had consulted
a specialist, who said that it resulted from 'an excess of electric vitality',
and that any attempt to stop it would be harmful. So they had let it
be. I have known no man of genius who had not to pay, in some
affliction or defect either physical or spiritual, for what the gods had
given him. Here, in this fluttering of his tiny hands, was a part of the
price that Swinburne had to pay. No doubt he had grown accustomed
to it many lustres before I met him, and I need not have felt at all
unhappy at what I tried not to see. He, evidently, was quite gay, in
his silence—and in the world that was for him silent. I had, however,
the maddening suspicion that he would have liked to talk. Why
wouldn't Watts-Dunton roar him an opportunity? I felt I had been
right perhaps in feeling that the lesser man was—no, not jealous of the
greater whom he had guarded so long and with such love, but anxious
that he himself should be as fully impressive to visitors as his fine gifts
warranted. Not, indeed, that he monopolised the talk. He seemed to
regard me as a source of information about all the latest 'movements',
and I had to shout banalities while he munched his mutton—banalities
whose one saving grace for me was that they were inaudible to
Swinburne. Had I met Swinburne's gaze, I should have faltered. Now

and again his shining light-grey eyes roved from the table, darting this way and that—across the room, up at the ceiling, out of the window; only never at us. Somehow this aloofness gave no hint of indifference. It seemed to be, rather a point in good manners—the good manners of a child 'sitting up to table', not 'staring', not 'asking questions', and reflecting great credit on its invaluable old nurse. The child sat happy in the wealth of its inner life; the child was content not to speak until it were spoken to; but, but, I felt it did want to be spoken to. And, at length, it *was*.

So soon as the mutton had been replaced by the apple-pie, Watts-Dunton leaned forward and 'Well, Algernon', he roared, 'how was it on the Heath today?' Swinburne, who had meekly inclined his ear to the question, now threw back his head, uttering a sound that was like the cooing of a dove, and forthwith, rapidly, ever so musically, he spoke to us of his walk; spoke not in the strain of a man who had been taking his daily exercise on Putney Heath, but rather in that of a Peri who had at long last been suffered to pass through Paradise. And rather than that he spoke would I say that he cooingly and flutingly *sang* of his experience. The wonders of this morning's wind and sun and clouds were expressed in a flow of words so right and sentences so perfectly balanced that they would have seemed pedantic had they not been clearly as spontaneous as the wordless notes of a bird in song. The frail, sweet voice rose and fell, lingered, quickened, in all manner of trills and roulades. That he himself could not hear it, seemed to me the greatest loss his deafness inflicted on him. One would have expected this disability to mar the music; but it didn't; save that now and again a note would come out metallic and over-shrill, the tones were under good control. The whole manner and method had certainly a strong element of oddness; but no one incapable of condemning as unmanly the song of a lark would have called it affected. I had met young men of whose enunciation Swinburne's now reminded me. In them the thing had always irritated me very much; and I now became sure that it had been derived from people who had derived it in old Balliol days from Swinburne himself. One of the points familiar to me in such enunciation was the habit of stressing extremely, and lackadaisically dwelling on, some particular syllable. In Swinburne this trick was delightful—because it wasn't a trick, but a need of his heart. Well do I remember his ecstasy of emphasis and immensity of pause when he described how he had seen in a perambulator on the Heath today 'the most BEAUT—iful babbie ever beheld by mortal eyes'. For babies, as some of his later volumes testify, he had a sort of idolatry. After Mazzini had followed Landor to Elysium, and Victor Hugo had followed Mazzini, babies were what among live creatures most evoked Swinburne's genius for self-abasement. His rapture about this especial 'babbie' was such as to shake within me my hitherto firm conviction that, whereas the young of the brute creation are already beautiful at the age of five minutes, the human young never begin to be so before the age of three years. I suspect Watts-Dunton of having shared my lack of innate enthusiasm. But it was one of Swinburne's charms, as I was to find, that he took for granted every one's delight in what he himself so fervidly delighted in. He could as soon have imagined a man not loving the very sea as not doting on the aspect of babies and not reading at least one play by an Elizabethan or Jacobean dramatist every day.

I forget whether it was at this my first meal or at another that he described a storm in which, one night years ago, with Watts-Dunton he had crossed the Channel. The rhythm of his great phrases was as the rhythm of those waves, and his head swayed in accordance to it like the wave-rocked boat itself. He hymned in memory the surge and darkness, the thunder and foam and phosphorescence—'You remember, Theodore? You remember the PHOS—phorescence?'—all so beautiful and vividly that I almost felt storm-bound and in peril of my life. To disentangle one from another of the several occasions on which I heard him talk is difficult because the procedure was so invariable: Watts-Dunton always dictating when I arrived, Swinburne always appearing at the moment of the meal, always the same simple and substantial fare, Swinburne never allowed to talk before the meal was half over. As to this last point, I soon realized that I had been quite unjust in suspecting Watts-Dunton of selfishness. It was simply a sign of the care with which he watched over his friend's welfare. Had Swinburne been admitted earlier to the talk, he would not have taken his proper quantity of roast mutton. So soon, always, as he had taken that, the embargo was removed, the chance was given him. And swiftly though he embraced the chance, and much though he made of it in the courses of apple-pie and of cheese, he seemed touchingly ashamed of 'holding forth'. Often, before he had said his really full say on the theme suggested by Watts-Dunton's loud interrogation, he would curb his speech and try to eliminate himself, bowing his head over his plate; and then, when he had promptly been brought in again, he would always try to atone for his inhibiting deafness by much reference and deference to all that we might otherwise have to say. 'I hope', he would coo to me, 'my friend Watts-Dunton, who'— and here he would turn and make a little bow to Watts-Dunton—'is himself a scholar, will bear me out when I say'—or 'I hardly know', he would flute to his old friend, 'whether Mr. Beerbohm'—here a bow to me—'will agree with me in my opinion of' some delicate point in Greek prosody or some incident in an old French romance I had never heard of.

On one occasion, just before the removal of the mutton, Watts-Dunton had been asking me about an English translation that had been made of M. Rostand's *Cyrano de Bergerac*. He then took my information as the match to ignite the Swinburnian tinder. 'Well, Algernon, it seems that *Cyrano de Bergerac*'—but this first spark was enough: instantly Swinburne was praising the works of Cyrano de Bergerac. Of M. Rostand he may have heard, but him he forgot. Indeed I never heard Swinburne mention a single contemporary writer. His mind ranged and revelled always in the illustrious or obscure past. To him the writings of Cyrano de Bergerac were as fresh as paint—as fresh as to me, alas, was the news of their survival. 'Of course, of course, you have read *L'Histoire Comique des États et des Empires de la Lune*?' I admitted, by gesture and facial expression, that I had not. Whereupon he reeled out curious extracts from that allegory—'almost as good as *Gulliver*'—with a memorable instance of the way in which the traveller to the moon was shocked by the conversation of the natives, and the natives' sense of propriety was outraged by the conversation of the traveller.

In life, as in (that for him more truly actual thing) literature, it was always the preterit that enthralled him. Of any passing events, of anything the newspapers were full of, never a word from him; and I should have been sorry if there had been. But I did, through the medium of Watts-Dunton, sometimes start him on topics that might have led him to talk of Rossetti and other old comrades. For me the names of those men breathed the magic of the past, just as it was breathed for me by Swinburne's presence. For him, I suppose, they were but a bit of the present, and the mere fact that they had dropped out of it was not enough to hallow them. He never mentioned them. But I was glad to see that he revelled as wistfully in the days just before his own as I in the days just before mine. He recounted to us things he had been told in his boyhood by an aged aunt, or great-aunt—'one of the Ashburnhams'; how, for example, she had been taken by her mother to a county ball, a distance of many miles, and, on the way home through the frosty and snowy night, the family-coach had suddenly stopped: there was a crowd of dark figures in the way . . . at which point Swinburne stopped too, before saying, with an ineffable smile and in a voice faint with appreciation, 'They were burying a suicide at the cross-roads.'

Vivid as this Hogarthian night-scene was to me, I saw beside it another scene: a great panelled room, a grim old woman in a high-backed chair, and, restless on a stool at her feet, an extraordinary little nephew with masses of auburn hair and with tiny hands clasped in supplication—'Tell me more, Aunt Ashburnham, tell me more!'

And now, clearlier still, as I write in these after-years, do I see that dining-room of The Pines; the long white stretch of table-cloth, with Swinburne and Watts-Dunton and another at the extreme end of it; Watts-Dunton between us, very low down over his plate, very cosy and hirsute, and rather like the dormouse at that long tea-table which Alice found in Wonderland. I see myself sitting there wide-eyed, as Alice sat. And, had the hare been a great poet, and the hatter a great gentleman, and neither of them mad but each only very odd and vivacious, I might see Swinburne as a glorified blend of those two.

When the meal ended—for, alas! it was not, like that meal in Wonderland, unending—Swinburne would dart round the table, proffer his hand to me, bow deeply, bow to Watts-Dunton also, and disappear. 'He always walks in the morning, writes in the afternoon, and reads in the evening,' Watts-Dunton would say with a touch of tutorial pride in this regimen.

That parting bow of Swinburne to his old friend was characteristic of his whole relation to him. Cronies though they were, these two, knit together with bonds innumerable, the greater man was always *aux petits soins*[1] for the lesser, treating him as a newly-arrived young guest might treat an elderly host. Some twenty years had passed since that night when, ailing and broken—thought to be nearly dying, Watts-Dunton told me—Swinburne was brought in a four-wheeler to The Pines. Regular private nursing-homes either did not exist in those days or were less in vogue than they are now. The Pines was to be a sort of private nursing-home for Swinburne. It was a good one. He recovered. He was most grateful to his friend and saviour. He made as though to depart, was persuaded to stay a little longer, and

---

[1] 'With delicate attention.

then a little longer than that. But I rather fancy that, to the last, he never did, in the fullness of his modesty and good manners, consent to regard his presence as a matter of course, or as anything but a terminable intrusion and obligation. His bow seemed always to convey that.

Swinburne having gone from the room, in would come the parlour-maid. The table was cleared, the fire was stirred, two leather arm-chairs were pushed up to the hearth. Watts-Dunton wanted gossip of the present. I wanted gossip of the great past. We settled down for a long, comfortable afternoon together.

Only once was the ritual varied. Swinburne (I was told before luncheon) had expressed a wish to show me his library. So after the meal he did not bid us his usual adieu, but with much courtesy invited us and led the way. Up the staircase he then literally bounded—three, literally three, stairs at a time. I began to follow at the same rate, but immediately slackened speed for fear that Watts-Dunton behind us might be embittered at sight of so much youth and legerity. Swin-burne waited on the threshold to receive us, as it were, and pass us in. Watts-Dunton went and ensconced himself snugly in a corner. The sun had appeared after a grey morning, and it pleasantly flooded this big living-room whose walls were entirely lined with the mellow backs of books. Here, as host, among his treasures, Swinburne was more than ever attractive. He was as happy as was any mote in the sunshine about him; and the fluttering of his little hands, and feet too, was but as a token of so much felicity. He looked older, it is true, in the strong light. But these added years made only more notable his youngness of heart. An illustrious bibliophile among his books? A birthday child, rather, among his toys.

Proudly he explained to me the general system under which the volumes were ranged in this or that division of shelves. Then he conducted me to a chair near the window, left me there, flew away, flew up the rungs of a mahogany ladder, plucked a small volume, and in a twinkling was at my side: 'This, I *think*, will please you!' It did. It had a beautifully engraved title-page and a pleasing scent of old, old leather. It was *editio princeps* of a play by some lesser Elizabethan or Jacobean. 'Of course you know it?' my host fluted.

How I wished I could say that I knew it and loved it well! I revealed to him (for by speaking very loudly towards his inclined head I was able to make him hear) that I had not read it. He envied any one who had such pleasure in store. He darted to the ladder, and came back thrusting gently into my hands another volume of like date: 'Of course you know *this?*'

Again I had to confess that I did not, and to shout my appreciation of the fount of type, the margins, the binding. He beamed agreement, and fetched another volume. Archly he indicated the title, cooing, 'You are a lover of *this*, I hope?' And again I was shamed by my inexperience.

I did not pretend to know this particular play, but my tone implied that I had always been *meaning* to read it and had always by some mischance been prevented. For his sake as well as my own I did want to acquit myself passably. I wanted for him the pleasure of seeing his joys shared by a representative, however humble, of the common world. I turned the leaves caressingly, looking from them to him, while he dilated on the beauty of this and that scene in the play. Anon he fetched another volume, and another, always with the same faith that *this* was a favourite of mine. I quibbled, I evaded, I was very enthusiastic and uncomfortable. It was with intense relief that I beheld the title-page of yet another volume which (silently, this time) he laid before me—*The Country Wench*. 'This of course I have read,' I heartily shouted.

Swinburne stepped back. 'You have? You have read it? Where?' he cried, in evident dismay.

Something was wrong. Had I *not*, I quickly wondered, read this play? 'Oh yes,' I shouted, 'I have read it.'

'But when? Where?' entreated Swinburne, adding that he had supposed it to be the sole copy extant.

I floundered. I wildly said I thought I must have read it years ago in the Bodleian.

'Theodore! Do you hear this? It seems that they have now a copy of *The Country Wench* in the Bodleian! Mr. Beerbohm found one there—oh when? in what year?' he appealed to me.

I said it might have been six, seven, eight years ago. Swinburne knew for certain that no copy had been there *twelve* years ago, and was surprised that he had not heard of the acquisition. 'They might have told me,' he wailed.

I sacrificed myself on the altar of sympathy. I admitted that I might have been mistaken—must have been—must have confused this play with some other. I dipped into the pages and 'No,' I shouted, 'this I have *never* read.'

His equanimity was restored. He was up the ladder and down again, showing me further treasures with all pride and ardour. At length, Watts-Dunton, afraid that his old friend would tire himself, arose from his corner, and presently he and I went downstairs to the dining-room. It was in the course of our session together that there suddenly flashed across my mind the existence of a play called *The Country Wife*, by—wasn't it Wycherley? I had once read it—or read something about it. . . . But this matter I kept to myself. I thought I had appeared fool enough already.

I loved those sessions in that Tupperossettine dining-room, lair of solid old comfort and fervid old romanticism. Its odd duality befitted well its owner. The distinguished critic and poet, Rossetti's closest friend and Swinburne's, had been, for a while, in the dark ages, a solicitor; and one felt he had been a good one. His frock-coat, though the Muses had crumpled it, inspired confidence in his judgment of other things than verse. But let there be no mistake. He was no mere *bourgeois parnassien*, as his enemies insinuated. No doubt he had been very useful to men of genius, in virtue of qualities they lacked, but the secret of his hold on them was in his own rich nature. He was not only a born man of letters, he was a deeply emotional human being whose appeal was as much to the heart as to the head. The romantic Celtic mysticism of *Aylwin*, with its lack of fashionable Celtic nebulosity, lends itself, if you will, to laughter, though personally I saw nothing funny in it: it seemed to me, before I was in touch with the author, a work of genuine expression from within; and that it truly was so I presently knew. The mysticism of Watts-Dunton (who, once comfortably settled at the fireside, knew no reserve) was in contrast with the frock-coat and the practical abilities; but it was essential, and they were of the surface. For humorous Rossetti, I daresay, the very contrast made Theodore's company the more precious. He himself had assuredly been, and the memory of him still was, the master-fact in Watts-Dunton's life. 'Algernon' was as an adopted child, 'Gabriel' as a long-lost only brother. As he was to the outer world of his own day, so too to posterity Rossetti, the man, is con-jectural and mysterious. We know that he was in his prime the most inspiring and splendid of companions. But we know this only by faith. The evidence is as vague as it is emphatic. Of the style and substance of not a few great talkers in the past we can piece together some more or less vivid and probably erroneous notion. But about Rossetti nothing has been recorded in such a way as to make him even faintly emerge. I suppose he had in him what reviewers seem to find so often in books: a quality that defies analysis. Listening to Watts-Dunton, I was always in hope that when next the long-lost turned up—for he was continually doing so—in the talk, I should *see* him, *hear* him, and share the rapture. But the revelation was not to be. You might think that to hear him called 'Gabriel' would have given me a sense of propinquity. But I felt no nearer to him than you feel to the Archangel who bears that name and no surname.

It was always when Watts-Dunton spoke carelessly, casually, of some to me illustrious figure in the past, that I had the sense of being wafted right into that past and plumped down in the very midst of it. When he spoke with reverence of this and that great man whom he had known, he did not thus waft and plump me; for I, too, revered those names. But I had the magical transition whenever one of the immortals was mentioned in the tone of those who knew him before he had put on immortality. Browning, for example, was a name deeply honoured by me. 'Browning, yes', said Watts-Dunton, in the course of an afternoon, 'Browning', and he took a sip of the steaming whisky-toddy that was a point in our day's ritual. 'I was a great diner-out in the old times. I used to dine out every night in the week. Browning was a great diner-out, too. We were always meeting. What a pity he went on writing all those plays! He hadn't any gift for drama—none. I never could understand why he took to play-writing.' He wagged his head, gazing regretfully into the fire, and added, 'Such a *clever* fellow, too!'

Whistler, though alive and about, was already looked to as a hierarch by the young. Not so had he been looked to by Rossetti. The thrill of the past was always strong in me when Watts-Dunton mentioned—seldom without a guffaw did he mention—'Jimmy Whistler'. I think he put in the surname because 'that fellow' had not behaved well to Swinburne. But he could not omit the nickname, because it was impossible for him to feel the right measure of resentment against 'such a funny fellow'. As heart-full of old hates as of old loves was Watts-Dunton, and I take it as high testimony to the charm of Whistler's quaintness that Watts-Dunton did not hate *him*. You may be aware that Swinburne, in '88, wrote for one of the monthly reviews a criticism of the 'Ten O'Clock' lecture. He paid courtly compliments to Whistler as a painter, but joined issues with his theories. Straightway there appeared in the *World* a little letter from Whistler, deriding 'one Algernon Swinburne—outsider—Putney'. It was not in itself a very pretty or amusing letter; and still less so did it seem in the light of the facts which Watts-Dunton told me in some such words as these: 'After he'd published that lecture of his, Jimmy Whistler had me to dine with him at Kettner's or somewhere. He said "Now, Theodore, I want you to do me a favour." He wanted to get me to get Swinburne to write an article about his lecture. I said "No, Jimmy Whistler, I can't ask Algernon to do that. He's got a great deal of work on hand just now—a great deal of work. And besides, this sort of thing wouldn't be at all in his line." But Jimmy Whistler went on appealing to me. He said it would do him no end of good if Swinburne wrote about him. And—well, I half gave in: I said perhaps I *would* mention the matter to Algernon. And next day I did. I could see Algernon didn't want to do it at all. But—well, there, he said he'd do it to please *me*. And he did it. And then Jimmy Whistler published that letter. A very shabby trick—very shabby indeed.' Of course I do not vouch for the exact words in which Watts-Dunton told me this tale; but this was exactly the tale he told me. I expressed my astonishment. He added that of course he 'never wanted to see the fellow again after that, and never did'. But presently, after a long gaze into the coals, he emitted a chuckle, as for earlier memories of 'such a funny fellow'. One quite recent memory he had, too. 'When I took on the name of Dunton, I had a note from him. Just this, with his butterfly signature: *Theodore! What's Dunton?* That was very good—very good. . . . But, of course', he added gravely, 'I took no notice.' And no doubt, quite apart from the difficulty of finding an answer in the same vein, he did well in not replying. Loyalty to Swinburne forbade. But I see a certain pathos in the unanswered message. It was a message from the hand of an old jester, but also, I think, from the heart of an old man—a signal waved jauntily, but in truth wistfully, across the gulf of years and estrangement; and one could wish it had not been ignored.

Some time after Whistler died I wrote for one of the magazines an appreciation of his curious skill in the art of writing. Watts-Dunton told me he had heard of this from Swinburne. 'I myself', he said, 'very seldom read the magazines. But Algernon always has a look at them.' There was something to me very droll, and cheery too, in this picture of the illustrious recluse snatching at the current issues of our twaddle. And I was immensely pleased at hearing that my article had 'interested him very much'. I inwardly promised myself that as soon as I reached home I would read the article, to see just how it might have struck Swinburne. When in due course I did this, I regretted the tone of the opening sentences, in which I declared myself 'no book-lover' and avowed a preference for 'an uninterrupted view of my fellow-creatures'. I felt that had I known my article would meet the eye of Swinburne I should have cut out that overture. I dimly remembered a fine passage in one of his books of criticism—something (I preferred not to verify it) about 'the dotage of duncedom which cannot perceive, or the impudence of insignificance so presumptuous as to doubt, that the elements of life and literature are indivisibly mingled one in another and that he to whom books are less real than life will assuredly find in men and women as little reality as in his accursed crassness he deserves to discover.'[1] I quailed, I quailed. But mine is a resilient nature, and I promptly reminded myself that Swinburne's was a very impersonal one: he would not think the less highly of me, for he never had thought about me in any way whatsoever. All was well. I knew I could revisit The Pines, when next Watts-Dunton should invite me, without misgiving. And to this day I am rather proud of having been mentioned, though not by name, and not consciously, and unfavourably, by Swinburne.

I wonder that I cannot recall more than I do recall of those hours at The Pines. It is odd how little remains to a man of his own past—how few minutes of even his memorable hours are not quite forgotten, and how few seconds in any one of those minutes can be recaptured. . . . I am middle-aged, and have lived a vast number of seconds. Subtract $\frac{1}{3}$ of these, for one mustn't count sleep as life. The residual number is still enormous. Not a single one of those seconds was unimportant to me in its passage. Many of them bored me, of course; but even boredom is a positive state: one chafes at it and hates it; strange that one should afterwards forget it! And stranger still that of one's actual happinesses and unhappinesses so tiny and tattered a remnant clings about one! Of those hours at The Pines, of that past within a past, there was not a minute nor a second that I did not spend with pleasure. Memory is a great artist, we are told; she selects and rejects and shapes and so on. No doubt. Elderly persons would be utterly intolerable if they remembered *everything*. *Everything*, nevertheless, is just what they themselves would like to remember, and just what they would like to tell to *everybody*. Be sure that the Ancient Mariner, though he remembered quite as much as his audience wanted to hear, and rather more, about the albatross and the ghastly crew, was inwardly raging at the sketchiness of his own mind; and believe me that his stopping only one of three was the merest oversight. I

[1] Cf. the last part of No. 29.

248

should like to impose on the world many tomes about The Pines.

But, scant though my memories are of the moments there, very full and warm in me is the whole fused memory of the two dear old men that lived there. I wish I had Watts-Dunton's sure faith in meetings beyond the grave. I am glad I do not disbelieve that people may so meet. I like to think that some day in Elysium I shall—not without diffidence—approach these two and reintroduce myself. I can see just how courteously Swinburne will bow over my hand, not at all remembering who I am. Watts-Dunton will remember me after a moment: 'Oh, to be sure, yes indeed! I've a great deal of work on hand just now—a great deal of work, but' we shall sit down together on the asphodel, and I cannot but think we shall have whisky-toddy even there. He will not have changed. He will still be shaggy and old and chubby, and will wear the same frock-coat, with the same creases in it. Swinburne, on the other hand, will be quite, quite young, with a full mane of flaming auburn locks, and no clothes to hinder him from plunging back at any moment into the shining Elysian waters from which he will have just emerged. I see him skim lightly away into that element. On the strand is sitting a man of noble and furrowed brow. It is Mazzini, still thinking of Liberty. And anon the tiny young English amphibian comes ashore to fling himself dripping at the feet of the patriot and to carol the Republican ode he has composed in the course of his swim. 'He's wonderfully active—active in mind and body,' Watts-Dunton says to me. 'I come to the shore now and then, just to see how he's getting on. But I spend most of my time inland. I find I've so much to talk over with Gabriel. Not that he's quite the fellow he was. He always had rather a cult for Dante, you know, and now he's more than ever under the Florentine influence. He lives in a sort of monastery that Dante has here; and there he sits painting imaginary portraits of Beatrice, and giving them all to Dante. But he still has his great moments, and there's no one quite like him—no one. Algernon won't ever come and see him, because that fellow Mazzini's as Anti-Clerical as ever and makes a principle of having nothing to do with Dante. Look!—there's Algernon going into the water again! He'll tire himself out, he'll catch cold, he'll—' and here the old man rises and hurries down to the sea's edge. 'Now, Algernon', he roars, 'I don't want to interfere with you, but I do think, my dear old friend,'—and then, with a guffaw, he breaks off, remembering that his friend is not deaf now or old, and that here in Elysium, where no ills are, good advice is not needed.

# Index

In accordance with the pattern established for the 'Critical Heritage' series, four indexes follow: (1) periodicals which are the sources of texts or illustrative material; (2) critics, reviewers, or authors of informal comments; (3) authors mentioned in relation to Swinburne; (4) a selective list mostly concerned with comments on volumes or individual poems.

References to texts included in this volume are cited by number rather than by pages and usually are immediately followed by pages in the Introduction mentioning such texts.

## I

## II

Critics, reviewers, and authors of informal comments

251

## III

Authors mentioned in relation to Swinburne, usually by way of comparison

## IV

A list of Swinburne's publishers precedes titles of volumes and poems that are the subject of special comment. References under *Dedicatory Epistle*, *Notes on Poems and Reviews*, and *Under the Microscope* include, however, numbers identifying selections from those works in this book.